Henry Clews

THE

WALL STREET

POINT OF VIEW

BY

HENRY CLEWS

GREENWOOD PRESS, PUBLISHERS
NEW YORK   1968

First Greenwood reprinting, 1968

LIBRARY OF CONGRESS catalogue card number: 68-28620

PRINTED IN THE UNITED STATES OF AMERICA

CONTENTS.

PART I.

WALL STREET ITSELF.

CHAPTER I.

CHAPTER II.

CHAPTER III.

iii

CONTENTS.

CHAPTER VII.

CHAPTER VIII.

PART II.

WALL STREET AND THE GOVERNMENT.

CHAPTER XI.

CHAPTER XV.

CHAPTER XVI.

CHAPTER XVII.

CHAPTER XVIII.

Devised and bequeathed to the Democratic party by the last will and testament of the last Democratic Congress. — The unfinished business of eight years of hard and anxious work in the White House. — Lincoln's views on the Constitution and the tariff.

CHAPTER XIX.

The invaders of our home markets repulsed. — Foreign manufacturers and the products of their pauper labor not in demand. — Definitions of revenue tariff and protective tariff. — The latter fairly provided for in the Dingley Bill, and wool restored to the farmers. — Home markets in preference to foreign. — How McKinley humorously caught the clothier member for Boston on the cheap clothing argument. — Home capital and home labor will get a chance for development, and the time of prosperity has come. — Practical outcome of the protection and free-trade doctrines considered. — The testimony on this subject of two eminent witnesses, James Buchanan and Grover Cleveland.

CHAPTER XX.

The immense showing of our foreign trade for the fiscal year ending June 30, 1898. — Our balance of trade far ahead of that of other years and twice the amount of any previous record. — This has been achieved under a protective tariff which free-traders thought was going to ruin the country. — How it tallies with the free-trade doctrine of the Cobden Club and that of its representatives in this country. — The immense increase in the exports of our manufactured goods. — Our wealth increases as our imports diminish, and as our exports increase. — We saved in 1898 an amount of money greater by half a billion of dollars than the national debt at the close of the Civil War by the much maligned protective tariff. — The greatest profitable import to us was gold, of which we had a balance of $105,000,000 for the year.

CHAPTER XXI.

CHAPTER XXII.

CHAPTER XXIII.

CHAPTER XXIV.

CHAPTER XXV.

CHAPTER XXXI.

PART IV.

WALL STREET AND INTERNATIONAL AFFAIRS.

CHAPTER XXXII.

CHAPTER XXXIII.

THIS BOOK

𝕴𝖘 𝕽𝖊𝖘𝖕𝖊𝖈𝖙𝖋𝖚𝖑𝖑𝖞 𝕴𝖓𝖘𝖈𝖗𝖎𝖇𝖊𝖉

TO THOSE

ABLE STATESMEN, POLITICIANS, FINANCIERS,

AND MEN OF AFFAIRS,

TO WHOSE CONSTANT GUIDANCE IS DUE THE ADVANCEMENT OF

OUR COUNTRY ALONG EVER-WIDENING PATHS OF

PEACE AND PROSPERITY

THE WALL STREET POINT OF VIEW.

PART I.

WALL STREET ITSELF.

CHAPTER I.

WALL STREET AS A GAUGE OF BUSINESS PROSPERITY.

What it is: its area, population, and institutions. — The difference between natural and artificial conditions, the latter being the false standard of judgment by outsiders. — People decry Wall Street speculation without a correct knowledge of its character. — The Street is not a gambler's paradise, but a place where hard, honest work tells. — It is a public benefactor and once, at least, saved the country. — The center to which the surplus money of the world flows for investment.

THE district known as Wall Street embraces more wealth in proportion to area than any other space of similar dimensions in the world. Considering even the mere thoroughfare known by that name and extending from Trinity Church to the East River, the same assertion holds good. This latter limit is the one mentally placed by the great majority of our people upon the financial heart of the country, that throbs with the daily ebb and flow of millions, infusing life into all our vast enterprises.

The Wall Street region includes in its wealthy grasp the large majority of New York banks and other financial institutions, including savings banks. It is the great center of the insurance companies, life, fire, and marine ; of the great Trust Companies which command thousands of millions of capital, and are the custodians of many of the largest and most wealthy estates in the country. Finally, the region known as Wall Street has virtually a contingent population of three millions, which is just about the census record of the thirteen original states when they cut lcose from Great Britain and asserted their independence. In addition to the financial institutions as above stated, Wall Street has banks with large capital connected with all foreign nations. China, no less that the comparatively contiguous London, is represented by banking institutions here.

It has been the habit of too many people — well-meaning people, too — to decry Wall Street as hurtful to the morals of the country and injurious to our best business interests, — all of which is mistaken. Wall Street has been very aptly described as the " business pulse of the nation," and that is what it is, in the truest sense of the term. As the mercury in the thermometer denotes the degrees of heat and cold, so do the fluctuations in the Wall Street markets show the rise and fall of the business activity of the country. Let there be any activity in mercantile or manufacturing circles, and it is immediately reflected in the Stock Exchange and the other exchanges where values are dependent upon business activity and financial confidence. On the other hand, causes that influence the outside world unfavorably have a depressing effect in Wall Street, and the prices of securities and products take a lower turn. These are the results when natural conditions are allowed to prevail. Of course there are times when speculative syndicates get control, and by their manipulations create artificial conditions and artificial results. Then it is that panics are liable to occur; in fact, I doubt if there has ever been a panic in Wall Street that was not due to the work of such manipulations. Wall Street is a place where the laws of cause and effect are conspicuously potent, and it is as impossible for any combination of men to resist these laws without making trouble as it is for a human being to defy the forces of nature. An irreverent operator in grain speculations, commenting once on the failure of a pool to put up the price of wheat and maintain it in the face of a big crop, said, "It is of no use trying to buck against God Almighty ; he can upset the bulls every time."

To the student of affairs there is more suggestive truth expressed in these few terse words of a disappointed speculator

than in whole columns of the tirades preached against Wall
Street's ways by those ministers who have only a superficial
idea of the subject they are talking about.   Wall Street is
not a gambler's paradise.   There is no place in the business
world where more hard work, closer calculation, keener insight
into affairs, and philosophical and conservative conclusions are
required than in the offices of its bankers and brokers ; there
is no class of men who watch events more closely than the
operators in its markets.   In the stress of war times it has
been to Wall Street that the government turned for help.   It
was from Wall Street that the assistance once came which
made a continuance of the government even a possibility, and
it has always been ready to respond to any call, when financial or business problems were to be met and solved.   It is
very true that men have taken a gambling advantage of opportunities afforded by this great market, but these are not the
men who have made it reflective of the business prosperity,
not only of this country but of other countries, — a place
where surplus money from all over the world flows for investment in the securities of the corporations which are dependent
upon the material development of the United States of America — the greatest land under God's sunlight.   No, we cannot
do without Wall Street.

How would our one hundred and eighty thousand miles of
railroads have been constructed without Wall Street?   These
great pioneers of development, prosperity, and civilization would
have remained exceedingly limited in their extent and scope if
the bonds to build them had not been negotiated by Wall Street
financiers.   Think of the fertile lands that have thus been
thrown open to millions from all nations of the globe, and the
enormous increase of wealth that has followed this opening of
vast national resources.   Then again, look at the army of well-
paid employés connected with the railroads themselves, who,
together with those who work in the interdependent trades, —
railroad building, car building, and railroad supplies of every description, — amount to nearly two millions.   While it is unfortunately true, as I have pointed out in my book, "Twenty-eight

Years in Wall Street," and in other publications, that disreputable railroad projectors and managers have, especially through the medium of construction companies, made railroads the means to their dishonest ends ; yet in spite of such abuses this vast railroad system, advanced and supported by Wall Street capital, has been the chief instrument for a national increase which has no historic parallel.

Not only is Wall Street indispensable to this country, but foreign nations also are feeling the benefit of its operations more and more every year. The London Stock Exchange and the Paris and Berlin Bourses would suffer if the New York Stock Exchange were to be closed for a week or even for a day ; the progress of great industries dependent on them would languish just as surely as our own railroad, telegraph, and other enterprises would suffer in the failure of the great financial fountain from which they draw their invigorating tonic. Enterprise everywhere would be depressed as if seized by a sort of financial paralysis. What folly is this enmity toward Wall Street ! Let us condemn and cut off its evil, parasitic growths, but let us recognize and glory in the fact that this great financial center is fast approaching the point at which it is destined to become the enormous clearing house of the world's enterprises and industries. In the course of evolution and a higher civilization we might be able to get along comfortably without Congress, but without Wall Street, never.

CHAPTER II.

THE STUDY OF THE STOCK MARKET.

The power of speculative fascination over a large number of people. — Bad results of adopting second-hand opinions. — The laws of speculation and investment must be studied profoundly. — Fact and rumor should be carefully distinguished. — Hard study of facts and realities generally leads to sound and accurate conclusions. — It is also necessary to study the circumstances and events which cause real values to fluctuate. — How natural laws eventually regulate values and reduce inflated ones to their true basis.

ANYTHING that is worth doing is worth doing well. In order to do anything well, one must study the subject thoroughly, not necessarily in books, because books are, except as to the laying down of principles, rather unsatisfactory teachers.

The stock market is a most fruitful and fascinating field of study. It attracts more influential and well-to-do men than any other arena of activity in American life, and of course a great deal of study is bestowed upon it. The reasons why the results of so much study are not always commensurate with the labor and time employed are numerous. Some of them are substantially as follows : —

People have preconceived notions. They are not willing to clear their minds of existing theories and bring themselves down to close dealing with facts. They are apt to base their conclusions on the opinions of others. Now, opinions as to the value of anything are sure to differ, and opinions as to future values differ still more widely, just as the spokes of a wheel are wider apart as you travel away from the hub. When you reach out into the future, you are getting away from the hub of the present. People are usually unwilling to act on conclusions that conflict with their desires, and that involve the acceptance of immediate losses. They resemble the wounded man who refuses to let the surgeon cut off his leg when he is told that amputation will probably save his life. They are apt to study in a superficial manner, without thoroughness, using scraps and smatterings of knowledge when even the most exact information is hardly sufficient.

Other reasons could be adduced, but they might be needless. A certain king excused the municipality of a town that neglected to fire a salute in his honor on their giving him the first one of fifty good reasons, — that they had no powder. The other forty-nine were suffered to remain undivulged. Enough reasons have been given here to explain why so many people fail to study the stock market successfully.

But while it is very easy to pick to pieces the various systems that are sure to win on the stock exchange, and to criticise the methods of study of the prejudiced, it is most difficult to lay down absolute rules for the successful study of the share market. One invariable rule there is, but it requires large capital and patience to practise it. It is this : Buy only what you can pay for ; buy when cheap and sell when dear. The veriest financial infants can see the force of this.

Yet even this precept has its weak points. For instance, how is a person to be absolutely certain that a given stock is cheap or dear at a given time? You say, by comparison? But if he compares the price with what it was at any past period, he must also be able to state all the facts that existed at that period having any bearing on this stock, and since these facts may run into the thousands as to number, and into all parts of the country as to place, our learner has a heavy contract on hand. Then, too, he must bring to bear a clear judgment, and a resolution such as soldiers exercise when they charge batteries, and he must be prepared next day to find out that he was wrong. After a careful and exhaustive search into all the materials at hand, he buys shares at, say, 60 per cent. of par, as being cheap at the price, and really worth more money, and next day they may be offered at 50. He then has really lost $10 on each share ; but if he holds the purchase, and it ultimately advances to par, he has gained $40 per share.

And suppose he sells on any given day at par, and a week after that the shares sell at 110, he then loses $10 per share. So that this " safe " road to success has its stumbling blocks as well as others, although they are not so dangerous.   In such a road there are no deadly pitfalls.   The men who travel it are not tempted to defalcations and suicides.

Horace Greeley once said that the way to resume specie payments was to resume ; and it might also be said that the way to study the stock market is to study it.   One distinguished and generally successful stock operator of the period is credited with being in daily receipt of numerous pieces of information from various parts of the country as to the condition of crops, weather, freights, passenger traffic, in short, all facts that go to make up the status of railroad enterprises.   These private bits of information are not open to the general public — they cost too much, and call for too much machinery ; but the bureaus of public information are continually sending out intelligence, and it is mostly trustworthy.   This class of facts must be distinguished from mere rumors.

Rumor is, as a rule, uncertain and untrustworthy.   It has been compared to an animated thing that begins its career by being small and compact, but as it stalks along it becomes larger and less definite as to form, until at last it is like a monstrous cloud that has neither shape nor consistency, and finally disappears, no one knows how or where.   But to study facts leads to generally accurate conclusions ; and accurate conclusions are apt to lead to wise transactions.

Thus, the fact of large harvests in the year 1891 in the United States, coupled with the fact of poor harvests in Europe in the same year, led to the conclusion that our grain would be in demand for foreign shipment, and that the earnings of our railroads would be increased.   The conclusions were sound and the earnings were increased, and judicious students of the market bought stocks for a rise.   Then the fact that stocks rose and kept on rising, coupled with the fact that the general public were buyers, and with the additional fact that the public prefer to be buyers and to buy at high prices, and not to buy at all unless prices are high, led these same judicious students to sell the same stocks during the prevalence of high prices, — both the stocks which they owned and large amounts which they did not own. Again, the study of facts led to wise conclusions, and these ended in successful results. Both as bulls and as bears the wise students have fared well. The careless and superficial public, coming in too late as bulls, found themselves at last compelled to become unwilling sellers at greater or less losses, in some cases so severe as to shatter households and drive citizens to ruin.

Thus the person who studies real values must not be content with that alone. He must also study the facts that in times of stress and storm make real values fluctuate as wildly in manner, if not in amount, as those of the most fanciful securities, and he must learn that no operation on margin is really safe unless the margin is large beyond the ordinary run, and is backed by equally large reserves. Some financial teachers lay it down that your risks should not exceed 25 per cent. of your capital. This is excessive prudence ; but the man who keeps half a mile away from the edge of a cliff will never fall from it. One who has studied the share market carefully has eventually found that if he is able to pay one half the market price of his holdings, he need have little fear as to the other half ; that is, on judicious selections of properties.

No mention is made here of shares that sell in December at 72 and in March at 30. Whoever buys such goods should pay for them and put them away, and let them incubate with such patience as is attributed to the hopeful setting hen.

The student of the stock market has at certain periods no easy task before him. Imports are sometimes large, and exports small. We sell to foreigners a million per week of cotton, and buy from them two millions per week of coffee, the cotton yielding us a small profit, the coffee yielding foreigners an immense profit. Other nations at times do not seem to prefer our grains to those of Russia and the East, despite those foreign markets of bewildering extent and good prices which exist, I fear, only in the imagination of free-traders. Then, too, the indebtedness of corporations and individuals acts as a constant menace to the natural tendency of loose capital to be lent out to useful enterprises.

Yet, at the bottom of all this turbulent mass of facts there are natural laws at work which, if we study them in relation to the objects which they control, will be found to be as sure in their operation as sunrise. The collapse of the iniquitous coal combination, as cruel as one to raise the price of water or air, was the result of natural law, and the same laws are busy to-day, and the facts are always with us. It is the business of the diligent to find them and to profit thereby.

Next to the unwisdom of selecting and following bad or incompetent advisers in matters of speculation and investment, there are also certain persons whom, if you wish to do well and make a fortune honestly, you should be careful to avoid. You will not always know them by their appearance ; in fact, that is often the worst rule to go by, for they are generally well disguised. It is in their walk, talk, and conversation that you will find them out, and, that this be the easier, I have made a collection of their characteristics, as follows : —

Avoid a man

    Who vilifies his benefactor ;

    Who unjustly accuses others of bad deeds ;

    Who never has a good word for anybody ;

    Who is always prating about his own virtues ;

    Who, when he drinks, habitually drinks alone ;

    Who boasts of the superiority of his family ;

    Who talks religion down-town in connection with his daily business affairs ;

    Who talks recklessly against the virtue of respectable women ;

    Who runs in debt with no apparent intention of paying ;

    Who borrows small sums on his note or check dated ahead ;

    Who won't work for an honest living ;

    Who looks down upon those who do ;

    Who imputes bad motives to those trying to do good ;

    Who betrays confidence ;

Who lies ;

Who is honest only for policy's sake ;

Who deceives his wife and boasts of it to others ;

Who chews tobacco in a public conveyance ;

Who gets intoxicated in public places ;

Who partakes of hospitality and talks behind his entertainer's back ;

Who borrows money from a friend and then blackguards the lender.

With a population of 80,000,000 people, which this country now has, it is easy to find associates in life without selecting men possessed of any of these characteristics, and life is the better worth living without them.

You will both save and make money by strict observance of this short catalogue of avoidances. You are not called upon to do anything or to risk any money in the exercise of this discretion. It simply consists in letting such people severely alone, and if you have been in the habit of being imposed upon by such characters, you will find your happiness as well as your treasury greatly increased by prudently avoiding them.

CHAPTER III.

MONEY AND USURY.

Various opinions regarding interest and usury. — Why should not compensation for the use of money be left to the freedom of contract untrammeled by restrictive laws? — Views of Lord Bacon and Lord Mansfield on usury and interest. — The word "interest" not known in Bacon's time. — All laws against usury capable of evasion. — Various rates and the laws of usury pertaining to different states. — Freedom of contract the true doctrine in money-lending and borrowing.

"MONEY and Usury" is a subject that has perhaps been more extensively discussed than any other within the sphere of trade and finance, and usury has been the fertile theme of a great amount of both sense and nonsense, as well as of a large number of foolish laws.

In times gone by the word "usury" was employed in the same sense as "interest" is now, and Lord Bacon, in his essay on usury, evidently attaches this signification to it, as he makes a distinction between high and low "rates of usury," and the context shows he was unacquainted with the term "interest." He criticises pretty severely the critics on usury, and says: "Many have made witty invectives against usury. They say that it is a pity the devil should have God's part, which is the tithe, that the usurer is the great Sabbath-breaker because his plough goeth every Sunday."

So we see from Bacon's opinion that the prejudice against paying for the use of other people's money is as old as it is unreasonable.

We have no record of any period when within the confines of civilization men were not in the habit of paying for the use of the property of other men ; in fact, such compensation marks the dawn of civilization — a time when it was discovered to be better to hire another man's goods or lands than to kill him for the sake of becoming their owner. An equivalent for the use of lands or buildings we style rent; for the use of chattels, hire; for the use of money, interest. One of the most noticeable facts about the last-named equivalent is that in almost all communities its amount, as related to the material for the use of which it is paid, has been made the subject of legislation. Laws have never been enacted regulating the prices of rents or of the hire of chattels, but statutes regulating the interest of money are beyond computation as to number, and their existence dates back to epochs beyond which public record and the memory of mankind run not to the contrary.

Since this is an undeniable fact, there must be a reason for its origin and its persistent vitality. May not this be the reason? — that money not being a commodity, but the representative of all commodities, capable of passing through all metamorphoses of lands, houses, cattle, grain — in short, of all transferable things whatsoever — may be said to have a value free from such changes as other commodities are constantly undergoing; therefore, while the owner of these may lawfully demand any price he pleases for the use of such property, and take all he can get, the owner of money must not demand or take more than a certain price, which price shall be stated by the lawmakers of the community. This is the probable basis of usury laws, though we should not assert that laws are enacted solely in order to assert a principle. As a matter of fact, they are kept on the statute books in deference to a sentiment which is supposed to pervade the public mind, that poor people must be protected from the rapacity of money-lenders.

It will not be difficult to show that the alleged principle on which usury laws are based is illogical; and further, that, as a matter of fact, these laws do not prevent poor borrowers, or borrowers upon hazardous pledges, from paying high prices for the use of money. That money is not a commodity because it is the representative and summary and equivalent of all commodities, is a conclusion which is not only open to doubt, but may be with reason flatly denied. That the greater includes the less is an axiom ; and if money includes all commodities, it must itself be the greatest of commodities. It is the nearest approach to an unchangeable measure of values that can be attained, but at the same time it remains a commodity, subject, as are other commodities, to the laws of supply and demand. In the varying conditions of trade, its use may at one time command interest, or usury, at a rate of but three per cent. per annum, while at another it may command six per cent. or more. These terms indicate the altered relation in its supply and demand, consequent upon the variations in production or consumption of other commodities. There is, indeed, no absolute measure of value except it be the general average resulting in society from the continually varying relations which commodities bear to each other in respect of prices. To-day a bushel of No. 1 winter wheat shall be exchangeable for a barrel of crude petroleum, or ten yards of sheeting, or one gold dollar ; to-morrow it shall be exchangeable for two barrels of crude petroleum, or fifteen yards of sheeting, or one gold dollar and a half. But we must have terms in which these fluctuations may be expressed, which shall form an understandable basis of exchange of products between individuals and among nations ; hence the elaboration of this means of facilitating commerce into vast monetary systems.

Money is not only an admitted equivalent for all commodities, but is itself a commodity and the greatest of commodities in this respect — that it is the most strongly desired, the most widely known, and the most universally possessed. As civilization has progressed, so has the necessity developed for such an equivalent in the most concentrated form, and one capable of easy transmission. Along with the social evolution of the most enlightened nations, has come, by successive steps, the adoption of the most precious available metal, gold, as the basis of this equivalent, and the most compact exchangeable representative commodity.

Some writers have asserted that money is not a commodity, because it is neither produced nor consumed. The objection to this statement is that it is not true. Money is both produced and consumed. It is first dug out of the earth, and afterward it undergoes a constant consumption by abrasion. It is estimated that the production of gold keeps but slightly in advance of its consumption year by year, while in the last twenty years the production of silver has been much in excess of the consumption. Therefore the relations of gold and silver have changed. Gold is dearer and silver is cheaper. This one fact shows that the precious metals used as money by the common consent of mankind are, in truth, commodities. Is it logical that the greater, the representative commodity should, in its operations, be bound by restrictive laws which have never been sought to be applied to the lesser commodities?

It would seem, therefore, that no reason worth the name exists why a person having money which he is able to spare to the uses of others, should not receive from them such compensation for its use as he and they may by contract agree upon. And all reasons urged against usury will be found to be either wholly sentimental or based upon misconceptions of the true functions of money.

History has already passed upon Napoleon's Berlin decrees, and his other laws against the use of, and traffic in, English merchandise; the witchcraft laws of New England have died; Quakers are no longer persecuted in Massachusetts and Connecticut; Great Britain has abolished all usury statutes; Connecticut has done the same, as well as many of her sister States; they never have disfigured the statute books of California; but in New York, the greatest of the States, the most commercial, the richest, the State where the fullest play should be given to the traffic in useful commodities, it is a crime to lend money on time at seven per cent. per annum !

Laws that regulate the rate of interest in cases where no contract is made, or on sums that have become overdue, are natural and reasonable; but no legislation can be seriously defended that attempts to prohibit one citizen from making any contract with another, touching useful commodities or services, which both agree to; still less where it brands one of the contracting parties with guilt and enables the other party to rob him with impunity, and even to procure his incarceration.

If we are wrong in this way of thinking, we prefer to be wrong in company with the enlightened sense of Great Britain, Connecticut, and California — to mention no others — rather than to be right in company with the antiquated sense of New York.

As to the many devices used to nullify these statutory trammels laid upon the freedom of man's dealings with man, Lord Mansfield, one of the great English judges of the eighteenth century, in delivering an opinion on usury, said: "Where the real truth is a loan of money, the wit of man cannot find a shift to take it out of the statute." Lord Mansfield, in his patriotic admiration of the English law which he, in common with Blackstone and some others, considered the "perfection of human reason," was doubtless sincere in the expression of this opinion, but there are very few judges in the present day who do not know that there never has been an usury law passed which human ingenuity has not found a method of evading. Many instances of such evasions and of a great variety of methods of evasion can be easily cited from the standard law books and reports, even from Lord Mansfield's day down to the present time.

Bacon, with his love for systematizing every subject which he handled, divided the arguments that prevailed in his time against and for usury, or interest, and states them as follows in his quaint but terse English. He says: "The discommodities of usury are, first, that it makes fewer merchants, for were it not for this lazy trade of usury, money would not lie still, but would in great part be employed upon merchandizing, which is the *vena porta* of wealth in a state; the second, that it makes poor merchants, for as a farmer cannot husband his ground so well if he sit at a great rent, so the merchant cannot drive his trade so well if he sit at a great usury."

It would seem that the borrowing of money at a high rate in our times works, as a rule, the very contrary to what many people in Bacon's day had estimated as the results. A man seldom borrows money at a high rate, or at any rate, now, without a fair prospect of investing it so as to have a profit after paying the interest. So the merchant never "sits at great usury," to use Bacon's words, unless he sees the means of paying the usury and realizing a surplus besides. Another reason assigned in the catalogue of Bacon's "discommodities" is "that usury doth dull and damp all industries, improvements, and new inventions, wherein money would be stirring if it were not for this slug."

This is a peculiar view of the results of borrowing. Consequences seem to be largely the contrary in our day. This power to borrow infuses activity into all the channels of industry and invention in which money is employed. Many of the projectors of our modern "sky-scrapers," for instance, can usually realize three or four per cent. profit between the money borrowed and that expended on the buildings. Of course it changes the nature of the transaction if the interest is larger than the profits of the business, but there are very few so foolish as to borrow under such conditions and at such ruinous rates.

Viewing the obverse side of the picture, however, Bacon's theories are more in consonance with present commercial practice and experience. But they all go to show, more or less, how narrow the basis of business, trade, and commerce was in the golden age of Queen Elizabeth and James the First, about three centuries ago, and they bring out in bolder relief the great progress that has been made since that time.

Bacon goes on to show that were it not for borrowing, "men's necessities would draw upon them a most sudden undoing;" and he concludes that "it is a vanity to conceive that there would be ordinary borrowing without profit, and it is impossible to conceive the number of inconveniences that would ensue if borrowing be cramped. Therefore, to speak of the abolishing of usury is idle. All states have ever had it, in one kind or rate or other; so that opinion must be sent to Utopia."

Such were the opinions of the great philosopher who has gained the credit of creating a revolution in scientific thought and who was chiefly instrumental in reducing the philosophic theories of centuries to the practical basis which has been at the bottom of all modern invention and discovery. "The key to the Baconian system of philosophy," says a great writer, " was utility and progress," and these have brought into being a world of business enterprise, and need for freedom in its transaction, not dreamed of in his time. The day is not far distant, I believe, when money will be bought and sold and rented out with as little restriction upon the parties to the contract as that pertaining to any other commodity.

CHAPTER IV.

THE RAILROAD PROBLEM.

Present status of railroads, and indispensable reforms in their management.
— Legislative requirements. — Railroad business as a gauge of prosperity. — Ten millions of people depending on them for a living. — Suggestions upon consolidation.— Hints for the regulation of directors. — President Ingalls's views on the evils of railroad management.

THE present status of railroads and the reforms necessary in their management, together with the legislation requisite to help to bring about these reforms, constitute one of the subjects of most extensive interest in this country at the present day. When railroads are prosperous, the whole country is prosperous, and not less than a seventh part of the population of the country is depending almost directly on them for a living. Therefore if such a calamity could be supposed as would bring the railroads to a standstill, not less than ten millions of people out of the seventy would be almost immediately brought face to face with all the horrors of famine.

Certain Western legislators never seem to think of this when they are doing their best to drive the railroads in their various localities out of business or into bankruptcy, nor does it ever seem to occur to these Solons that they themselves would be among the greatest sufferers by the strict execution of the laws which they are annually striving to promulgate.

One of the first things that Congress should deal with, and that without delay, as regards the railroad problem, is the enactment of a pooling bill that will allow freedom of contract between and among railroad corporations. If there were a well-defined and liberal national law to this effect, then the State legislatures would be powerless to shackle commerce, for the Constitution of the United States makes full provision against

18

such interference in Article I., section 10, clause 1, which says : " No state shall make any law impairing the obligation of contracts." This clause in the Constitution would squelch all the vicious attempts of the anarchistic railroad-wrecking legislators throughout the entire West, or wherever the spirit of populism might desire to destroy property and rob the owners thereof of their just rights.

The loose and somewhat hostile laws of Congress, and their still more hostile interpretation by the Supreme Court, in one instance at least, have hitherto stood in the way of the application of this clause in the Constitution against mischievous State legislation in the matter of railroad corporations. Hence the necessity of a national law to make effective this constitutional provision which the Fathers in their wisdom inserted in the supreme law of the land, in the interest of personal freedom, and to conserve the rights of private property.

The question of railroad consolidation is one that is largely occupying the minds of railroad managers, and those who have large interests in railroad securities. One railroad magnate of great experience in building railroads and saddling most of the expenses on the government, thinks that it would be a good thing if consolidation were carried so far as to concentrate the whole railroad property of the country in the hands of not more than three corporations. What a tremendous number of rotten organizations this one would contain, — probably enough to wreck them all ! In such an arrangement many wealthy and well-to-do stockholders would in all probability be reduced to poverty, and ultimately the three big concerns might have to go into the hands of receivers, thus throwing the great aggregate system into bankruptcy.

Consolidation cannot fail to be beneficial where connecting roads extend on parallel lines, and all are naturally working toward the same end ; namely, the transportation of freight and passengers from one prominent and opulent town to another. Particularly is this the case where some rich valley or system of valleys indicates the course of travel and commerce between these points ; and for an illustration we may take the New Yc :

Central, which is the most brilliant instance of successful railway consolidation known in the United States.

At the time when this arrangement was effected, the plan of introducing branch roads from comparatively thinly settled and barren districts had not been exploited to any noticeable extent, nor has this particular road favored such a plan. Its acquisition of the ill-starred West Shore Road was a necessity; it was consummated with reluctance, and only because the directors believed that the destinies of our imperial State would eventually grow in opulence sufficiently to make the transaction productive. It was legitimate because it "had to be," and there is no danger of such another enterprise. The topographical formation of the State is such that no competing trunk road can be laid between Albany and Buffalo, and no capital or charter could be procured to construct a fourth line between New York City and Albany. Both sides of the Hudson River are now occupied, and the Harlem road is sufficient for the rich and level counties that extend between the eastern bank of the Hudson and New England. The system, therefore, is, humanly speaking, complete; and, although on its central and westward divisions it may yet absorb laterals, its comparative permanency and necessary conservatism tend to give it the confidence of investors, and to make it as it has been termed, "the 'consol' of the market."

It strengthens our position that while this great process of consolidation took place, attended by a continual increase of market value of shares, two other roads — one partly, the other wholly in the same State — which attempted absorptions equal in magnitude, but wanting in the elements of prudence and rationality, experienced such depressions of share values as seriously to disturb the money market and ruin thousands of small holders. The stock of one of these great roads sank to $30\frac{7}{8}$ in 1877; that of the other to $25\frac{1}{2}$. Both have since recovered to above par, but the operation has been slow and painful, and during a period of years their stocks were footballs and speculative traps, the tools of gamblers, instead of the useful servants of the community, and the secure refuges of finance.

When we go westward and look at the outcome of consolidation, we find different conditions and less prosperous results. The real logic of the case has been neglected or contemptuously thrust aside, and steps have been taken which no arguments could justify. The directors of the main lines in these cases have proceeded not in the direction of the interests of their stockholders, but in that of bargains and deals with the officers of unprofitable connecting and lateral roads on the principle of spoliation and a division of the spoils.

These transactions have been numerous and of enormous magnitude, but they have been all pretty much alike, so that when we describe one we describe all. Given, a useful, well-constructed dividend-paying road ; a body of people with some capital and political influence aided by some of the directors of this prosperous line ; these construct a branch road to some outside point, — the more important such point the better, but that is of small consequence. The road gets itself built, it is bonded for more than it cost, and it cost twice as much as it ought, since the constructors were all together in the ring and favored one another. Then the capital stock is fixed at so much, and this is mostly distributed among the constructors. The road then, swelled to a fictitious price of three or four to one, and not worth much to start with, is ripe for absorption and consolidation. Its directors and those of the main line meet, confer, and vote the measure through. They all profit by it, more or less, but their profits are enormously in excess of the trifling losses due to the shrinkage of values of the shares of the main line. A director of the main line may perhaps lose $20,000 on a thousand shares, but what is that when compared to a gain of hundreds of thousands in his holdings of the branch road whose liabilities are assumed by his victimized corporation? Such a director would not be equal to the demands of his covetousness if he had not sold thousands of shares short, in anticipation of the fall which the transactions of himself and his associates were inevitably bound to produce.

This is not a fanciful picture. On any railroad map the expert in railway affairs can trace out such main lines, each with its connecting branches or suckers, many of them worthless and many others worse than worthless, which lose themselves at the further end in hypothetical towns and barren wildernesses, and are all grouped together under the specious names of former profitable and well-managed railroads. A road may have been originally the A. & B. and have paid full dividends, so full that it may have been advisable to double the volume of stock in order to keep the price of shares at something like par, but not too much above it. Even when thus watered it has been excellent property, safe for investors, desirable collateral for bank loans, creditable to its managers, and useful to the public. To-day it masquerades under the name of A. & B., or perhaps A. B. & C., but it is not either, because it is so much more. It has swallowed so many indigestible morsels of useless and unprofitable branches that all the letters of the alphabet would be required to particularize them ; it has guaranteed all their bonds, and has exchanged its own scrip for theirs, so that its own share of capital is in excess of value to that extent that it represents only the phantom equity that trails along at the heels of a fourth or fifth mortgage. The shares that were once a firm property at par are tossed about the market at all prices from 70 to 20 ; dividends are scaled down from 7 per cent. to 4, then 2, then passed temporarily, then passed indefinitely ; a floating debt of unknown amount is created ; its paper — known as " railroad paper " — is to be found by the ream in the portfolios of note brokers ; and when it fails to get itself sold at 6 or 8 per cent. it lets itself out at 10 or 12. Capitalists and banks are invited to make bids on private terms. Every banker knows that railroad paper is frequently negotiated at 18 per cent., and although the proceeds ostensibly go to bona-fide holders for value, no one doubts that the treasury of the road that makes such ruinous discount of future earnings is the real borrower. Then come income bonds, " subordinated and unsubordinated," debenture bonds, all the delusive schemes on which bankrupt concerns float along, until receivers are appointed and honest management is enforced. The court imposes an assessment, and it is announced as a great success that the A. B. & C. is now earning fixed charges !

Such is consolidation run mad, and such is its tendency when not restrained by natural causes or by honesty on the part of managers. Can we expect any other results ?

And speaking of honesty on the part of managers brings me to another important part of the subject under consideration. That is the necessity of a protective system of committees, chosen by the stockholders of every railroad, to investigate the management, have its accounts audited periodically by trustworthy experts upon a plan that would exclude the possibility of collusion, and have the reports of these committees reported to a central association, also chosen by said stockholders, at reasonable intervals. This would in time reform and thoroughly eradicate most of the evils now complained of, and make the railroads still more potent instruments for developing material prosperity through our unlimited resources.

In a discourse by M. E. Ingalls, President of the " Big Four," C.C.C. & St. Louis Railway, delivered at Purdue University, Indiana, many of the evils of railroad management, and the needed reforms, are set forth in a very succinct manner, and exhibit the thorough grasp that Mr. Ingalls has taken of the subject. After adverting to the immense increase and power of these properties, and showing what they have done for the nation in affording greater facilities for travel, decreasing freight rates on the average to four fifths of a cent per ton per mile, and on the great products such as wheat, corn, cotton, iron, and coal to half this rate, he goes on to show that after the panic of 1857, stocks of many of the railroads that had formerly been paying dividends went down to 10, and in some instances 5 cents on the dollar. He then describes the advent and methods of the promoter who obtained charters, issued stocks and bonds on prospective roads, and how the holders of these presumable securities felt when the day of reckoning came and they were unable to meet the interest. It was in this state of affairs that Western hostility was engendered toward promoters and contractors and railroad managers in general, and thus the

Granger movement of the seventies had its origin. After it had spent its force, Congress passed the Interstate Commerce Law in 1886, making the difficulties even greater than did the State laws. By this law, pooling or the division of business in certain equitable proportions was prohibited ; while it is the judgment of railroad managers that in no other way than by such divisions can permanent and fair rates be obtained. One effect of the law is that the big shippers can evade it and undersell the small shippers, driving them out of business ; and the same rule holds with communities, — the building up of Chicago, for instance, and the breaking down of places like Lafayette.

Mr. Ingalls advises that it is necessary to build five thousand miles a year in short and inexpensive lines, as feeders to the main systems. He concludes that in a few years we will require two hundred and fifty thousand miles of main lines to accommodate one hundred million population, which will be an increase of 40 per cent. over the present mileage. But we require new legislation of a fairly liberal character to achieve this end.

One point in Mr. Ingalls's recommendations is worthy of special note ; that is, the issue of debenture bonds on the English plan instead of mortgages. This would put a stop to the immense reorganizations which during the past few years have involved one fifth of the whole railroad property of the country, and would prevent the stockholders from being wiped out in times of trouble. There is no foreclosure in England. When the company defaults on the interest of the debentures, a receiver is appointed to take care of the profits, but the stockholders retain their interest in the property.

It is easy to see, therefore, that if we should adopt the English system, the occupation of our numerous railroad wreckers would be gone ; and if they should turn their attention to the calling of the highwayman, it would involve a considerable enlargement of our prison accommodation. In their new occupation they could hardly count on the immunity that is now extended to them by the custom which has been in vogue for forty years, gaining strength and power all the time.

I am glad to find that the plan of extension which I have been advocating in the newspapers and periodicals for years in preference to that of consolidation, is commended by Mr. Ingalls. The operation of consolidating down to two or three corporations, or probably one, as Mr. Huntington recommends (in the belief perhaps that the Pacific roads should be the nucleus of the one), would in all probability result in government ownership. This would suppress competition, deteriorate values, rob many thousands of stockholders of a portion of their property, and destroy the chief stimulus for railroad extension and railroad enterprise, thus throwing a wet blanket on every kind of business connected with railroad traffic, — and what business is not so connected? In fact, it would probably create one of the worst panics we have ever experienced ; and finally it would greatly embarrass the government itself, which would not be able to make railroad revenues and expenses balance. Then would come the oppression of extra taxation, either in the shape of an addition to the internal revenue already swelled to unreasonable proportions, or perhaps an income tax.

There would be no end to the trouble caused by the government ownership of railroads. But there is no chance for such a consummation in this generation.

CHAPTER V.

MANAGEMENT OF OUR INDUSTRIAL ENTERPRISES.

The relation of the financial management of these institutions to their success or failure. — They should be compelled to make periodical statements of their condition as quasi-public concerns. — The origin of corporations and their beneficent purposes. — They are powerful in the present day, if properly managed, for the production of wealth and the promotion of the best interests of society. — A public and periodical system recommended for the examination of accounts by experts trained for the purpose. — Under proper management, the whole community might share in the great advantages which these industrials are capable of conferring on the public at large.

IN considering the great subject of industrial enterprises, the first thing that naturally strikes the prudent man of general business, is the character of the financial management of these institutions.

Usually, the management is most faulty in its failure to make periodical statements of their condition, and the favored few in the inner confidence of the managers have advantages in the general market to which they are not justly entitled.

The fact that industrials are possessed of double attributes, of public and private nature combined, opens the way to abuse of official power, which may frequently happen with an honest purpose but with an intense desire to assert private independence against what may be regarded as public intermeddling with private affairs. An inability to perceive fine distinctions between two sets of obligations of this dual character and the natural tendency in human nature to follow the selfish purpose in the first instance, may lead to official delinquency toward the public interests, where the original intention was only a matter of self-assertion or a sensitive desire to stand upon personal dignity and personal rights. But after such a habit of action has been some time indulged, it may assume a grosser aspect in which delicacy of feeling and lofty notions of self-respect play but little part, the change in the man's nature or the management's nature and principles having been wrought through an appeal to his avaricious propensities, and so blunting his perceptions that he becomes incapable of drawing a fine distinction between *meum et tuum*.

Unfortunately, it is such a spirit that pervades the management of many of these industrials, in consequence of which they have been viciously deflected from their true intent and purpose. This deflection has occurred through ignorance of the end in view, or in forgetfulness that to aim at the greatest good is often the best means of attaining one's own individual benefit. In truth, avarice is seldom capable of adopting any broad view, and this vice is one of the worst influences with which the industrials have had to contend, and there seems to be but one power that can prevent its invading both public and private rights. I have no contention with those who hold the doctrine of moral suasion in cases of this kind ; I am considering the practical phase of the subject, and I fear that nothing but the strong arm of the law will be found satisfactorily effective. Of course the moral sense is an important factor to cultivate in maintaining the laws of society and business equity, but where this quality becomes atrophied, as in many cases of industrial management, the ends of justice require firmer measures of reform.

In plain terms, it is utterly useless to preach the moral law to a man who has an idea that he is doing an able and meritorious act in laying schemes to plunder his neighbor in a way that the latter cannot detect or expose because the methods adopted are such as the public have been taught to think consistent with good business methods. Nor will the doctrine of passive submission help that neighbor to secure his rights. It will only render him more liable to be victimized.

The corporation idea when applied to industrial enterprises was, and is, calculated to confer the greatest benefits on humanity that human ingenuity and energy can bestow. Rightly applied, it is the most effective instrument for moving the forces that produce wealth and happiness; and there is no happiness in poverty nor morality in destitution, no matter what theorists may say. The existence of the corporation is absolutely necessary in this age of progress and development, to give inventions a chance of exhibiting their capacity and of conferring their illimitable boons and blessings upon mankind. It enables an aggregate of individuals to put their capital and energy together so as to act as one gigantic individual and to overcome obstacles that can be put aside by no other means. It is the practical faith in our day and generation that removes mountains.

But still this naturally benevolent giant is not infrequently possessed by the vile demon of avarice to which I have just referred, and the problem is how to exorcise the demon. Our legislative machinery should, in my opinion, be equal to this task. The periodic examinations of the financial management of all industrial enterprises can readily be made effective to cut off the opportunity for plunder. I admit that this treatment is suggestive of very radical measures; but "desperate cases require desperate remedies" is a medical adage quite applicable to business maladies.

Now comes the most delicate part of my task. There is no use in firing bullets in the air and losing ammunition upon game that is beyond our range. We must give cases in point, rather than generalities; we must point out the very concerns in which the faulty secretiveness exists, and without beating about the bush. A few of the most conspicuous of these are briefly termed in the everyday language of the stock exchange: "Tobacco," "Leather," "Whiskey," "Ice," and "Sugar."

If these, and others similar to them, had been subjected to the ordeal of a thorough investigation by expert accountants, and their true financial condition laid before the public, an innumerable number of serious losses would have been prevented from falling upon innocent and worthy people, nor would the enterprises in question have been exposed to the reproach now cast upon them by victims and others.

Some people draw a distinction between dishonest and unwise methods in the financial management of such properties, and many methods are indeed unwise without being at all dishonest or criminal. Ultimately, however, they wreck the property just the same as in the cases of Cordage, Whiskey, and of numerous railroads, a mere catalogue of which would extend this chapter far beyond the limits of its allotment.

There are also many in the railroad list furnishing illustrations of similarly faulty financial methods. Some of these have exhibited peculiar methods, if not delinquencies, in bookkeeping, which should have undergone more rigid investigation than they have received; and the guilty parties should have been held responsible for their acts, which brought about the financial downfall of so many great railway corporations in the memorable panic of 1893.

The investigation of the refunding committee of the Pacific railroads at Washington brought out most remarkable evidence from one of the principal witnesses, who stated that the books connected with the construction of the road had been burned or destroyed as useless trash involving the superfluous expense of room rent, though they contained the record of transactions involving hundreds of millions of dollars, a record which became absolutely necessary to a fair settlement between the government and its debtors. Also, the fact was put in evidence that a certain party in interest had testified before another committee, on a former occasion, that he was present when $54,000,000 of profits were divided equally among four partners, himself and three others. None of the books of record containing this valuable information escaped from the flames.

Now, under a system of public examination as often as once a year at least, by experts trained for that special purpose, no such valuable evidence could be destroyed, and I believe that industrials would be capable of fulfilling the highest aims of their beneficent purpose as originally conceived by their first organizers; that is, to cheapen production, in order that consumers might reap by far the larger portion of the profits derivable from this cause, after a fair remuneration to management and shareholders.

Though it would take volumes to ventilate this subject fully, yet I think the matters to which I have referred and the means of reform which I have suggested, strike at the root of some of the worst abuses relating to the speculative management and manipulation of industrial securities. The "scoops" which have become so frequent and so terrible a scandal in speculative circles, and which have brought such unmerited odium on the legitimate business of Wall Street, would be hardly possible under a system of surveillance with a syndicate of expert, honest, responsible accountants as the keystone of its arch, and under government or state supervision.

The more attentively and closely this subject is examined, the more clearly does it appear that the place of financial management in the industrial organization largely determines its success or failure. The power and ability of the capital to increase are liable to be crippled in every attempt if the financial management is slow to perceive the requirements for this end. The surplus must be carefully watched, and not wasted in superfluous expenses ; for it is through the persistent law of aggregation by means of the surplus that the industrial concern achieves its great development and expansion over other methods of enterprise.

Not the least important advantage resulting from prudent, honest, and capable management is in preventing state interference beyond the limits of salutary supervision, as before indicated, and in leaving no excuse for state control, which might prove destructive of the highest aims of the legitimate industrial, and deprive it of its greatest potentialities.

CHAPTER VI.

CONCERNING TRUSTS AND CORPORATIONS.

Trusts are transformed into corporations and doing business legally. — How corporations with large aggregations of capital make everything cheaper for consumers and purchasers generally. — Amazing decline in prices and railroad rates, while wages are higher than ever and the number of employés increased. — The power of consolidations and corporations for increasing wealth, national and private, and making everybody more prosperous. — Interesting confession of F. B. Thurber, the *ci-devant* anti-monopolist. — He gives cogent reasons for his change of heart, and shows the great benefits corporations confer upon the people. Farmers and cotton growers more prosperous than ever, and why ? — Coöperation the coming power in the competitive struggle, which will also solve the problem of socialism. — Enough of remedial legislation already provided to give relief in almost any supposable case.

TRUSTS, as such, are virtually things of the past. Those who are fighting them now are merely battling against the wind, for the so-called trusts have nearly all been reorganized as corporations, and as such are now presumably perfectly legal, if they ever were otherwise ; for investigating committees created for the purpose of finding causes or excuses to dismember, dislocate, and otherwise maltreat these institutions, have been thus far powerless to accomplish their purposes. What they have achieved in the way of side issues, I do not know ; but it would be unfortunate if all their arduous labor and patriotic exertions to protect the people from some imaginary foe should have been spent in vain. When now they clutch ferociously at a trust, as Macbeth grappled desperately for the dagger in the air, behold, it has vanished, and become metamorphosed into another thing, called a corporation, which the law expressly allows, and which, instead of being in restraint of trade, has been wisely designed for the promotion of prosperity and general business, in which the entire community will share ; and instead, therefore, of the trust being " against public policy,' the corporation is right in the line of that policy, and calcu-lated to confer the greatest good on the greatest number.

These important changes in the programmes of the trusts might wisely have been discovered before the special committee of New York was appointed on this subject, thus saving money to the treasury of this State ; but that is a question between the people and their representatives.   If the former want informa-tion in this expensive manner and are willing to be taxed to pay for it, that is their right; but I cannot help thinking that i we had the Swiss referendum, and the people were fully in-formed thereby as to what their money was being spent for they would be likely to object.

In the formation of a corporation men have a right to com-bine or unite their capital, skill, knowledge, and experience fo the purpose of engaging in the manufacture or sale of any article of commerce that the community may require, and which i not injurious to the health, happiness, and general comfort o the people.   These business institutions may be organized in any State, without violating the law or infringing the rights, o any citizen.   There need be no conspiracy about the operation unless the parties to the agreement prefer plotting and doing things in secret which can just as well be transacted openly but it is hardly likely that Catilines would be found in grea abundance among men whose chief desire is to form a kind o partnership for doing a legitimate business.

As a matter of fact and of history, the combinations called " trusts," wherever backed by large capital, expert skill, and great business ability, have conferred material benefit on the community at large and almost invariably insured the promo-tion of prosperity on a durable basis.   They have furnished the people with many of the commodities of civilized existence a much lower prices than formerly, not only without decreasing the wages of labor, but in many instances increasing them, and eventually extending the field for a larger number of employés

Sugar, india-rubber goods, tobacco, leather, and a grea

variety of other commodities are cheaper than at any former period of the country's existence, and wages are higher here to-day than ever they have been except in war times; in fact, almost double those paid in any other country.

As long as these corporations, combinations, trusts, or whatever people may choose to call them, furnish the community with goods cheaper than they can be obtained elsewhere, and do so within the lines of the law, they not only may be endured, but instead of being a curse to society, as some people seem to regard them, can be safely looked upon as a great blessing. It may happen that a few people will at first be incommoded by their methods of doing business, but it is difficult to effect any change or improvement for the good of the many which will not cause temporary inconvenience, and, in some instances, suffering, to a few.

Now, it is easy to discern that the young and ambitious man with moderate or perhaps small capital who aspires to go into business for himself finds his way barred by these corporations. He cannot compete with them. The only resource for young men of some capital who contemplate business careers is to get together and form combinations of their own. Nothing can compete successfully with combinations except new combinations, and these will put new life and energy into the general coöperative movement.

Coöperation needs no socialistic impetus. It can start on the present foundation which civilization, however imperfect thus far, has laid, and go on building up with the best materials it can command. Brain is as important as capital, and those who serve the people best will win. If, then, secure in their monopoly, their service deteriorates, new rivals will not be lacking to displace them. This point is generally overlooked by those who pose as anti-monopolists: that when the so-called monopoly begins to advance the price, it immediately invites competition for which the brains and the capital will be ready as soon as the profits of the business are large enough to arouse cupidity.

Of course the corporations already in the field, composed of a few members, or which combine now or shall combine in the future with comparatively few members, have some advantage over the new coöperationists with presumably smaller capital; but it has been demonstrated in Great Britain that such coöperation can be made to compete with most of the big moneyed concerns in existence.

Similar conditions prevail in farming as those adverted to in the case of corporations. A young man going West would be foolish if he undertook alone to cope with established methods. He would find at the end of his first harvest that the sale of his crops had not come near to covering the expense of production, and probably that the very necessities which the farm and the garden had supplied to his own table had cost him about twice the amount for which he could have bought them in the next market town. The mammoth appliances made necessary by the latest inventions in the art of agriculture have rendered individual enterprise with small capital almost futile, and such attempts at competition ridiculous. Without the means of keeping abreast of the times in the art of invention and being able to procure the latest labor-saving machinery, competition is out of the question in farming as in many other pursuits. So the advice of Horace Greeley, " Go West, young man," has no longer the significance it possessed when that veteran journalist and philosopher was in the habit of imparting it.

Railroads afford the most conspicuous example of the formation of big corporations with which no individual power can compete ; and even where governments in Europe have tried to compete they have failed to make money. It is to be hoped that the experiment will never be tried here, as there is no necessity for taxing the people to invest their money in enterprises that would be almost certain to leave the taxation a permanent burden on the country.

One of the most significant examples of change of heart as to the morale of railroad corporations and combinations was afforded in the testimony of Mr. F. B. Thurber before the Lexow committee. About a dozen years ago he was a leader among anti-monopolists, and spent about $100,000 in printer's ink paper, and otherwise, in addition to much valuable time in opposing trusts, monopolies, combinations, and corporations. After the experiment had cost him a vast deal, he discovered that many of the combinations which he had been so strenuously opposing, while working in their own selfish interests, were also doing great work for the benefit of the whole community. They had builded much better than either they or Mr. Thurber knew, though their building was all the result of efforts for self-aggrandizement.

This is an important illustration of the principle, that in the aggregation of wealth devoted to the promotion and development of great enterprises for the purpose of enriching its members and with little or no desire on their part to benefit the many, the latter have one of the best guaranties possible that they will be taken care of. Wealth cannot possibly combine and go into any business that will largely increase its returns without conferring much greater benefits upon the community than if the wealth in question had remained in its isolated fragments where it would in all probability have been spent without any extensive distribution.

The aggregate is likely to be directed by chosen brain power, skill, and experience, and is almost certain to increase and multiply by the innate power and conditions of its very existence and employment.

Apropos of this benign and universal principle, which seems to work about as independently of the purposes and desires of interested individuals as the law of gravitation, I here introduce the testimony of Mr. Thurber in corroboration of this and other matters of interest on the point at issue. It must be regarded as disinterested in view of his former attitude, and he is a man of great intelligence, well versed in politics and economics, of thorough practical capacity, an expert accountant, and possessed of extraordinary executive ability in business, so that his conclusions, based on his protracted experience and irrefragable statistics, can hardly be erroneous. When on the stand he referred to the fact that the consolidation of railroad organizations was the most conspicuous example of the working of the so-called trusts. Explaining the success of this experiment, and the former fears excited by it, Mr. Thurber said : —

"There was a fear in the public mind, in which I shared, that these combinations and consolidations would result in exorbitant rates for transportation and to the detriment of the public interest. What the result has been is shown by the following extract from a report adopted by the National Board of Trade at its annual convention in 1896: ' The average charge for sending a ton of freight one mile on thirteen of the most important railroads in the United States during 1865 was 3.08 cents; in 1870, 1.80 cents; in 1875, 1.36 cents; in 1880, 1.01 cents; in 1885, 0.83 cents; in 1890, 0.77 cents; in 1893, 0.76 cents; in 1894, 0.746 cents, and, in 1895, 0.720 cents. These railroads performed one-third of the entire transportation of 1893, and, from the figures given, it appears that 0.72 cents would pay for as much transportation over their lines in 1895 as could have been obtained for 3.08 cents thirty years earlier.' "

The witness produced a tabular statement showing the influence of the Standard Oil combination on the prices of refined illuminating oils, per gallon, exported from the United States, 1871 to 1896. The prices represent the market value of article at time of exportation : —

1871	25.7
1875	14.1
1880	8.6
1885	8.7
1890	7.4
1895	4.9
1896	6.8

He also produced the following table, showing the variations in the price of sugar for a number of years : —

Average price.	Cents per pound.		
	Centrifugals (raw).	Granulated (refined).	Difference.
1879	7.423	8.785	1.362
1885	5.729	5.441	.712
1887	5.245	6.013	.768
Average 9 years . .	6.807	7.905	1.098
1888	5.749	7.007	1.258
1890	3.451	6.171	.720
1893	3.689	4.842	1.153
1895	3.258	4.140	.882
1896	3.631	4.539	.908
Average 9 years . .	4.291	5.272	.961

On the general principles of aggregation, as he has found them, Mr. Thurber testified : —

" A combination of capital in any line temporarily exacts a liberal profit ; immediately capital flows into that channel, another combination is formed, and competition ensues on a scale and operates with an intensity far beyond anything that is possible on a smaller scale, resulting in the breaking down of the combination and the decline of profits to a minimum. The only trusts which have succeeded for any length of time have been those which have been conducted on a far-sighted basis of moderate margins of profit, relying upon a large turnover, and the economies resulting from the command of large capital intelligently administered. The truth of this is illustrated by innumerable failures in trust organizations, recent illustrations of which are the Strawboard Trust, the Starch Trust, the Wire Nail Trust, and the Steel Trust. There are trusts so-called in nearly every branch of business, and there are good and bad in all, but the good so far predominates that such aggregations of capital should be encouraged accompanied by safeguards against abuses. The only additional safeguards needed are for stockholders and investors, whose interests are often sacrificed through lack of publicity. So far as the interest of consumers is concerned, it is amply protected now ; first, by competition, as I have shown, and, second, by the common law, which, if invoked, will nullify any contract in restraint of trade, and under existing statutes any unreasonable combination is subject to indictment for conspiracy.

"The popular hostility to trusts is due principally to lack of knowledge of their economic effects, and these are gradually becoming better known. There were just enough abuses attending them to give an excuse for sensational journalistic denunciation, and this has caused undue prejudice. A great politico-economic question like this should be considered dispassionately and all sides of it carefully investigated before conclusions are reached. The result of my many years' study of it has been to modify materially the views I entertained in the beginning.

"While within the limits of a hearing like this it is impossible to discuss exhaustively all the varying phases of so large a subject, I have endeavored to present to your committee the thoughts which have come to me in a somewhat extended observation and study of the phenomena attending the great economic revolution now in process of development, with the hope that they may have suggested some points which are worthy of further consideration and which may aid your committee in arriving at wise conclusions."

Senator Lexow wished to know whether the witness favored legislative supervision of prices. In answer to questions, Mr. Thurber said that he believed that competition against the American Sugar Company was increasing and would continue to increase.

Mr. Thurber did some sums in arithmetic to show that the price of granulated sugar was 6.77 cents per pound for five years preceding the Trust, and for the first five years subsequent it was 5.97.

"Do not the large dividends," asked the Assemblyman Mazet, "prove that the consumer does not get the whole benefit?"

"Certainly," was the reply.

"In my own business," he said, "I would never again incorporate if it could be carried on individually." He admitted that speculation in stocks was possible when they were listed, but added that thousands of corporations did not list their stocks. He cited the Standard Oil Company as a conspicuous example of a company whose stock was not used for speculation.

One of the most important points in the testimony of Mr. Searles, the Secretary of the American Sugar Refining Company, in favor of the plan of combination, was that which he gave regarding the way in which consumers were benefited by the competition of the company against London speculators. He was very positive as to the evil arising from the attempt of legislation to drive capital from the State, and contended that combinations were more helpful than injurious to the interests of labor. He said : —

"Our prices are controlled largely by the London market, which is distinctly a speculative market. The speculators there speculate against the needs of the world. They say that the American Sugar Refining Company will have to have so much sugar. We will hold this sugar until we make them pay our price. This is speculation against our country's need for the commodity. Now, with our vast capital, we have been able to go to other markets ; we have been able to go to the uttermost parts of the earth, and to purchase our supply before it got into the hands of this speculative market. In that way we have time and time again beaten that market out, and the price of sugar has thus been kept low. If in place of this great combination of ours, this aggregation of capital, there had been fifteen or twenty smaller concerns, no one of them would have been able to go to the lengths that we were able to go, and they would all have been held up by the London speculators. This is one of the most important of the benefits that the consumer has received."

He was asked whether he thought that his organization was a philanthropic organization, and answered : —

"I have distinctly stated to you that we are in no wise a philanthropic organization. We are an organization in business for the purpose of making money. We find that the greatest profit is in the reduction of the price of our commodity to the lowest possible point, because that very largely increases the consumption. Where we make less a pound we make more pounds and more profit. In telling you the advantages of this combination, however, I have omitted to tell you one of the most important things of all — that is, the value of the combination of technical knowledge and the ability of the people who conducted the business when it was cut up. At the time that the trust was organized each concern had appliances that were considered secret. All of them were of considerable value. When the trust was organized, and the heads of the various concerns came together, all of these valuable appliances were combined, and their use was extended to all the plants. There was a combination of all the knowledge and the technical skill, and it was all utilized for the common good."

When asked if combinations of capital made labor suffer, he replied : —

"They certainly do not. There is a law, let me tell you, sir, higher than the State of New York. That is the law of supply and demand. No trust has ever been yet organized, no corporation has ever been created, and there never has been any combination of capital of any sort big enough to violate that law. As I told you, hundreds of millions of dollars are in New York waiting to be put into industrial pursuits ; but if all the hundreds of millions were put in one industry, the violation of the law of supply and demand would bring about the destruction of all the wealth. The consumer is amply protected by the operation of this law, just as the combination of capital is held in check by it."

I think the best and strongest side of the so-called " trusts " is very ably and clearly stated in these two citations. It may be said that Mr. Searles is an interested party, but the same criticism will not hold good in the case of Mr. Thurber ; for while admitting the success of the principle of combination and its soundness in theory, he still seems to adhere inwardly to his old love of individual independence in doing business. This would seem to amount to the fact that he does not love his share of the combination profits less, but his individuality more, and does not in any respect shake the force of his opinion and arguments in favor of the combination scheme of doing business.

The prices to which the products of these corporations have been reduced in a comparatively short time, leave the opponents of the consolidation methods without any solid ground to stand upon. The chief argument used from time immemorial has been the danger of the corporations charging exorbitant prices when they are able to control the situation ; but except in a few isolated instances, which are the exceptions that only prove the rule, they do not succeed in controlling the situation, and the foregoing statistics of constantly declining prices are the best answers to all such objections and fallacious arguments. Would any of the objectors to railroad consolidation wish to go back thirty years and pay three cents per ton per mile instead of three quarters of a cent, for the sake of having the corporation system changed into the old plan of individual ownership and competition? To state this question clearly is to answer it. Would anybody, except a few people on Staten Island, who have been born there, lived to a ripe old age, and expect to die there, as some of their ancestors have done, without ever seeing New York, agree to go back to the old passenger rates, with all the inconvenience attending the system? No. People who are in the habit of using railroads do not wish to go back to the conditions which prevailed thirty years ago, and which, without corporations, would doubtless prevail still to a very considerable degree. People in general, in all lines of business, are better off now than then. If the changes at first threw some out of employment, the improvement and extension in almost every sphere of human energy and industry have ultimately given employment to many times more than suffered any deprivation from the change which brought general prosperity.

Some people, it is true, may have suffered temporarily from this very prosperity, which included in its capacious scope the cheapening of all products by improved machinery. The farmers have occasionally been complaining as sufferers from this cause, and under the bad advice of selfish politicians and ignorant legislators have been instrumental in causing much mischief and seriously retarding the growth and advancement of some of the western and northwestern States ; but the malcontents, in this province of industry, are now reduced to a few impotent and harmless grumblers, who have not been able to take advantage of the progress and discovery of the age, and think that the march of intellect and invention should wait until they get sufficiently animated to join the procession. Such processions, however, do not wait on laggards. They are on forced marches to wider and more promising fields of discovery, and the laggards must take care of themselves as best they can, or suffer the consequences. Surely the farmer is better off to-day with wheat 70 cents a bushel in Chicago than he or his predecessor was during the period prior to the war, say from 1855 to 1860 inclusive, when the average price for six years was $1.69, and the highest in 1855, $2.43½. When he takes into account the reduction in transportation charges, the facilities for much larger production, and the cheaper rates at which he can buy everything he needs (under a Republican administration, at least), he is in a much better position than his father or his grandfather was in ante-bellum times when, not "George IV. was king," but General Jackson; or at more recent dates which we could name. Farmers are better off and more independent, viewed as a confraternity or brotherhood, than any other secular denomination of our citizens; and this applies, of course, in especial degree to those who have kept abreast of the times in making use of modern inventions.

Let us take a cursory glance at the cotton planter, for instance. He is better off now than when "cotton was king." Cotton was formerly sold at 9 to 10 cents a pound. In 1833–1842 inclusive, the average price was 12 cents; in 1843–1846, it fell to 6½, but again, in 1855–1860, it rose to 10½. Now it is around 6½ and 7 cents, and occasionally higher or lower. But the immense increase in production through machinery, and the utilization of portions of the product that were formerly discarded as refuse, such as cottonseed oil, coke, etc., by which means the producer is enabled to realize about a cent and a half per pound, brings the net return to the producer up to about the old standard.

It seems to me, so far as the corporations are concerned with the investigating committees of this State, that the latter are too zealous in explaining with exactitude the letter rather than the spirit of the law.   Section 7, relating to "combinations," for instance, reads as follows : —

" No stock corporation shall combine with any other corporation or person for the creation of a monopoly or the unlawful restraint of trade or for the prevention of competition in any necessary of life."

There is a foot-note to this section in the statutes which reads thus : —

" This section is not intended to prevent the consolidation of corporations engaged in the same business.

" Cameron *v.* N. Y. & M. V. Water Company, 62 Hun., 269.

" 16 N. Y. Supp., 757.

" 42 N. Y. St. Rep., 912."

Now, the sugar corporation and others similarly organized contend that they have rendered full compliance with the terms of this section and in accordance with the decisions herein cited.   They allege that the field is open for competition, and show, as in the case of the London speculators in sugar and the perpetual formation of competing sugar corporations, that they themselves do not control the trade, and that, so far from aiming at higher prices, they have consistently held to the principle in theory and demonstrated it in practice that they have been constantly aiming at and actually reaching lower prices, and that in the success of this operation they have found their highest profits.

Now, where do the objections come in, if these conclusions are demonstrable?   It is for the reader to see whether the so-called trusts or the investigators have made out their case.   I have presented their best arguments as plainly as I know how, and I leave the inference to the reader.

One thing appears pretty clear.   There is no wrong which these corporations are capable of inflicting for which either the common or the statute law, or both, do not provide a remedy, a sufficiency of the latter for this purpose being already on the statute books.   Then why require more laws until these are tried and found wanting?

CHAPTER VII.

THE ART OF MAKING AND SAVING MONEY.[1]

Numerous opportunities for making money. — How to embrace them, and
how to begin the work of accumulation. — It is easier to make than to
save money. — The small beginnings of prominent millionaires, and how
they made their fortunes. — Industry, perseverance, honesty, and thrift
must be associated with the methods of all who aspire to success in life.
— Necessity has been the great stimulus in the eminent examples here
cited. — Prudence, forethought, and sage advice required for successful
investment. — Begin right, early in life.

IT does not require a great genius to make money. The
accumulation of wealth is, after all, an easy matter. It
does not require education, breeding, or gentle manners, and
perhaps even less than people imagine has luck anything to do
with it. Any man or woman may become wealthy, if he or she
begins aright. The opportunities for gathering the nimble
dollar are very numerous in this country. But there are certain fundamental rules that must be observed.

The first step to acquiring a fortune lies in hard work. I
could give you no better advice than that given by Poor Rich-
ard : " Save something each day, no matter how little you earn."
Cultivate thrifty habits. Make your toil count for all that you
can. Always save some portion of your wages, and then be on
the alert for investment. If you do this wisely, your money
will begin to accumulate, double, treble, and in a few years,
perhaps, you may be a millionaire.

The beginning is the most difficult. Lay a good foundation
for your fortune. Be brave, be generous, be helpful, be honest,
do not overwork, keep in good health, cultivate your mind, be

[1] This chapter was published originally in an article in the *Ladies' Home
Journal.*

pure, and to these add thrift, and you need not fear. You cannot fail.

I would say to all fathers and mothers, teach your children the value of money. When they are old enough, make them understand the worth of a penny. From the child's savings-bank in the play-room to the millionaire's bank account is not a long step. It is a short and easy span.

Keep a bank account.

When you have saved one hundred, or two hundred, or five hundred dollars, look about for a good investment. Do not take up this or that scheme at a venture, but examine it carefully, and if you see your way clear, put your money into it. Real estate is usually a good investment. More money has been made in real estate than you could estimate in a day. A first mortgage is, in nine cases out of ten, safe. But take advice on the subject before you invest. Go to some good conservative man and get his views. I should advise the same course if you should put your money in stocks or bonds, or railway shares. In fact, I should urge, before you invest a penny, that you get the best counsel on the subject to aid you in taking the right course.

If your first investment prospers, by careful management, and by always being on the alert, you can increase your fortune by reinvesting your profits.

A man who had only a few hundred dollars left out of a fortune, called one day at a banking house and asked to see the manager, who was a man of conservative mind and fully acquainted with the best and most profitable investments. Throwing down his roll of bank notes, he said : " Invest this for me. Use your pleasure with it. I'm going to the country for the remainder of the summer. I will leave my address with you, and you can let me know what you do with it." The man walked out, and was not seen again for many months. His money was judiciously invested on his carte blanche order, and began to accumulate. The house duly informed him, according to its business methods, of his good luck, but nothing was heard from him for some time. Some months afterward he presented himself at the banking-house, rosy health beaming in his face, well dressed and portly. The manager failed to recognize him at first, but when his memory was refreshed he recalled the circumstances of the case. This was an example of a man who more than doubled his savings by simply taking the advice of an experienced and reliable man. And this is not an exceptional case.

How did Samuel J. Tilden attain his elevated position and immense fortune? Simply by the exercise of thrift and industry, together with a certain degree of common sense; added to the capacity for taking advantage of the chances thrown in his way, and his cleverness in turning them to the best account.

It will not do for any one to sit down and wait for the coming of wealth and fortune. Industry, persevering and untiring, is essential to the accumulation of money. I have myself some little knowledge of the toil attendant upon the amassing of wealth, and I have the highest respect and sympathy for the man who, in the face of adverse circumstances, turns his pennies into dollars, and his dollars into millions.

The life of Commodore Vanderbilt affords singular scope for reflection on the immense possibility of a great business capacity to amass a great fortune in a few years, especially in this country. From being the possessor of a row-boat on New York Bay, he rose in sixty years to be the possessor of $90,000,000. William H. Vanderbilt, his son, obtained $75,000,000 of this, and largely increased the fortune before his death.

It has been truly said that any fool can make money, but it takes a wise man to keep it. William H. Vanderbilt's ability was signally displayed in keeping intact this great fortune, besides adding as much more to it. I make special mention of Mr. Vanderbilt because he was not a speculator, in the true sense of that term. He was, first and for all time, an investor. And every man in this great Republic has the privilege of walking in his footsteps.

Collis P. Huntington came to New York when a boy of fifteen, without a penny. His father was a farmer and small manufacturer. The youth early showed great shrewdness in business, and unlimited energy and resolution.   But success is not usually attained without long and persistent effort, and this Mr. Huntington found to be the case.   After years of hard work his fortune was made, and now he is worth about $30,000,000. He is still, however, a hard worker, and employs, directly or indirectly, thirty thousand men.

Leland Stanford received an academical education and commenced the study and practice of law.   At twenty-eight years of age, a fire wiped out his law library and other property, which led him to the West in search of better fortunes.   Here his native shrewdness and energy asserted itself, and soon the dollars began to multiply.   When he died he was worth from $25,000,000 to $30,000,000.

Darius O. Mills is one of the most notable figures daily seen down town in New York.   He was born in a small town on the Hudson River some sixty years ago, and began life in very humble circumstances.   His courage was equal to that of a Richelieu, and his caution, conservatism, energy, and industry were all fully developed.   He has always been dependent on his own exertions, and has fought his way up in life by sheer force of his own keen intelligence and undaunted enterprise. In the battle of life he has achieved signal success.   He is worth about $40,000,000.

John W. Mackay was born in the humblest circumstances in Dublin, Ireland, some fifty-five years ago.   Coming to this country very early in life, he worked for a time on board ship. During the years that followed, in whatever occupation he engaged, he labored industriously and faithfully.   He saved his money, and watched his opportunity, which so very few people do.   He is now twenty times a millionaire, and all by reason of hard and continuous effort and thrift.

The late James C. Flood was once a poor boy of New York City, and became worth more millions than can be exactly estimated.   He made his money by shrewd and successful investment, and by the exercise of energy, self-reliance, and thrift.   His rise was remarkable, but he showed himself equal to the surprising good fortune which attended his strange career. And that was no small thing. It is a great matter to be able to view one's success without any untoward feeling of exultation.

The wealth of the Astors is remarkable for the way it has been kept intact, and for the steady augmentation which is taking place. The elder Astor made a mint of money out of the fur trade, and would have continued in that business, but he found that investment in real estate was vastly more profitable. The family has steadily adhered to this line of investment through four generations.

George Peabody was a poor Massachusetts boy who, by hard industry, rose to be one of the great millionaires of his day. His fortune at one time exceeded $10,000,000, and during his lifetime he gave away more than· $7,000,000 to charitable purposes. His millions were acquired by the saving of pennies, and by the exercise of thrift, honesty, and persevering effort.

Alexander T. Stewart, "the merchant prince," amassed his millions by close attention to business and by the aid of shrewd common sense and thrift. He was reputed to be one of the three wealthiest men in the United States, Commodore Vanderbilt and John Jacob Astor being the other two. He left an estate exceeding $25,000,000.

Peter Cooper had a hard time getting an education. He was born in New York, one hundred years ago, and at the age of seventeen was apprenticed to a shoemaker. He tried his hand at several trades, and got together a comfortable fortune of about $6,000,000, through unremitting toil, conscientious devotion to duty, and economical habits.

August Belmont came to New York poor, and lived to be worth millions. Prudence, acuteness, and sagacity were the instruments by which his wealth was accumulated. His successful career is an illustration of the fact that this country affords a fine opportunity for the intelligence, thrift, and industry, not only of native Americans, but of the Republic's adopted citizens.

Cyrus W. Field is another apt illustration. He has been termed a locomotive in trousers. The simile serves to convey an idea of the indefatigable energy of the man. His indomitable resolution and his energy of character placed him high among the distinguished men of the age.

Vice-President Morton received his business training in the dry-goods trade. Then he became a banker. In his youth he had to shift for himself. Necessity is the stimulus that men of real ability require. He amassed his large fortune by tireless effort and the exercise of shrewd common sense.

Russell Sage, as a boy, was employed in a village store. His business aptitude early manifested itself, and in six years he bought out his employer. He is one of the largest capitalists in the country, and all his millions have been rolled up by energy and thrift.

John Wanamaker, Chauncey M. Depew, James M. Brown, Anthony Drexel, Moses Taylor, George W. Childs, J. Pierpont Morgan, and a host of others, are men who have fought their way to prominence and affluence by sheer force of integrity, pluck, intelligence, and industry.

The lives of all the men mentioned in this chapter are instances of what can be attained by any boy or man in America. They are eloquent testimony of the truth that industry, perseverance, honesty, and thrift can accomplish anything. A man who is wise, careful, and conservative, energetic, persevering, and tireless, need have no fear of his future. But there is one other thing. He must have a steady head, one that can weather the rough sea of reverses, from which no life is altogether free, and one that will not become too big when success attends his efforts.

Keep out of the way of speculators. Take your money, whether it be much or little, to one whose reputation will insure you good counsel. Invest your money where the principal is safe, and you will get along.

But do not forget the acorns. See that you begin aright early in life. Save your money with regularity. By so doing, you will more than save your money ; you will make money.

CHAPTER VIII.

BUSINESS EDUCATION.

How the business prospects of young men of the present day compare with those of twenty-five or fifty years ago. — A much better start in life possible now than then, as proved by historical facts. — The young man of to-day as compared with his grandfather at the same age. — How millionaires of old were made, and how young men now want to become millionaires by jumping over the intermediary steps and omitting the hard work. — Certain delusions about business success criticised and some cordial advice vouchsafed. — Opinions old and new on college and classical education and the value thereof in a business career. — Macaulay's views.

THE question is frequently put to me: "Do you think there are as good chances now for young men to make their way in life and for some of them to become wealthy, as in the past, say from a quarter to half a century ago?"

Yes, I should unhesitatingly answer, the opportunities are quite as favorable, and in many instances much more so; but as to the young men themselves, that is the question. In fact, the start in life for a young man fifteen years of age is much easier now than it was then. For instance, the parents of such a youth who were intent upon getting him a start in an office in former times were obliged in most instances to pay fifty dollars the first year for the privilege. At the end of the second year he received fifty dollars, and fifty dollars advance for every year afterward until the end of his fifth year, which completed his preliminary business education, or rather his apprenticeship.

Then, of course, he was employed according to his value as estimated by his ability and the use which he had made of his five years' experience. Our young man of the present day enjoys the distinction of entering upon business without any idea of apprenticeship, and instead of his parents having to advance any money to his employer, the latter gives him three dollars a week to start with, and before he has spent two years at the business he may — very often unwisely — strike for seven, ten, or perhaps fifteen dollars a week, in many instances. These aspirations would never have entered the head of his grandfather before he had attained his majority and cast his first vote, while he never knew the taste of tobacco, much less thought of "pooling for drinks," as many of the young office boys do now. It was not from such young men as these, but from the training of half a century ago, that the old millionaires who are now the envy of our young men, were made.

But the young men of our time want to get wealthy suddenly. They want to reach the goal of their ambition by some imaginary rapid-transit route, and to escape the toil and patient waiting to which their forefathers were subject.

Science, it is true, has made rapid strides since the old fellows laid the foundation of their large fortunes, but in all its discoveries science has never yet found the method of dispensing with toil of both brain and muscle in the incipient stages of accumulating wealth.

The few who are born to wealth hardly need to be considered. The accumulators among those are comparatively few, — the Vanderbilts, the Goulds, the Astors, and a few others in the Western world being conspicuous exceptions to the general rule of squandering rather than augmenting the wealth left by the hard-working and humble ancestors. In Europe, the Rothschilds and the Barings are prominent exceptions. They, too, made more of what was left them, but, in the majority of instances, the proverbial wings seem to attach themselves magically to the hardest earned accumulations. Most frequently, before the third generation has enjoyed its share, and often sooner, they are recklessly distributed to the millions.

This law of distribution affords one of the most remarkable examples of the irony of fate, manifesting its workings and results by inscrutable methods. In the periodical distribution of wealth, the highest order of intelligence rather than the blind happenings of chance would appear to be behind the active and mysterious agencies which carry out what seem in most instances to be the beneficent designs of Providence. No benevolent institution could do the scattering abroad of this surplus wealth in a more general or a more equitable manner, —no, not if all the benevolent institutions in the country should form a grand trust or corporation with the design of engaging in the dissemination of riches.

Many young men, as well as some old ones, are under the delusion that the big fortunes now in existence form mountains in the path of modern individual enterprise, which can never be ascended by the present generation, except by lucky chances in speculation, such being the methods, as they presume, by which these mountains attained their present altitudes. Some of the more foolish ones would like to see these stupendous heights above the surface of general prosperity demolished by terrific and destructive forces, ignorant or unmindful of the fact that they constitute the chief fund from which capital is drawn for the development of all great enterprises and for the advancement of civilization.

It is necessary that people should be admonished of this fact, especially people of a speculative turn of mind, as the delusion when nurtured is liable to lead its possessor into all kinds of excesses where there may be any apparent promise of profit. They must be constantly reminded that these men whose prosperous ventures in speculation about which they have been reading, had long and toilsome uphill work before they were able to approach the big deals in speculation and investment for which they became celebrated. They should read the text with the context. For instance, when they reflect with great avidity on the immense stroke of luck which attended the bold speculations of the eminent sire of the house of Vanderbilt, they should not omit the account of his hardships for a living in all kinds of weather in Staten Island waters in a row-boat, to purchase which he had earned the money by digging and planting, early and late, a potato garden. These young men, however, want to start with the command of fleets bearing argosies to and from every foreign shore, as the Commodore did afterward. But they must go through the old preliminaries, unless they happen to be sons or grandsons of others like him; even then they cannot afford constant, luxurious repose, but must look diligently after the wealth of which they are virtually only the trustees.

The retention and increase of these acquisitions impose a very heavy burden on the mind, which only a few are able to bear without breaking down as Robert Garrett did.

When young men read about Jay Gould having made big deals in Erie and other stocks, and a fortune sometimes at a bound, by getting hold of two or more broken-down railroads, putting them together and making a good one out of them, perhaps they say to themselves, "Go and do likewise." But they find their own commands hard to obey, chiefly because they want to take hold of that million of dollars at once without having a dollar of their own, and when they fail in coming up to this impossible idea, they despair of doing anything. These over sanguine youths might find some consolation, or at least a salutary lesson in humility, by turning back to another scene in the checkered career of Mr. Gould when he was working for low wages in a country grocery store, studying at night the art of surveying, and even in his sleep dreaming of a method of increasing his small earnings by the invention of that famous mouse-trap.

If the youths in question should become envious of old Daniel Drew when they think of the time that he made millions in Erie by his paper-mill, which turned out the certificates of stock faster than Vanderbilt could purchase them with all the money he could command and borrow, they will find a cooling and tranquil influence exercised on the passion of envy when they picture this fortunate man in early life, when he was a drover suffering untold hardships and miseries, driving his cattle from the West over the Alleghany Mountains in the dead of winter, overtaken by snow-storms, and with no covering to shield him from the blizzard.

Instances of ordeals of similar severity in the lives and experience of the greater number of those who have made large fortunes might be cited in sufficient number to swell this volume to several times its purposed dimensions, and all going to show that these men have been nothing but hard-worked helots for the benefit of others, and principally for the benefit and pleasure of posterity, while in their own lives they were constantly subjected to the vilification and abuse of their envious contemporaries.

The wealth-producers in question are in general the unconscious and undesigning instruments, in the economy and design of nature, for human evolution to a higher plane of existence. Without them it would seem that the condition we term civilization would come to a standstill or probably retrograde. As a rule, they are charmingly unconscious of what they are doing, but their works follow them all the same.

Such are still the chances for a young man succeeding in life and making a large fortune ; though, after all, the latter should not be the highest object of human ambition. Success depends, as I have said above, on the young man himself. Of course, circumstances may either favor a man or be very much against him, yet favorable circumstances will avail little or nothing if the individual himself lacks the ability to take advantage of them. If a man has sufficient energy, fixity of purpose, patience, self-denial and self-control, frugality, and economy, he can acquire a competence, or a moderate fortune, except in those rare cases where sickness or misfortune follow him so persistently as to make it impossible ; and this is as true at one period of the world's history as another. It was the case twenty, thirty, forty, fifty years ago, and it is the case now ; and just so it will be fifty years or a century from now. The exercise of the qualities that win fortune will win it in any age.

No young man should ever despair or be discouraged in the pursuit of wealth so long as he retains the full use of his faculties, provided those faculties are up to the average. That is all that is necessary. It does not require a genius to make a fortune. In fact, the rare individuals with genius are not famous in this line with perhaps the exception of Thomas A. Edison and a few others. Geniuses seem to know things by instinct, except the secret of accumulating wealth, and this latter, after all, is a very ordinary faculty, and does not require a man to be more than a fair scholar, as is proven by the lives of some of our greatest fortune-builders. This species of architecture requires only the exercise of ordinary endowments, directed by common sense and a due regard to the first law of nature — self-preservation.

I have described elsewhere to some extent the apparent difficulty presented to individual enterprise on the part of young men emerging into business life when they find opposed to their comparatively small means large aggregates of capital managed by corporations or so-called trusts, and I have suggested the remedy : viz., to adopt the tactics of their competitors. Let such young men get together and form combinations of their own to go into such lines of business as may be suited to their tastes and capacities. There is no limit to the size of possible combinations, and consequently no limit to their possible aggregate means for doing business. The remainder is a question of skill, experience, and enterprise. In large combinations, of course, harmony is all-important. But there is nothing in business that a few people with a few million dollars can do but what a few hundred people with the same number of millions of dollars can do just as well. The same salaries which are paid to the employés in a corporation composed of a few millionaires will afford fair wages to all the capitalists of a coöperative concern, and will help materially in the struggle by enabling them, if necessary, to undersell their competitors. If not pressed, it need not force the competition, but can place the money which might go in that way to the surplus account of the company for further extension and betterments. There are five of these coöperative companies in England, paying almost as large dividends as any of our corporations.

Some eminent authorities differ regarding the best field for youthful enterprise. Dr. Chauncey M. Depew thinks a man has the best chance in a young community, whereas Russell Sage, while he does not attach vital importance to environment, thinks it is better for a young man to remain in a big place, if he happens to be there. For my own part, I think the secret of success lies most in the ability to turn the circumstances of the surroundings to the best account, and the man who has the elements of success in his nature and character need care much less for the place in which his lot may be cast than for the adaptation of his means to the end of success in that place. He centers his whole attention and best efforts on the latter, and does not whine over something that he does not possess. The best evidence that a person can give of his ability to do well in some other place is to succeed where he is. The world in general rejects all suppositions or contingent evidence in forming its opinion of his capacity. It simply looks at the result in the abstract. It has no time for excuses.

If a man's character and ability, for instance, has been put to the test as a financier or an expert in finance, in a position where there was scope for the fullest demonstration of the highest faculties in this field, and he has wholly failed to manifest any such ability, it is useless, and not only useless but ridiculous, to tell the people that he is an accomplished college professor and a mathematician second only to Sir Isaac Newton.

Reviewing briefly the list of successful men, it strikes me that the most brilliant examples made no point of the field of their operations and adventures, and in the majority of cases it would seem that they had little or no choice in the matter. Those who would succeed must cultivate the habit of feeling at home wherever their lot is cast. Emerson in his essay on "Self-Reliance," which every young man should read and every traveler also, makes some signally good remarks on this phase of success and contentment. He says : —

"It is for want of self-culture that the idol of traveling, the idol of Italy, of England, of Egypt, remains for all educated Americans. They who made England, Italy, or Greece venerable in the imagination did so not by rambling around creation as a moth around a lamp, but by sticking fast where they were, like an axis of the earth. I have no churlish objection to the circumnavigation of the globe for the purposes of art, of study, and benevolence, so that the man is first domesticated, or does not go abroad with the hope of finding somewhat greater than he knows. Traveling is a fool's paradise. We owe to our first journeys that place is nothing."

In the spirit of the philosopher of Concord, let young men, and all men, try to imagine that "place is nothing," and that it behooves them to exert their individuality and most vigorous exertions for their best interests, irrespective of place and surroundings. In other words, let them be themselves and put forth their best energies for their own good and profit, while being careful at the same time to respect the rights of others.

It is pertinent to state here that modern girls have a great advantage over the girlhood of their grandmothers. The vocations of the male sex have been thrown open to them, with very little of the old prejudices remaining, and they are enabled to compete with their brothers in almost every walk of life, except that they do not, as a rule, make good speculators, and comparatively few of them, luckily, see any attraction in the stock market.

When referring to this subject in my former book and in various magazine articles, I have spoken of college education and its inadequacy to form the minds of youth for the struggles to be encountered in the arena of practical business life. I find that time and experience are bringing many people over to this opinion who were formerly greatly in favor of college education.

The conversion of college graduates and classical scholars to this view is not by any means a new thing, though some people talk as if it were. It is toward half a century since Lord Macaulay, himself a very distinguished classical scholar, wrote his famous essay on "The London University," in which he showed that the time-honored classical education of that day was, in a large measure, utterly useless in fitting a young man for practical business; and though Macaulay was an admirer of Greek, almost to the point of adoration, he greatly deplored the time that was spent studying that famous tongue, even in the old universities, to the neglect of a thorough training in English and science which would far better qualify a man for the business by which he is to earn his living and make his way in the world.

Many professors and presidents of colleges are convinced of the insufficiency of the existing system, but are shy and slow about confessing that they have been so long on the wrong side ; while some of them have become such an integral part of the system that it would almost be like dislocating an arm or a leg to disturb them in the serenity of their ancient notions. Another reason that comes home to them still closer is that the change would deprive many of them of the means of living. But with most it is mere timidity of declaring any change of opinion that would conflict with the old conservatism, grown hoary under the patronage, protection, and indorsement of the most eminent scholars of centuries.

CHAPTER IX.

FALSE MEN AND METHODS ON THE STREET.

Modern and ancient opinion on this subject compared. — How it manifests itself in Wall Street affairs. — The inherent capacity to resist the evil tendency. — Fortunes that are made by degenerates and regenerates contrasted.

ONE of the popular subjects of the day is the theory of degeneration, which has been imbued with new life by that voluminous and somewhat eccentric author, Max Nordau.

In all that has been lately written, very little has appeared to modify the earliest opinions on this question. The Creator Himself made the discovery of human degeneration at an early period, according to the record of Moses, who told the matter candidly in the following terms : "And God saw that the wickedness of man was great in the earth, and that every imagination of the thoughts of his heart was only evil continually. And it repented the Lord that he made man on the earth, and it grieved him at his heart." Surely there can be no stronger testimony to man's degeneracy than this.

It has been with a deep sense of my own incapacity to cope with the mysteries of this question that I have made several references to it for some years past at the request of certain journalists and newspaper proprietors ; but any opinion, no matter whence it emanates, provided the source is only human, must be of a speculative character.

In Wall Street affairs we have many examples of the degenerates ; but they do not belong to the ranks of the genuine business men, and, such as they are, they seem to be now in a fair way of being expelled from what is known as the Wall Street district. They are, for the most part, simply confidence

men who have not had any Wall Street training or experience, and do not require it, since their game for making money
is entirely outside of, and antagonistic to, genuine Wall Street
methods. Their system is one of misrepresentation and
deliberate lying. They personate Wall Street methods to outsiders, and by this means get people in various parts of the
country to send them money for the ostensible purpose of spec-
ulating and investing in stocks, but the alleged purpose is never
put into operation. The money is pocketed by the confidence
operators, but no stocks are bought in good faith, and fresh
victims are sought through similar false pretenses by advertis-
ing in the Sunday newspapers and by sending circulars offering
large monthly dividends and professing to have a " system " of
speculation that cannot fail. Then there is another class of
more clever swindlers who occasionally give the victim some
chance, with the ultimate design of leading him further on and
bleeding him more copiously.

These are the financial degenerates of our day, often found
in the midst of our honest business life and operations, of
whom we must beware, and concerning whom we wish to warn
people who are ignorant of their deceptive and insinuating
methods.

A feeling of regret cannot always be repressed at the view of
the broken-down merchant, and small, timid, impecunious speculators who frequent the bucket shops, so called, in hope of gain.

The proprietor's game is, on the face, fair enough ; but the
customer is so intent on digging his own pit that he fails to
calculate the chief factor involved. The margin required is
1 per cent., and you pay one eighth commission to come in and
one eighth to go out. Therefore, when you lose a dollar you
lose a whole dollar ; when you win a dollar you collect 75 cents.
The odds of 100 to 75 are thus continuously against you.

Again, the customer goes wholly on guess work. If he were
to toss a copper as to whether to buy or sell, he might be right
something like half the time, but if the odds are 1 to 2 that a
stock will move in a given direction and also 1 to 2 that a
guesser will guess right, the guesser starts in with actual odds

of 4 to 1 against him.   The bucket-shop customer may not be familiar with this element of probabilities, but the mathematical professors lay it down, and Mr. Proctor mentions it in his treatise on gambling, and the prosperity of the bucket shops seems to bear it out as a truth.

In some of these byways of finance you can buy one share. In others, where five shares are the smallest gamble, two, three, sometimes five small speculators will share in a five-share lot. These facts are not stated as evidences of depravity nor as the basis for sneers at honest and laborious poverty ; they only tend to show that where people are unable to dig large holes to bury themselves in they will dig small ones.

A pitfall in the regular stock market is the small margin system.   There are indeed advocates of this system, on the ground that where the market goes against you it is better to lose 1 or 2 per cent. than 5 or 10.   And where a speculator is in close touch with the exchange this may answer.   On the exhaustion of his margin he may re-margin, or may let the stock alone until a proper time comes to buy in again.   But if the speculator has other affairs, this system is eminently a pitfall.   Let him buy into a stock at 75 at 5 per cent. margin, which is the smallest that any reputable broker will accept, even on stop order.   It is quite upon the cards that the said stock will drop to 72, or 71, or 70, within a few hours, or even half hours, and then rally again to cost price or above.   In such a case, with a proper margin he would not be injured ; but with a slim margin he has lost his total investment.

As a matter of fact, men who speculate on small margins, 2 and 3 per cent., acquire reckless and unreasonable habits of dealing, and degenerate into actual gamblers.   They are almost certain to be losers also, because the same odds operate against them that we have seen operating against the bucket-shop players.   Brokers' commissions, one eighth each way, must be paid. On 1 per cent. margins the odds are 100 to 75 ; on 2 per cent., 100 to $87\frac{1}{2}$; on 3 per cent., 100 to 92 ; whereas the operator who puts up 10 per cent. margin has only odds of $2\frac{1}{2}$ per cent. against him, with a fair prospect in any ordinary condition of the market of not being sold out for want of margin. The man who puts up 16 per cent. usually has another 10 per cent. in reserve, which is almost sure to carry him out in the end to a profit.

One of the deepest, most precipitous pitfalls is dug for the unwary by the professional point-giver. King Solomon is reputed as saying in the Book of Proverbs, " Surely in vain is the net spread in the sight of any bird," but the people who slide numerously and with alacrity into the holes dug for them by the givers of points seem to gainsay the wisdom of Solomon.

The point-giver is of Protean build. Sometimes he makes your acquaintance accidentally, as it were. Sometimes he brings a letter of introduction from some person who does not thoroughly know him. Then, again, he advertises. When he advertises it is done in something like the form of one of these announcements, which can be cut by the dozen out of many Sunday newspapers : —

CONFIDENTIAL CLERK to prominent operator knows of good dividend paying stock that will yield good profits. Address Profits, 185, —— office.

A Great Opportunity for making money in stocks. For particulars address Active, box 202, —— office.

A. — WANTED — Party with capital to take advantage of my reliable information on stock market. Address Success, box 24, —— office.

If you address either of these ingenious gentlemen, he will call upon you if he thinks you are worth calling upon, and after some conversation touching the necessity of caution and confidence on both sides, and the superior sources of information enjoyed upon his side, he will tell you to go at once to your broker and buy X, Y, Z shares. That is, unless he has just advised some other person to buy X, Y, Z ; in which case he will earnestly urge you to hasten, without loss of time, to sell X, Y, Z. As for the profits, in all cases he is to have half the net gain, and he leaves it to your honor to let him know what the amount of the gain is.

If ten persons act upon his advice, five will gain and five will lose. The losers he has nothing to do with, he would prefer not to see them; but he has the names of the winners in his memorandum book, and he rarely fails to collect from them. This pitfall looks like a shallow artifice, and it is; but a great many people slide down its sides in the course of any given year. Else how should the professional point-giver flourish as he does, and have so much cash wherewith to advertise in the Sunday newspapers? Among the degenerates that infest Wall Street, that class which has been running at intervals which are known as " discretionary pools " is one of the most atrocious. Their depredations, it would seem, have been most conspicuous among savings banks depositors, to whom they make special appeals in their circulars, showing the profits derivable from their guaranteed two per cent. a month, compared with the small interest paid by the savings banks. These land sharks were making very bold and profitable invasions on the deposits of many savings banks throughout the country when the police raids some time ago put a partial stop to their fraudulent operations; but they are not all dead, and new adventurers of a similar character are springing up every day in all parts of the country.

One of the worst, deepest, most dangerous, and most frequently tumbled into of all pitfalls of Wall Street is dug by operators themselves, and seems to be the result of a weakness of the human mind, which leads it into the practice of taking small profits and large losses.

A speculator puts up 10 per cent. margin and buys X, Y, Z at 75. The shares fall to 74, 73, 72, and so on. Now, if he knows the property to be sound and really valuable, there is no reason why he should relinquish it merely because the market price is lower than it was. On the contrary, if he can afford the cost, it may be policy for him to buy another lot at 70, and even another lot at 65, besides protecting his first purchase.

But suppose he is merely the kind of speculator whose gains proceed from turning a small capital frequently, is it not his most obviously plain course of action to drop his purchase at 73 and take chances of buying in again? Most of us would say, "Yes, by all means." But as a matter of fact he will not drop out until the 10 per cent. margin is exhausted. On the other hand, if X, Y, Z had gone up to 77 or 78 and then shown a tendency to sag off, this same operator would at once have closed the transaction, thus showing a willingness to gain by twos and threes and lose by tens.

An English novelist once wrote : "There are at this moment 10,000 Englishmen wandering homeless and penniless over the continent of Europe because they would not lead trumps at the proper time !" So any well-informed broker can say of his own personal knowledge and experience, "There are thousands of American citizens who are to-day poor because they would not cut short their losses and let their profits run on."

There is also another dangerous pitfall which men dig for themselves ; namely, the belief that because a certain description of shares mounts and soars above previous calculations of the general market, therefore it is desirable to buy into it after it has mounted during a long period of days. This belief is almost universal, and yet it directly contradicts our experience and the laws of nature. We know that the higher the wave gets, the weaker it is at the top, while its base is always strong ; and we also know that whatever goes up has a tendency to descend again, and that the time always comes when the holders of any commercial property, no matter how desirable, prefer money to property.

Still, the majority of outside operators regard the market as strongest when prices are up and weakest when prices are down, and act accordingly ; whereas those who know, base their actions on the firm truth that the market is never so weak as when it is high, and never so strong as when it is low ; being, in fact, like that ancient wrestler who, whenever forced down by his antagonist so that his body touched the ground, immediately received from Mother Earth a redoubled allowance of strength.

Some men are born degenerate, some achieve degeneracy, and some have degeneracy thrust upon them ; and one is likely to meet these three kinds of degeneracy in Wall Street. I think, however, that of all the class, those who achieve degeneracy are in the majority, since " evil communications corrupt good manners." Most men are born with a capacity for doing good, and they are capable of acting an honest, straightforward part in business, if they will only exercise that faculty. Money gained by crooked business methods does not make its possessors prosperous for many generations, seldom even for one ; and I believe, if the statistics on the subject could be fully ascertained, it would be seen that the number who adopt surreptitious means, no matter how well concealed, to succeed in life would show far more failures in their ranks, perhaps ten times more, than those who fail while seeking fortune by honest methods. The fortunes made by degenerates are usually built upon sandy and shifty foundations, while those that are amassed by their opposites, the regenerates, the good, and the true among mankind, are founded upon rock of the most adamantine quality.

CHAPTER X.

PANICS AND THEIR INDICATIONS.

The causes which usually give origin to panics described. — How these great upheavals in business and finance may be partially avoided and their consequences alleviated when they do occur. — Greater elasticity in the methods of banking required to enable the banks to meet emergencies. — These institutions have in recent years done well when not handicapped by law. — They should be permitted to make more liberal use of their reserve to relieve financial distress. — How banks and business men should coöperate in times of impending crisis. — The forecast of the panic of 1893.

MY belief in prophecy generally resolves itself into the fact that there is a great deal of repetition in all history, and by watching the present, storing the mind with a careful knowledge of the past, and collating the facts thus in possession, a pretty good idea of the future may in many instances be premised without any pretensions to supernatural power. When events turn out in accordance with the general tenor of any instance of forecast, that is irrefutable evidence that the reasoning has been practically correct, irrespective of the principle upon which it may be based.

I shall reproduce here the greater portion of an article which I wrote by request and which was published January 13, 1893. In this I stated the conditions which underlie panics, and the deductions were unhappily exemplified in the panic of 1893, which soon began. The article was as follows : —

The query now being asked on all sides, " Will there be a panic in 1893 ? " should impress business men and financiers with the fact that certain peculiarities in the development and trade of the United States render our markets more exposed to peril than those of any other nation, and make the question of panics a peculiarly American one, as we shall see.

The financial crises known as panics are commonly spoken of as freaks of the markets due to antecedent reckless speculation; as being controlled in their progress by the acts of men and banks who have lost their senses, but above all as being easily prevented, and as easily cured when they happen. These are the notions of mere surface observers. They may be in a measure true when applied to the markets of some of the older countries, whose business moves in long-established grooves and embraces but little of the risk attendant on new enterprises. In France and Germany, for example, the hazards of business are almost entirely confined to the accidents of political events, and such nations are exempt from panics due to purely commercial causes. Panics in the United States are due principally to causes from which European countries are exempt.

We are still a nation of pioneers. Nearly fifteen millions of people are added to our population every ten years. This new population has to subdue new territory. New lands have to be cleared, new mines opened, new railroads built, new banks created, new industries established, and new corporations founded. These new ventures are necessarily in a measure experimental. Some of them fail utterly while others succeed magnificently. They require large outlays of capital in advance of obtainable results. In many cases these outlays are met by borrowing, the loan being secured by liens upon the uncertain undertakings, and therefore lacking the stability of value that attaches to well-developed investments. We have thus a ceaseless stream of new issues of stocks, mortgages, and commercial paper, comprising a large amount of outstanding obligations, liable, from the uncertainty of their basis, to wide fluctuations in value. Then we have also a large amount of obligations issued against enterprises, which, though not properly new, are still in an experimental stage, and the value of which is, therefore, subject to wide fluctuations. Issues of this character naturally appeal to the adventurous instincts of our people and cause activity in speculation.

The action of commerce, like the motion of the sea or of the

atmosphere, follows an undulatory line.   First comes an ascend-
ing wave of activity and rising prices ; next, when prices have
risen to a point that checks demand, comes a period of hesitation and caution ; then contraction by lenders and discount-
ers, and then a movement, in which holders simultaneously
endeavor to realize, thereby accelerating a general fall in
prices.   Credit thereupon becomes more sensitive and is contracted ; transactions are diminished ; losses are incurred
through the depreciation of property, and finally the ordeal
becomes so severe to the debtor class that forcible liquidation
has to be adopted, and insolvent firms and institutions must be
wound up.   This process is a periodical experience in every
country, and the sharpness of the crisis that attends it depends
chiefly on the steadiness and conservatism of the business
methods in each community affected.

In times of crisis, the obligations of the enterprises so numerous in this country suffer instantly from the uncertainty about
their intrinsic value.   Holders are anxious to get rid of them ;
banks which have advanced money on them call in their advances, and they become virtually unavailable assets.   Every
panic that has happened since the beginning of the era of railroads in this country has been intensified many fold by the
sudden shrinkage in the value of this class of assets, and it is
precisely here that the aggravation and the chief danger of an
American panic centers.   Risks and panics are inseparable
from our vast pioneering enterprise, and all we can hope is
that they may diminish in severity in proportion as our older
and more consolidated interests afford an increasing power of
resistance to their operation.   I am disposed to think that in
the future the counteraction from this source will be much
more effective than it has been in the past.   The accumulation
of financial resource available for market purposes at our
monetary centers is increasing at a very rapid rate.   Evidence of this is seen in the fact that while the magnitude of
our corporate undertakings is augmenting every year, we are
also every year becoming less dependent on the money markets of Europe, and our large corporate loans are now made

principally at home. These accumulations impart elasticity to our financial system and serve as a buffer against great financial disturbances.

I cannot refrain from expressing the opinion that there are permitted to exist in this country conditions which needlessly aggravate the perils of financial upheavals, when they occur. In every panic much depends upon the prudence and self-control of the money-lenders. If they lose their heads, and indiscriminately refuse to lend, or lend only to the few unquestionably strong borrowers, the worst forms of panic ensue. If, on the contrary, they accommodate to the fullest extent of their ability the larger class of reasonably safe borrowers, then the latter may be relied upon to protect those whom the banks reject, and thus the mischief may be kept within some bounds. Everything depends upon anxiety being held in check by an assurance that deserving debtors will be protected. This is tantamount to saying that all depends on the calmness and wisdom of the banks. They may easily mitigate or aggravate the severity of the crisis according as they are prudently liberal or blindly selfish. It is, perhaps, safe to say that the banks never do all they may, but the banks of New York must be credited with having shown great sagacity in troubles of this kind within the last twenty-five years. They have largely succeeded in combining self-protection with the protection of their customers, and the precedents they have established will go far toward breaking the force of any further panic.

Unfortunately the law imposes restraints upon the national banks which seriously interfere with the wise discretion of those institutions. As the law now stands, the banks are liable to be wound up at the order of the government if they permit their lawful money reserves to fall below 25 per cent. of their legal deposits. This establishes a " dead line " which is so dreaded when approached that it becomes almost a panic line. When that limit is reached, the banks are compelled to contract their loans, and, under certain conditions, the contraction of loans means forcible liquidation without regard to consequences. Thus the very contrivance designed to protect the banks becomes a source of serious danger to their customers and therefore to the banks themselves ; and in times of monetary pressure it is the most direct provocative of panic. Were the banks allowed to use their reserves under such circumstances, a fund would be provided for mitigating the force of the crisis and the danger might be gradually tided over ; but as it is, the banks can do little or nothing to avert a panic ; on the contrary, the law compels them to take a course which precipitates it ; and when the crash has come, they have to disregard the law and do what they can to repair the catastrophe that a preposterous enactment has helped to bring about. This is one of not a few restrictions upon our national banks which should be stricken from the statute book.

It was chiefly due to the prompt and liberal policy of the banks that the panic of 1884 was so short lived and so narrowly circumscribed. The results of the timely action taken by the managers of these institutions in that crisis prove that panics can be arrested by proper methods, and that quick and determined action is indispensable in the incipient stage of the emergency. If bank presidents could be relied on by the business community to act promptly and in unison with the business men, as they did in this instance, threatened panics need have but little terror for the people who now live in constant dread lest an outburst of business disaster may be sprung upon them at any time in any decade. In the early history of panics, bank managers, as a rule, have acted without system, without judgment, and almost entirely without any well-defined plan of action. There has been an astonishing lack of vigor in their methods and purposes.

If the panic of 1873 had received the same vigorous treatment at its beginning as that of 1884, it could just as easily have been checked as the latter, and the entire country would have been saved in a great measure from the depressing effects of that serious collapse and its attendant disasters, which caused a state of general prostration for five or six years succeeding. These years, from a business standpoint, appear as a blank in the history of the country's progress. It was the disturbing element of panic makers, who generally constitute one of the most potent factors of disruption to be dealt with in seasons of business trouble, that caused the greater part of the mischief at the time of Jay Cooke's failure in 1873. The holders of Northern Pacific bonds, finding then that the security was no longer equal to that of government bonds (as they had been taught to believe), but was apparently worthless, became panic stricken at their losses, and were all transformed into panic makers, infusing the spirit of distrust into every one with whom they came into contact, until, like a fatal virus, their terror inoculated the whole country, spreading business disaster far and wide.

It is to be hoped that in future legislation on currency reform, ample provision against the emergencies liable to arise out of panics will be regarded as of the very highest importance.

Referring to my own forecast of the panic of 1893, I think I may afford to lay modesty aside in view of the value of the facts.

The following communications were written a few months prior to the outbreak. Then was the calm before the storm, but the rumblings of distant thunder were occasionally heard, for hearing which I do not take any special credit to myself or pretend that I have sharper ears than other people. There was a host of bankers and brokers in Wall Street and elsewhere who heard those rumblings as well as myself, but only a few of them spoke out their minds freely, and fewer still took it upon themselves to caution and advise those at the helm of state. The storm burst at length in tremendous fury on the heads of all the people of the nation, but directed its most destructive bolts against the larger financial centers, of which Wall Street, of course, was the chief.

I had taken especial pains at the time to warn the Treasury through President Cleveland regarding the impending danger, and to suggest how it might be averted. I wrote to him as follows : —

"NEW YORK, March 28, 1893.

"MR. PRESIDENT : — In view of the fact that the United States Treasury gold balance is now so low, while the gold balance in the banks is in a far more satisfactory condition, it would appear advantageous to strengthen the Treasury gold balance through a negotiation of bonds. The banks, I find in a canvass I have made amongst many of the large ones, are perfectly willing to part with $25,000,000 of their gold for bonds, as they are anxious to do all in their power to uphold the government credit. Such a negotiation as this could be better effected now than later on, and its moral influence would be to restore confidence, now on the wane, in the ability of the government to continue gold payments.

"Respectfully yours,

"HENRY CLEWS."

The time at which this letter is dated was very opportune for obtaining enough of gold through the channels indicated therein, and a loan of twenty-five millions then would have been more efficacious in allaying the excitement and impeding t.   :niv 'han four or five times that amount a few months later ; and, moreover, one hundred millions could have been more easily obtained then than twenty-five millions at the later date. History will bear me out, I think, as regards the relative conditions of the money market and the borrowing power at these two dates.

Mr. Cleveland, however, did not seem to pay any attention to these suggestions. Why did he not ? Simply because the result of their operation would have been in conflict with his political policy at that time, which was to let things severely alone, so that some pressure might come to teach Congress an " object lesson " which would force it to repeal the silver purchasing clause of the Sherman Law. That law, he seemed to think, was at the root of all the financial evil and distress with which the country was then visibly menaced. The gathering clouds which contained a terrific storm had already begun to darken the horizon and threatened, momentarily, to burst ; and if Mr. Cleveland could have foreseen the fury of that financial gale, I am certain that he would have used the best means at his disposal to weather if not to avert it.

An adherent of Mr. Cleveland has asked me this question : " Do moderate men think Cleveland deliberately and purposely brought on the panic, to teach Congress by an object lesson ? "

I answered : " He said so himself, and took great pride in this theory at the time, on the principle of making a law obnoxious by executing it. He has never said he was sorry for it."

I do not wish the reader to imagine that I think there was any feeling of malevolence in Mr. Cleveland's desire to bring about a panic just as an " object lesson " to Congress, for the purpose of urging that honorable body to repeal the obnoxious clause of the Sherman Silver Act. He had no conception of the baneful results that were inevitable from his more than executive action. He could start the panic, but could not stop it at pleasure. His course of procedure in the matter reminds me of a story that is told about a raw recruit in the English army. On his advent into barracks the first thing that attracted his attention was the cannon, a specimen of which he had never seen before. He was an Irishman. So he said to the comrade to whose care he had been consigned and who explained the nature of the destructive weapon, " I would like to see how she shoots. Will you charge her ? " The comrade consented and put in the ordinary charge of powder, but, when he was about to apply the match to the touchhole, he recollected that there was no ball in the cannon, and that he could not give Pat a full and satisfactory illustration of its power without that necessary adjunct. " Oh, never mind," says Pat ; " what's the use of wasting a ball on a try shot ? I'll put in me head, and you shoot aisy."

So Mr. Cleveland thought he could shoot easy, but the range of the panic was a long distance one, and went far beyond his calculation. While it would be impossible to estimate the numbers of killed and wounded by that shot, it is safe to say that there have been very few, if any, pitched battles in the whole range of ancient and modern history so expensive as Mr. Cleveland's " try shot " at Congress.

PART II.

WALL STREET AND THE GOVERNMENT.

CHAPTER XI.

WASHINGTON DOMINATION IN FINANCE, SPECULATION, AND BUSINESS.

Some inquiry into its nature. — Assumes the complexion of a centralizing bureau of financial information with a censorship attachment. — The attempt of the political power to override the financial, a failure. — All financial roads lead to Wall Street. — New York destined to be the world's center of finance. — Politics cannot rule finance except on a very broad basis. — Some sapient object lessons from the Constitution in their application to statesmanship, politics, and finance. — Justice Story's opinions of the duties of a President in giving information and counsel to Congress. — The immense powers of the President in these matters, and the requisite qualifications to enable him to advise. — His great and varied responsibility. — The " duty of a President " is more than " executive." — A nice distinction between advice and the power of initiating measures in Congress. — The object lesson for the people in the Washington domination, and its issue.

THE Washington domination, which had such a blighting influence on speculation and business interests generally during the greater portion of the last Democratic régime was so potent and peculiar in its nature and results that I think it is entitled to very serious inquiry with regard to its causes. Some of these may be at least surmised, if not demonstrated, by a careful study of our governmental policy during the period of the abnormal conditions which so thoroughly upset the conventional methods of Wall Street.

The humiliation of the spectacle was sad, but it did not seem to strike many of the people in that light. The necessities of the case were all they appeared to regard, and they servilely conformed to them. The power was apparently too strong to be opposed, and the authority too autocratic to be disputed. It seemed very like a manifestation of hypnotic influence on a large scale.

At one time the government assumed the complexion of a centralizing bureau of financial information with a censorship attachment, and though there was no censorship publicly established, yet it was presumable that the news went through a secret sifting process under the surveillance of a senatorial clique before it was given out for general distribution. If you wished to avoid irreparable mistakes, you were obliged to take your cue, humbly, from the seat of government, while you had to be careful to observe the adage, " Least said, soonest mended."

Washington statesmen were at that time more conspicuous in the eyes of the business public, and especially in senatorial circles, than they had ever been before during the history of the Republic. Presumably it may be only a symptom or characteristic of progress ; for I believe that, without close intimacy and contact with Wall Street, it is impossible for the government to exhibit a healthy condition in some of its most important concerns. In fact, if it were cut off from Wall Street, emergencies would be liable to arise almost at any time that would place it in a state of helplessness though not of " innocuous desuetude " ; for if the government were stranded for want of money, the consequence would be appalling to the nation.

It is fairly inferable, and in many instances it has been demonstrated, that government is largely dependent on Wall Street in all financial emergencies, and when the powers at Washington assumed the ascendency, it seemed to the apprehension of acute financiers and old habitués of the Street that the natural order of things had been reversed, and in fact that " the tail was wagging the dog."

It was partly, therefore, through failure of recognizing this dependence of government on the great center of finance and attempting, instead, to exercise a domineering policy through the chicanery of a political clique, that this temporary domination was established. It was eventually a failure, and then the true attitude of the financial power had to be recognized *nolens volens*.

As all roads in the old world were formerly said to lead to Rome, so all financial roads in America must inevitably lead to Wall Street. There is no way but this ; and it is within the range of possibility, I may say probability, that at the end of a similar period in the unexplored future, when the Greater New York buildings shall have covered Long Island, Staten Island, the greater part of New Jersey, and extend, perhaps, even unto the Adirondacks, Wall Street will still maintain its prestige as the great loaning and financial center. Yes, more, — New York may then be the financial center of the world ; for Macaulay's New Zealander will, perhaps, have arrived in the English metropolis long ere that date, and taken his stand on London Bridge to sketch the ruins of St. Paul's.

Owing to the legislative delays in regard to the repeal of the Sherman Silver Law, as well as disappointed expectations regarding an anticipated bond issue that would have brought partial relief if it had been negotiated at an earlier date, people were kept in a highly agitated and nervous condition during the entire summer of 1893. There had been so much weary waiting and worry, and the agony had been so long drawn out, that when the relief came in November, six months too late, it was no relief at all, for the worst had been done.

If Mr. Cleveland had dealt with the subject in a more positive manner in his inaugural address, that might have helped to turn the tide of adversity before its power had become disastrous, but an intense aversion to the silver cranks took possession of his mind and prevented him from taking the much wider view of the situation which the emergency required.

When the President called the special session of Congress on November 1, 1893, he had no idea of the extent to which his " object lesson " would spread before the end of the year, nor of the devastation that would follow it. I will even venture to assert that if the advice given in a bulletin, which I published

about the middle of that August, had been taken by the Administration, the ravages of the then existent panic would have been
neither so extensive nor so pernicious as later developments
showed. The following is a copy of the bulletin : —

"AUGUST 14, 1893.

"The object lesson which was an attack against silver, really
caused the panic, the incentive being to affect legislation so as to
bring about the repeal of the authority of the government to purchase silver. Instead of any attempt being made to stop the panic,
it was permitted to make headway to the point of exhaustion, the
entire country being absolutely covered by it. Senator Hoar recently
said over his signature, that if President Cleveland had declared in
his inaugural address that the full power vested in him should be
used to keep the gold and silver money of the country of equal value,
it would have prevented the panic. I believe that to be true. Or
if, at the time Europe commenced to draw our gold away on account
of a scare which was founded on the fear that we were going to drift
to a silver basis, the President had authorized the sale of only a
moderate amount of United States bonds for gold, his action would
have been accepted both at home and abroad as an evidence that our
government had entered the world's contest for gold. That alone
would have saved us from the panic ; but the President did neither
of these two things, and thus caused an abandonment of all hope of
relief from the administration ; so the panic has had to continue, as
a natural sequence, to the point of exhaustion. The only hope left
is that wise legislative action will come from Congress. It is for that
reason that the assembling of Congress has been so universally
desired. To restore confidence, therefore, is now the task which
that august body has in hand. It has a patriotic work to do, and
party animosities should not be permitted to crop out in any
direction."

Notwithstanding the plentiful advice which came not only
from Senator Hoar and myself, but also from other quarters,
the panic materialized because the Administration did not
recognize the important fact in the healing art, that prevention
is better than cure.

It may be interesting to examine also how far the Administration was in harmony or otherwise with the requirements of the

Constitution on that occasion. The third section of the second article of the Constitution of the United States makes the following provision with regard to the powers of the President. It says : —

" He shall from time to time give to the Congress information of the state of the Union, and recommend to their consideration such measures as he shall judge necessary and expedient. He may on extraordinary occasions convene both Houses, or either of them, and, in case of a disagreement between them, with respect to the time of adjournment, he may adjourn them to such time as he shall think proper. He shall take care that the laws be faithfully executed ; and shall commission all the officers of the United States."

It will be observed by a careful reading of this section that it confers immense powers. The Executive is the sole judge of the expediency of the measures which he may think proper to recommend to Congress. It is understood as a matter of courtesy that he will consult the Cabinet on such occasions, though the section does not say so. The powers which it thus confers were widely conceived and considered by the Fathers, and according to Chief Justice Story were most beneficent in their design. Commenting on the section just quoted, that eminent jurist says : —

" The first part, relative to the President's giving information and recommending measures to Congress, is so consonant with the structure of the executive departments of the colonial and state governments, with the usages and practice of other free governments, with the general convenience of Congress, and with a due share of responsibility on the part of the Executive, that it may well be presumed to be above all real objection. From the nature and duties of the executive department, he must possess more extensive sources of information, as well in regard to domestic as foreign affairs, than can belong to Congress. The true workings of the laws, the defects in the nature or arrangements of the general systems of trade, finance and justice, and the military, naval and civil establishments of the Union, are more readily seen by, and more constantly under the view of the Executive, than they can possibly be of any other department.   There is great wisdom, therefore, in not merely allowing, but in requiring, the President to lay before Congress all facts and information which may assist in their deliberations, and in enabling him at once to point out the evil, and to suggest the remedy.   He is thus justly made responsible, not merely for a due administration of the existing systems, but for due diligence and examination into the means of improving them."

It will thus be seen, by an intelligent reading of the section itself, and a clear conception of Justice Story's remarks thereon, that one of Mr. Cleveland's favorite maxims, "The duty of a President is simply executive," hardly covers the case.   Though he has not the power of initiating measures in Congress, his authority in the way of advice comes so near it that the "middle wall of partition" which divides the two is transparently thin.   Still, it is manifest that the Fathers must have intended to make a very clear distinction between the assertion of the one-man power and the "giving Congress information of the state of the Union," as well as the "recommending such measures as the President might consider expedient."

In his closing remarks on that part of the Constitution which defines the "rights, powers and duties" of the executive department, Justice Story draws the following inferences and conclusions, which are worthy of being preserved in letters of gold : —

"Unless my judgment has been unduly biased, I think it will be found impossible to withhold from this part of the Constitution a tribute of profound respect, if not of the liveliest admiration.   All that seems desirable in order to gratify the hopes, secure the reverence, and sustain the dignity of the nation, is, that it (the executive department) should always be occupied by a man of elevated talents, of ripe virtues, of incorruptible integrity, and of tried patriotism ; one who shall forget his own interests, and remember that he represents not a party, but the whole nation ; one whose fame may be rested with posterity, not upon the false eulogies of favorites, but upon the solid merit of having preserved the glory and enhanced the prosperity of the country."

What a valuable lesson for all who aspire to the presidency is contained in the noble and comprehensive language of the scholarly jurist, whose works shed durable luster on the bench of the United States Supreme Court which he adorned. The criticism of Ben Jonson regarding William Shakespeare, in literature and the drama, may very appropriately be applied to Joseph Story in law, jurisprudence, and ethics. "He wrote not for the age, but for all time."

But to return to the question of Washington domination, as evidenced in the latter years of the Democratic régime. I think I have clearly shown that the assumption of the power which established for a time that domination over financial concerns and Wall Street affairs originated in a false and mistaken notion of both the legislative and administrative functions of a great republic. The experiment in both departments has been a costly one, but it is now perhaps worth more than it cost to the people of this nation, besides being of great benefit to all who read our political history.

CHAPTER XII.

THE CHIEF MAGISTRATE.

Qualifications indispensable for the highest office in the land. — Neither a
towering genius nor an offensive partisan fit for the position. — The ultimate and crucial test of the popularity of a President and his consequent
success, is the material prosperity of the country. — He has to bear the
brunt of bad times, no matter how able and good he may be. — Failure
of Webster, Clay, and Calhoun to reach the goal of their ambition. —
The nation sensitive on a President's errors in finance and currency. —
Parallel between Jackson and Cleveland. — Origin of the National Banking System.

WHEN we pass beyond the requirements cited by Chief
Justice Story, opinions differ as widely as the poles
regarding the requisite qualifications of the man who aspires to
be the Chief Magistrate of this country. Yet there is only one
opinion respecting certain essential qualifications among all rational men, irrespective of politics or previous training.

These essentials are frequently expressed more clearly nega-
tively than positively. For instance, there is a deep-rooted
prejudice against those individuals who for want of a better
name are called geniuses. In the ordinary English dictionary
the word "genius" is defined thus: "Natural endowment,
natural faculty or aptitude of mind for a particular study or
course of life, uncommon powers of intellect, and especially of
inventive combination, a man endowed with such powers,
peculiar character." The word, though Anglicized, is purely
Latin without change of spelling. So, turning to the Latin
dictionary, we find the definition as follows: "Genius, a good
or evil demon attending each man or woman, or on mankind
in general, either to defend or punish them." The word

"demon," spelled "dæmon" in Latin, and in Greek "daimon," simply means a spirit, without designating its quality, but in our modern theology it means an evil spirit.

The common and general acceptation of the term "genius" is a man who can accomplish extraordinary things without appearing to make much effort, and who is sometimes without much education. The genius seems to possess by mysterious innate faculties what but few others can aim at by long and laborious exertion, and a characteristic of the real genius is that his judgment in matters peculiar to himself is generally almost unerring. Hence the ancient Greek theory and the modern Christian doctrine, that there are always two spirits contending for the control of the individual.

It is passing strange, however, that the people of the United States should seem disposed to ignore a genius in their choice of a President, and it is paradoxical also, for the reason that George Washington, the first President, was undoubtedly a genius in the truest sense of the term ; and the five succeeding Presidents, John Adams, Thomas Jefferson, James Madison, James Monroe, and John Quincy Adams, were geniuses of different orders and varieties, but all on a pretty high plane. To John Quincy Adams succeeded General Jackson, and he was a genius of such an extraordinary type and so eccentric that to put him in the same category with the others would play havoc with all the rules of comparison. Without means and without education, by force of his indomitable will and fierce, untamable spirit, he elevated, or rather forced himself, step by step, to a judgeship and then to the presidency. The last step was not so extraordinary as the preceding ones, for, as the hero of New Orleans, Jackson became a popular idol, and the memory of all his savage deeds was cast into oblivion by that overwhelming victory ; while the man who supplied the sinews of war for the achievement and mortgaged his estate to do it is hardly ever mentioned in connection with that glorious and final triumph over British ascendency. Had not James Monroe, then Secretary of War, supplied the cash to equip the expedition, Jackson's heroism would have been ineffective, and Pakenham with his Peninsular veterans would have borne victorious laurels back to England.

After Jackson, the geniuses appear to have stood aside as presidential candidates until Abraham Lincoln loomed up, a giant, and with nothing of education but self-culture. That acquirement was his, however, to a high degree ; and in this he was unlike Jackson, with whom letters were either secondary or ignored — though "Old Hickory" was not blameworthy for not cultivating a capacity and a kind of talent which he never possessed. If he had been the other kind of man, perhaps the battle of New Orleans might have gone the other way ; whereas, if Lincoln had gone to the front and attempted to meet Pickett's charge at Gettysburg, or tried to beleaguer Vicksburg, instead of permitting Grant to do so, slavery in this country might be a recognized institution to-day. But the "daimons" that rule the destiny of war decided matters otherwise, and we can only abide by the results, and in the strength of our national optimism go on our national way rejoicing.

The prejudice, therefore, against the selection of a genius for President would seem to have its origin in the apprehension that he would be likely to do something extraordinary that might embroil the country in war or other trouble, and, not being subject like an ordinary man to the will and disposing power of others, the step for him to a despotism would not be far, as in the case of Napoleon when, after the fashion of Roman generals, he made his election as First Consul of France a stepping-stone to the Empire. A cardinal objection to a genius for most practical purposes is that he is too self-willed. Otherwise he would not be a genius.

There is some reason in this view of the case, but there is another cause at the bottom of the prejudice. The genius would not be likely to tolerate the political oligarchies that feed and exist on the gullibility of the rank and file of the voters. This is probably the chief reason why the strong man is feared in the presidency, while, if he is only a bogus genius and is trying to play the part without the capacity, he is a proper object to inspire alarm in the voters, and the independent suffragists should spurn the charlatan. But so long as "dark horses" are fashionable at conventions, and the secret caucus is the "power behind the throne," it is difficult sometimes to avoid mistakes in this direction. The first half dozen Presidents had no need of caucuses and other modern methods in politics. They had nearly all gained a great reputation as statesmen, with extensive experience both foreign and domestic. They were, most of them, profound scholars, for their times, and though several had been raised in the lap of luxury, they never shirked the very hardest labor and fatigue incident to the duties of the office. In fact, in every office which they had filled prior to the presidency, they had been found to be harder workers than those obliged to toil for a living from their earliest boyhood.

Another qualification for President is that he should not be an "offensive partisan." On this subject George Washington has left on record some of the best counsel to be obtained in all the annals of political wisdom. Speaking of "combinations and associations" organized for party purposes, the first President deplores their tendency to strike at the root of some of the fundamental principles of a stable government. He says : —

"They serve to organize faction, to give it an artificial and extraordinary force — to put in the place of the delegated will of the nation the will of a party, often a small but artful and enterprising minority of the community, and, according to the alternate triumphs of different parties, to make the public administration the mirror of the ill-concerted and incongruous projects of faction rather than the organ of consistent and wholesome plans digested by common councils and modified by mutual interests."

If this party spirit, denounced in these strong terms by the Father of our Country, is such an evil factor in politics generally, it must be very bad when manifested in a candidate for the chief magistracy ; and the aspirant possessed of tendencies so dangerous to the peace and safety of the nation should be shunned by all good people who wish to see our political institutions brought up to the full measure of purity and permanency.

In pursuing this subject still farther, the man who was "first in the hearts of his countrymen" adduces the idea that republics, above all other kinds of government, have most to fear from this "offensive partisanship." In his remarks he displays at once the deep insight of the philosopher, the breadth of vision peculiar to the statesman and diplomatist, and the keen perception of the practical politician. Therefore, Washington decidedly was a genius, as judged by this expansive range of mental vision and faculty for combinations. He says : —

"The spirit of party, unfortunately, is inseparable from our nature, having its root in the strongest passions of the human mind. It exists under different shapes in all governments, more or less stifled, controlled, or repressed, but in those of the popular form it is seen in greatest rankness and is truly their worst enemy. The alternate domination of one faction over another, sharpened by the spirit of revenge natural to party dissension, which in different ages and countries has perpetrated the most horrid enormities, is itself a frightful despotism. This leads at length to a formal and permanent despotism. The disorders and miseries which result, gradually incline the minds of men to seek security and repose in the absolute power of an individual, and sooner or later the chief of some prevailing faction, more able or more fortunate than his competitors, turns this disposition to the purposes of his own elevation on the ruins of public liberty."

A careful study of these precious words of Washington will partly explain, even in our times, why a genius, in the present condition of political parties with their factions and their jealousies, is not a desirable person for President. In the first instance, the right kind of genius, which presupposes moral worth of the highest type, could have little or no sympathy with constituents of this character, and opposing repellent forces are generally mutual in their action and reaction. These considerations and causes may, to some extent, account for the failure of Henry Clay, Daniel Webster, John C. Calhoun and others, to reach the goal of what was popularly supposed to have been their life-long and highest ambition. It is probable, however, that there is a great deal of popular misconception about the depressing effect that the disappointment left on the minds of these great statesmen. It is often flippantly remarked that Webster died of grief, from discomfiture and from pondering on his blighted hopes, but it appears that Webster was a man of too many intellectual resources to succumb to grief on this account, and he lived up to the Scriptural limit of three score and ten, while his great contemporary, Clay, died the same year (1852) at the ripe age of seventy-five. Both obtained renown that any President might envy, and several did envy.

The probability is that the fame of Webster rests on a more secure basis than it would had he reached the presidential chair. The durable reputation which his last great patriotic speech in the Senate on the Missouri Compromise gained for him, could hardly have been enhanced by any presidential honors.

In order to be a popular President the incumbent of that office must be a diplomat of such a character as to enable the country, if possible, to be at peace with all other nations, except when a real *casus belli* arises, and then the people should be fully satisfied as to the justice and expediency of their side of the dispute, as in our late war with Spain. An error in diplomacy is a most fruitful cause of business depression and financial disaster, as our international business relations now stand. It is therefore fatal to the popularity of a President, as all the blame falls on him owing to his prominence no matter who else should justly share it ; popular fury must have an object to aim at, and the most shining mark it can select is the Executive of the nation. The public do not take time to measure and calculate nice distinctions. The question for the majority of them is : Does this affair in politics or diplomacy make it harder to get along in the world and obtain a living? When international trouble is threatened, all are pinched before they get time to think why, and it is with the common laborer as with the wealthy financier. When the landlord calls for his rent at the first of the month, and the wife tells her husband about it, the latter asks : " Why, what is the meaning of this? He never used to be this way before, if it ran on into the next month."

" Well, he says he needs the money," she replies.

This conversation has hardly been concluded when the little girl comes in from the grocery store, and says, "Here's the grocer's bill, and he says he wants the money right off."

" Why, what's the matter with him? Does he think we are going to run away ? "

Johnny next arrives from the butcher's, and says : "The butcher told me to bring the money with me the next time I came. He says he can't give any more trust."

By this time husband and wife are both terribly confounded, and begin to imagine that some enemy is playing a practical joke upon them. Then it begins to dawn gradually upon the mental vision of the husband that he has heard some talk about a war message, and that, he thinks, has given rise to all the trouble. But this is not all. When the husband comes home from his work on Saturday night, he hands his money over to his wife as usual. She looks at it, and says : " Where is the rest of it ? " He answers, " That's all I got. The boss says money is tight. He has laid off one third of the hands, and others with myself will be put on half time next week."

The speculator calls on his broker, and says, " How about those shares ?"

" What shares?"

" Oh, you know."

" Let me see," says the broker. " What margin had you up ? "

" Five per cent.," confidently replies the customer.

" Yes, my dear sir," sorrowfully rejoins the broker, "but that stock has declined ten points."

" And am I wiped out? " queries the irate customer.

" Well, of course," says the broker, "you're no tyro in dealing in stocks, and you were notified like others that more margin was required if you desired to hold on to your purchase."

The customer, after being partially convinced that the broker has done his duty in the premises, restrains his ire and begins to ask about the cause of all the trouble.

"Well," replies the broker, who is in sympathy with the Administration, "you have heard about that matter in which our national honor was involved — "

"National honor be blowed!" ejaculates the furious customer, again lapsing into his tone of irritability and abuse. "I want my money back."

"Well, you see," continues the broker, "a difference of opinion arose between our Secretary of State and Lord Salisbury, the Premier of Great Britain, and — "

"Ah! Now, my dear sir, what are you giving us? I have nothing to do with politics or the foreign affairs of the government, and I don't see how it can affect stocks and my margin in that way."

The experience of the banker is the same. A man calls for an accommodation, and offers collateral similar to that which has been taken without hesitation on other occasions. When the cashier asks him for more or some of a better quality, he is surprised, and feels offended that his credit is beginning to be held cheap. When he is told that securities have depreciated within a day or two since his last visit to the bank, he can hardly realize it. Thus it is that the collapse in confidence extends its influence throughout all the ramifications of trade, both small and great, and the blame everywhere is hurled at the head of the President. The people quoted as examples, together with a great many others, some of whom are far more intelligent about cause and effect, can see only their own side of the question and the side that affects their pockets.

It is an old saying that the nearest way to a man's heart is through his pocket, and there may be a mutual attraction between the two that science has not yet discovered, even by the aid of the X-rays. However this may be, the influence over the feelings is stronger than any other of an earthly nature.

There is an old proverb frequently quoted referring chiefly to newly married people whose worldly goods are scanty. It says, "When poverty comes in at the door, love flies out at the window." The same idea would seem to hold good in reference to patriotism. A man can sing the "Star-Spangled Banner," or "Hail Columbia," with far more gusto after a good beefsteak, than when he is on short rations. It is difficult to attune the mind to the sympathetic air of a national anthem under the last named conditions. Although the mind has great power over the body, usually, the animal part of our existence is liable to succumb when not duly nurtured, and its influence then on the mental part of our organization is not the most salutary.

But nothing can explain to the people a failure of prosperity that has happened through any incapacity on the part of the Executive to deal with the currency system. The people, it would seem, have always shown the deepest displeasure toward a President guilty of any shortcoming of this character. It was so in the time of General Jackson, whose two terms stand out in bold relief both for signal and successful achievements as well as for conspicuous errors, failures, and defeats. The worst of the general's mistakes, perhaps, from the point of view now under consideration, was his stubborn opposition to the renewal of the charter of the United States Bank, which had done very fair financial service for thirty-six years, considering the times and the difficulties in banking in those days. The charter had four more years to run when Jackson was elected the second time, in 1832, and both Houses of Congress passed a bill to renew it. This was vetoed by the President, who also was guilty of the high-handed act of removing the funds to certain favorite State banks, against the most solemn and eloquent protests of Daniel Webster and others in the Senate, who declared that the act of removal was an illegal encroachment.

Jackson, however, insisted on having his own way, and the result of withdrawing so much money from an institution that had the confidence of the greater number of the people and putting it into several other concerns that were not generally regarded as trustworthy, had its inevitable result. A panic ensued, followed by widespread financial disaster, and the President's pet banks began to inflate their paper and were unable to meet the runs on the money that had been taken from the big bank and deposited with them. Jackson afterward recovered a part of his popularity by the determined stand he took against John C. Calhoun and his confrères on the subject of "nullification"; but people retained a horror of him and were possessed with dread lest he might, by some mishap, get another opportunity of tinkering with the public finances.

There seem to be some points of parallelism between General Jackson and Mr. Cleveland, both in the circumstances of their advent to office and in their arbitrary methods. They both sailed into office on the crest of the highest wave of popularity, and their interference with the legislative branch of the government turned the tide of that popularity.

But the evil that Jackson did in the financial affairs of the nation lived after him. Jackson left his opinions on finance to Van Buren as a legacy which was afterward the chief instrument in creating the panic of 1837, which has been fully described in my book, "Twenty-eight Years in Wall Street." A makeshift Treasury Bill was passed which afforded temporary relief, but every effort to restore the charter of the United States Bank was defeated by the presidential party.

Financial hope gleamed for a short time above the horizon of party spirit when, after the election of William Henry Harrison in 1840, Daniel Webster was appointed Secretary of State, and a bill was passed by both Houses, providing for the restoration of the charter of the United States Bank; but Harrison died a month after his inauguration, and Vice-President Tyler succeeded him in the presidency. Tyler had inherited the legacy of political State banking, by a kind of law of primogeniture, from Father Jackson through his politically adopted heir, Van Buren, and so he vetoed the bill. While this bank was not all that could be desired, yet it was much better than the State banks by which it was superseded.

It thus will be seen, from the foregoing instances and comments, that the Chief Magistrate has far greater power in
ordering the financial affairs of the nation than is commonly
supposed. He seldom keeps within the limits of purely executive duty ; circumstances seem to force him farther, often, perhaps, in spite of himself.

CHAPTER XIII.

THE CLEVELAND ADMINISTRATION — FIRST TERM.

An excellent beginning with the best intentions. — Large promises, but small performances. — Purposes regarding Civil Service Reform. — The theory was Jeffersonian, but the condition was Jacksonian. — The famous "Tariff Message" of Mr. Cleveland. — "A Condition, not a Theory." — How the purchase of a yard of calico confounds his theory and pet arguments in favor of free trade. — Mr. Cleveland's free-trade principles would bestow our home markets on foreign manufacturers and reduce our own workmen to indigence.

GROVER CLEVELAND made a good beginning as Chief Executive. He was a devoted advocate of Civil Service Reform, and I have no doubt that at first he thought his administration capable of making his theory and practice harmonize. The keynote of his avowed policy in that particular was embraced in the following sentence from his letter of acceptance for the first term: "The selection and retention of subordinates in government employment should depend upon their ascertained fitness and the value of their work." The whole gravamen of Civil Service Reform is contained in this sentence, and the merit system is clearly set forth.

But Mr. Cleveland did not think that this expression of his views and intentions was quite strong enough to make clear his hatred of official bossism and political corruption, and, in a speech made some time afterward, he put himself on record in a way that could leave no doubt in any candid mind that, so far as he was concerned, the mere office seeker should have no show in his administration and the political trickster no "pull"; and that the time-honored Jacksonian doctrine, "To the victors belong the spoils," should henceforth be regarded as a relic of semi-barbarism, having no place in an enlightened political system.

Mr. Cleveland said : " Let there be an opportunity offered to the people for a change of parties of such a kind that the victors must give up all idea of a general distribution of offices among their adherents, and the people will joyfully agree to it."

" A Daniel come to judgment," or words to that effect, cried many who heard or read that speech. " Here is a man," they said, " for the first time since the days of Lincoln who has the courage to combat the spoils system."

The post-office was the place where the first test came, in the attempt to work out Civil Service Reform practice in accordance with the theory ; and it must be admitted that the test proved a failure, though Civil Service Reform rules and principles were respected in some cases by virtue of what is known as the four-years' rule. For instance, Mr. Pearson remained postmaster at New York. The main pretext for displacing post-office officials was "offensive partisanship," a phrase which has become universally applicable to cases of prejudice in politics.

Then from the post-office department a system of espionage spread all over the country, until politics and political patronage in this country sank to a low condition of degeneracy. The office-seeking politicians bore down upon the administrative forces, which were unequal to successful resistance. Whole departments were demoralized and broken up to serve the rapacity of the office seekers ; and even a large number of the employés of the railway mail service were discharged through the secret espionage plan, and their places filled by others.

A prominent Southern senator and his following constituted one of the strongest forces with which the President had to contend, in their interference with his nominations and in various irritating ways known only to the trickery of professional politics. This Southern faction had great influence throughout the entire term, and exercised their power for mischief in tying the President's hands by interfering with some of the most important functions of his office. We can now see that there were many extenuating circumstances surrounding some of his actions, where a superficial observer might imagine the President was blameworthy. This was notably the case in dealing with the Southern faction, which took great pride in its influential power, and whose methods must have been very irritating to Mr. Cleveland.

The theory of the Cleveland administration in its official appointments was Jeffersonian, its motto being, "Is he honest, is he capable?" The practice, however, was largely Jacksonian, its motto being, "To the victors belong the spoils."

Let us now glance at Mr. Cleveland's famous tariff message of December, 1887, for which it is claimed he was personally responsible. When that document appeared it gave rise to a flood of criticism, both favorable and hostile. It was considered one of Mr. Cleveland's best literary efforts, and some of its sharp hits have had a wonderful currency in the newspapers, particularly the saying, "It is a condition which confronts us — not a theory." The condition was too much money in the Treasury. That condition has not given any trouble since a short time after that message. The great difficulty for a few years past has been a deficit in the Treasury, and the problem has been how to meet it. It was reserved for the McKinley administration to solve that problem.

The burden of the tariff message was an overflowing Treasury, which was constantly becoming more plethoric, and, like the Augean stables, filling up twice as fast as it was emptied. Our presidential Hercules, as stated in the message, did all that was in his power to remedy the situation. He bought bonds, and did everything in that line which the law allowed. Still the currency surplus would not down, but kept accumulating until it had reached the dangerous figure of $140,000,000, when Mr. Cleveland scented panic in the air. There would surely be a commercial smash-up, he soliloquized, if that Treasury were not depleted or at least a vein opened somewhere to relieve the congestion. The Treasury's great need was really gold and not currency at this time. The trouble lay in a redundancy of the former and a dearth of the latter. A high tariff, in Mr. Cleveland's opinion, was responsible for the desperate condition of affairs, and, according to the message, the country was on the very brink of commercial ruin. This was the honest theory of the President, and, irrespective of politics, he had a host of followers of the same financial belief.

That message was, as I have suggested, more remarkable for its literary excellence than for the soundness of its economic views. It is partly as a literary and partly as a historic documentary reminiscence that it seems worth analyzing now, for its economic views are somewhat unique, and show how much Mr. Cleveland had to learn upon the tariff question. No doubt he has profited by the two great object lessons, the McKinley Bill and the Wilson Bill, which he has in some measure been forced to study since then.

To show how mistaken his notions were regarding the practical result of tariff laws, I quote the following from the message : "These laws, as their primary and plain effect, raise the price to consumers of all articles imported and subject to duty, by precisely the sum paid for such duties. Thus the amount of the duty measures the tax paid by those who purchase for use those imported articles."

Mr. Cleveland could have had this argument answered practically and refuted by the simple operation of purchasing a yard of calico at 5 cents, and then looking in the list of tariff prices, and finding that the tariff upon a yard of calico was 6 cents. Of course Mr. Cleveland would say he must pay 11 cents for it. " Oh, no," the dry-goods man would answer, " we don't charge two prices. This is a one-price house." The dry-goods man might further reply : " It is a condition that confronts us — not a theory. Your theory is 11 cents ; our price is 5." The same rule applies in the majority of instances.

Mr. Cleveland made a mistake in thinking that the consumer pays the tariff tax, when it is really the producer or the seller who pays it, or it may be divided between producer and consumer. But it would be much more difficult to make Mr. Cleveland or any free-trader understand this than the calico transaction, which is simple and easily demonstrable.

Here is another point on which Mr. Cleveland required enlightenment. He said : " Nor can the worker in manufactures fail to understand that while a high tariff is claimed to be necessary to allow the payment of remunerative wages, it certainly results in a very large increase in the price of nearly all sorts of manufactures, which, in almost countless forms, he needs for the use of himself and family."

This is another instance in which the " condition " is at variance with the theory. There may be a few instances in which " the tariff results in an increase in price," but the rule is by no means general, and the increase is not " large," and where it does exist, the higher wages cover it several times over. Under any approach to free trade, the " increase " in the foreign goods would soon be twice as much. This has been often demonstrated, and was first clearly explained to the people of this country by Horace Greeley more than fifty years ago.

Mr. Cleveland seemed to have got it into his head that our manufacturers are grinding monopolists, and that they corral very large profits, quite forgetting, apparently, that foreign manufacturers are not better than they in this respect, and perhaps not so good. Under his system of " reduced taxation," as he called it then, we would permit the British manufacturer to take the profits instead of our own manufacturer. It is easy to see the great difference it makes to us as a people in having the money we pay for clothing and many other necessities spent in this country instead of its being spent abroad. The money spent here goes to enrich us all permanently, and we get what we need for it besides ; but what goes abroad we derive no further benefit from, and it impoverishes our country to the extent of that sum. The most unpatriotic people, therefore, are those who purchase foreign goods (except upon reciprocity principles), provided they can get what they want at home.

The theory and ideas of tariff reform, according to the free-traders, would munificently bestow our home markets, which take 90 per cent. of our products, upon the competing foreigner, without any compensation, except, perhaps, a cheaper suit of clothes once a year or so, which the impoverished laborer would hardly be able to purchase, as all his surplus wages would be divided between the foreign manufacturer and the pauper employés of this foreign protégé of our free-traders. I know that Mr. Cleveland would never admit that he is in favor of free trade out and out, and he may honestly believe that he is not; but no fair-minded person can read his messages, his severe criticisms against protection, and his bitter denunciations of its adherents, without being forced to the conclusion that he is one of the most uncompromising free-traders. His saving remnant of protection suggests the Kentucky colonel's mixture of water with his whiskey. The Kentuckian had a deep-seated prejudice against taking his whiskey straight, or at least of being considered to do so, and when he would fill his glass of Bourbon to the very brim, he would say to the waiter, " Now, John, take that glass, keep a steady hand, mind you, and just pour in one drop of water, just one drop." Mr. Cleveland's alleged remnant of protection, whatever it is, is like the Kentuckian's drop of water, which he mixed with his Bourbon in order to preserve the consistency of his prejudice.

CHAPTER XIV.

THE HARRISON ADMINISTRATION.

Its influence on some of the consequences of the Baring panic. — The absence of " Jingoism " was a conspicuous feature of the Harrison régime. — Harrison as an orator. — His Western trip compared with the Eastern trip of Bryan. — His astonishing familiarity with all the States and their conditions, and his magnetic power over audiences, as displayed in Western cities. — A thorough politician and a far-seeing statesman. — His coöperation with James G. Blaine in devising the wise policy of reciprocity which was spoiled by the Democrats.

THE Baring failure, though its influence for universal evil was checked (as shown in another chapter) by the able management of Mr. Lidderdale, who was the chief instrument in adroitly using the power and funds of the Bank of England to avert a very extensive panic, was nevertheless followed by an unhappy aftermath, the effects of which were severely felt on this side of the Atlantic.

Things might have been much worse here, however, except for two fortunate circumstances. One of these was the sound condition of our banks and the systematic management of the Clearing House which, in any threatened emergency or extraordinary tightness in the money market, issues certificates to tide over the trouble. The other circumstance was that we were blest with one of the best administrations that we have had since the days of Washington and Lincoln.

The Harrison administration stands out in bold relief as one of the greatest in the history of the Republic. It was characterized by honesty and economy. In it Jingoism was conspicuous by its absence. It was too thoroughly American for that, and it sought no recognition from abroad. It did not seek to elevate itself into public notice by any display of cheap sensationalism. It was thoroughly unostentatious, and, avoiding all entangling alliances according to the advice of Washington, attended strictly to domestic business, which it looked after with constant assiduity.

The last year of the Harrison administration, 1892, was one of the most prosperous in the history of the country, and, if General Harrison had been reëlected there is every reason to believe that the same conditions would have continued. It would have been a continuous chain without a break ; but when Harrison left the White House the scene was changed.

General Harrison had not long taken his departure when the ominous forebodings of the Wilson Bill took hold of the minds of the people. What was the result ? Our manufacturing industries were paralyzed, we had another panic on our hands, and the struggle against the malign influences of free trade went on until McKinley was elected.

With regard to General Harrison himself, he is a man of unique personality and fine culture, a profound lawyer and an eloquent orator ; yet he was never known to parade any of these gifts or attainments. His modesty in this respect has seldom been excelled by any one in an eminent office. His speeches are marvelous for their variety ; wherein they differ from Bryan's, which always harp on the same theme. But General Harrison is unexcelled in versatility even by Horace Greeley. That Western trip of thirty days in the spring of 1891 has no parallel in the annals of electioneering speeches — which they virtually were.

General Harrison traveled, just as Mr. Bryan did, throughout the whole West and South ; he covered more ground than Mr. Bryan in the same time, was equally ubiquitous, and made about as many speeches ; but here the comparison ends.

The speeches were of a different kind. In every separate State General Harrison displayed an intimate knowledge of that State and its people, with their habits and customs from the earliest times, as if he had been born there and lived among them all his life. Not only in variety, but even in mere number of addresses, Harrison leaves the free-silver orator far in the distance. He made nine speeches in one day, for instance, in

San Francisco without repeating himself, and one of them was a banquet oration, regarded by both Republican and Democratic papers as one of the greatest oratorical efforts ever heard in that city.

One very conspicuous point in General Harrison's visiting trip was the sudden and strong attachment of the people to him, which thus displayed the powerful magnetism of the man. He had a rare felicity in complimenting the people on the good points exhibited in their State, and of making them feel satisfied with their lot and location. A good illustration is from a little speech in Ashland, Oregon, as follows : —

"My friends, you have a most beautiful State, capable of promoting the comfort of your citizens in a very high degree, and, although already occupying a high place in the galaxy of States, it will, I am sure, take a much higher one. It is pleasant to see how the American spirit prevails among all your people, love for the flag and its constitution, those settled and permanent things that live, whether men go or come. They come to us from our fathers and pass down to our children.

"You are blessed with a genial climate and most productive soil. I see you have in this northern part of California what I have seen elsewhere — a well-ordered community, with churches and schoolhouses, which indicate you are not giving all your thoughts to material things, but are thinking of those things that qualify the soul for hereafter. We have been treated to another surprise this morning in the first shower we have seen in California. I congratulate you that it rains here. May all the blessings fall upon you like this gentle rain."

The chief qualities that characterize this speech are simplicity, terseness, directness, and a thorough appreciation of his audience. General Harrison has been charged with being cold, but the sympathetic tone in which he addressed the people of Ashland would seem to disprove the imputation. He may be cold toward those who would be incapable of appreciating his warmth, and between whom and himself there is no natural sympathy.

Let us now regard General Harrison as a politician and a

statesman.   He is a man of remarkable candor and courage.
This was displayed very prominently in his letter of acceptance,
in which he refused to follow slavishly the platform of the party,
but boldly expressed his own independent opinions.   Candidates for the highest office in the land, or, indeed, for any office,
are usually afraid to venture on such a course of action ; but in
the case of Harrison it was made clear that he was a thorough
politician as well as a far-seeing statesman.   It might be said of
him, in fact, as a great Englishman, Viscount Bolingbroke (St.
John), said of Dean Swift ; " Turn him to any course of policy,
the Gordian knot of it he will unloose, familiar as his garter."

To show the depth of President Harrison's political insight,
there probably could be no better testimony than that of James
G. Blaine.   Commenting on the political sagacity in General
Harrison's letter of acceptance, the man of Maine said : —

" The position of the candidate, as defined by himself, is of far
more weight with the voters, and the letter of acceptance has come
to be the legitimate creed of the party.   Notoriously, little heed is
given to an exposition of principles by the committee on resolutions,
and less heed is given to resolutions when submitted to the convention at large.   This springs naturally from the fact that great
haste characterizes the preparation of the platform, and if one man
of the committee has any political hobby that he wishes to incorporate, he has little trouble, from the general inattention of the
members, in compassing his end.   Conventions often embody issues
which are impracticable, and occasionally that are mischievous and
embarrassing."

General Harrison cleverly evaded the hobbies of the convention, while he paid due respect to the main features of the platform.   This was respectful to the convention.   Mr. Cleveland, on
the contrary, in his acceptance took no chances.   According to
Mr. Blaine he made the platform himself, quite ignoring the
convention.   It must be remembered also that Mr. Cleveland
was consistent in the maintenance of this independent policy
to the end of his administration.

The policy of President Harrison toward the South was of
the most conciliatory character, and in no instance, perhaps,

did his wisdom and prudence shine more brilliantly.   His suggestion to Congress that provision be made " for the appointment of a non-partisan commission to consider the subject of
apportionments and elections in their relation to the choice of
federal officers " was a master-stroke of policy, especially at the
time when Democratic politicians were attempting to inflame all
the hostile passions of their party against the Federal Election
Bill.   President Harrison's wisdom was further shown in this
matter by urging upon Congress the passage of a law which
would give to the Supreme Court the appointment of the non-
partisan commission.   This took the wind out of the Democratic sails and bereft several prominent journals of their best
material for criticism, as well as many politicians of a prolific
subject for discussion.

Any review of that administration would be incomplete without a reference to those significant commercial projects contemplated by President Harrison and his brilliant minister,
Secretary Blaine.   I refer to the plan of reciprocity treaties
wherever they could be profitably negotiated.   Before the end
of his administration the enterprise was well under way ; it had
worked admirably and profitably in Cuba and in the Windward
and Leeward Islands ; it had begun to manifest its good influences in South and Central America, and was materially lessening the balance of trade against us in those countries.   But the
succeeding Democratic administration did not see the incalculable benefits to be derived from this great movement in trade
and commerce, partly through inappreciation of its commercial
importance, and partly, perhaps, through partisan prejudices
because Secretary Blaine and President Harrison were its original projectors.   It is sad to think that partisanship should block
the way of progress in some of the most benignant and patriotic enterprises ; but perhaps such things must be while two
political parties of generally opposite views seem necessary to
carry on the government and to maintain those checks and balances indispensable to its stability.

CHAPTER XV.

MR. CLEVELAND'S SECOND ADMINISTRATION.

How Mr. Cleveland acquired the character of an independent candidate. — Success of his fiscal policy, especially regarding the surplus revenue and the depository banks. — Making himself "solid" with bankers and financiers. — How it was that he was beaten by Harrison in 1888, but vanquished him in 1892. — How he lost his popularity by the irreparable errors of the two object lessons. — Remarks on his sound money views and his indomitable perseverance. — Utterly failed to understand the tariff question.

IF Mr. Cleveland had prudently followed up during his second term a few of the strokes of wise policy and, in several instances, the good guiding and prudent management which characterized his first administration, he might have gone down to posterity in the odor of political sanctity; but his two famous object lessons were two unfortunate departures.

These two object lessons were Mr. Cleveland's personal interference with the repeal of the purchasing clause of the Sherman Law of 1890 relating to silver coinage, and the Wilson Tariff Bill.

In order to understand fully the nature of Mr. Cleveland's second administration, it is necessary to recapitulate a few important points intimately connected with his first.

After the nomination for his first term, though a Democratic nominee, he owed his election chiefly to those deserters from the Republican party who were designated "Mugwumps." His peculiar relationship to these independent voters made him in reality an independent President. He therefore acted upon the principle that he was the people's President without regard to party lines, and this idea seemed to inspire him with a feeling that, like Napoleon, he was a man of destiny.

After Mr. Cleveland was inaugurated for the first term he

found an overflowing Treasury, with a consequent dearth of money outside. Owing to the contraction in circulation caused by this surplus, there were ominous forebodings of panic in the air. Mr. Cleveland first did all he could, as noticed elsewhere, in the way of buying such bonds as the government under existing legislation had authority to purchase, but all to very little purpose. He then wisely resorted to the depository banks, putting the surplus there, and the strain was soon relieved. He even had the number of these banks increased for the purpose of putting the money into circulation.

The situation was more alarming than many people think, for dangers of this kind cannot be thoroughly estimated until after the danger is past. Considerable money was required at a certain time, then not far distant, to move the crops, which that year gave an ample yield ; while money in Wall Street and throughout the country was becoming very stringent, and very hard to obtain. Hence is seen the financial wisdom manifested by Mr. Cleveland in augmenting the number of the depository banks. He issued an order through his able Secretary of the Treasury, Daniel Manning, to the effect that all money due the government thereafter should be paid into these banks, and kept in circulation, instead of having it remain uselessly in the government vaults ; an action which had an immediate and soothing effect upon public feeling, restored confidence in business circles, and enabled the crop movement and other enterprises to go on without interruption.

The banks, meanwhile, accumulated $60,000,000 in deposits to the credit of the government, and had this money gone into the Treasury instead of the depository banks, we should probably have witnessed in Wall Street and throughout the country one of the worst panics on record. Mr. Cleveland and his Secretary of the Treasury gained great praise for the masterly manner in which the finances were managed at that critical period, and the credit is all the more due to them both, inasmuch as it was a new experiment in government financiering on so large a scale, and the necessity was sprung upon these two officials quite unexpectedly.

The popularity which Mr. Cleveland suddenly and unexpectedly acquired by this able operation put him and his independent party away ahead, and made him, if possible, still more independent of the Democrats. The confidence on the part of the public had developed considerably beyond even what it had been at the time of his election, and everybody seemed to feel that all matters financial, internal and international, were safe in his hands. In fact he had become dangerously popular, if he had been a man imbued with one-man power ambition.

This public feeling continued unabated and even waxed warmer quite up to the time of his second inauguration, and it was not therefore to be wondered at that a vast number of the people of the country wanted him again for President. Practically he was forced upon the convention which his managers carried by a *coup*, and secured his nomination in the face of all the opposition that an antagonistic party machine could concentrate against him. It was demonstrated to his own satisfaction and that of the public that the people were with him at that convention, and in such victorious circumstances, against such odds in the convention, why should he not have continued to feel that he was backed by the people, and not by politicians? Can it be matter of surprise that he fought the politicians all through his second term of office, neither asking nor giving quarter? He thus succeeded in making enemies of nearly all the powerful leaders of the Democratic party. " We love him for the enemies he has made," said one enthusiastic adherent; but harmony between him and those prominent leaders who in a well-regulated administration should uphold the hands of the President was out of the question. On the contrary, the antipathy was mutual and bitter, and discord was the natural result. The administration was divided against itself, and it could not stand.

It was mainly due to these unfortunate relations between the Executive and the Democratic party that it became possible at the Chicago convention of 1896 for Altgeld, Tillman, William Jennings Bryan, and a few others of that ilk, to capture the convention and steal the machine of the party. The dissensions between the Democratic leaders and the Executive enabled free-silver cranks, anarchists, socialists, and others belonging to the revolutionary fraternity, to take advantage of the situation. Moreover, quite a number of sound-money men became silverites at this convention, not from any conviction that the theory was correct, but out of sheer antipathy to Mr. Cleveland. According to the adage, some of them were ready to cut off their noses to spite their faces. The opinion seemed to prevail, at least in inside circles, that the silver plank was inserted in the Democratic platform chiefly for the purpose of heading off the designs of Mr. Cleveland for a third term, as he was famous for springing surprises.

In reviewing Mr. Cleveland's administration, it must be borne in mind that the prime cause of commercial misfortune lay in the reversal of national policy. The country was thriving under institutions that had been built up as the result of the politico-economic experience of thirty-two years' rule of the party previously in power. The inevitable result of a reversal of governmental policy is in the upheaval of business, which must needs be entirely readjusted to new methods and conditions, with, in many instances, disastrous consequences.

Mr. Cleveland obtained an immense vote in his third campaign, in 1892, from those who remembered his energetic struggle to reduce the surplus, and his able management in preserving the country from panic during his first administration. They naturally favored him for another term, being assured that the same shrewd and sagacious policy in finance would direct and inspire all his efforts and actions in that department of the government. He retained this popularity and his hold on the people, notwithstanding his temporary defeat in 1888 and the Harrison interim ; and he came up, after a long rest, in 1892, potent and debonair, with the same old clientele considerably augmented, as the darling of the people, and as independent as ever of the machine Democracy. In fact, he had kicked the machine out of his way again, just as he had in 1884 defied John Kelly and Tammany Hall.

It may seem somewhat strange that Mr. Cleveland carried his popularity over those four years despite all the allowance that must necessarily be made for secret electioneering in the meantime ; and the most puzzling part of it appears to be that he could not beat General Harrison in 1888, but vanquished him by the large majority of 132 in the electoral college in 1892. In 1888 General Harrison had a majority over Mr. Cleveland of only 65 in the electoral college. It will be remembered that he severely denounced a tariff reform of greater protection to American industries during his first term, and especially in his message of 1887. This was undoubtedly displeasing both to wage earners and their employers. And it was this revulsion of feeling against Mr. Cleveland's language toward protectionists and his strong free-trade proclivities that worked against him in his unsuccessful campaign against General Harrison.

How President Harrison in his turn lost his hold and failed to succeed for a second term is a long story, not in place here. Briefly, it was an inauspicious time, and a large number of voters who knew little or nothing about finance were easily persuaded that the President and Congressman McKinley were largely to blame for the Baring panic. This was one element which contributed to the defeat of General Harrison. "Now," said the independent followers of Mr. Cleveland and the stump spellbinders, " didn't we tell you what protection and the McKinley Bill would bring upon the country?" This seemed plausible under the circumstances, but it was only part of the story. There was considerable solidity behind Cleveland. The wealthy financiers, bankers, and others remembered his wise policy in establishing the additional depository banks and filling them with government money, and they had faith in him for this reason, a circumstance which alone brought a large contingent of the money power to his back, and contributions to the campaign fund were on an unusually liberal scale. Added to these facts, Mr. Cleveland was sound on the money question, an uncompromising gold monometallist ; and, as he was bold and firm even to the verge of obstinacy, he was properly considered an excellent choice to withstand the hosts of free-silverites whose clans were then gathering with hostile intent and preparing all over the West for a fierce fight.

Another thing which favored Mr. Cleveland was the patent fact that President Harrison and his managers did not make as much out of their opportunities as they might have done. If Mr. Harrison had taken up the question of Civil Service Reform, for example, in which the first Cleveland administration failed, and made strenuous efforts to carry out its legitimate purposes, he might have been more popular for the second term than Mr. Cleveland. But where President Harrison made his greatest mistake was in his manifestation of jealousy against Mr. Blaine. If he had magnanimously left the field clear for Mr. Blaine's candidacy, that most popular man in the Republican party, as well as the favorite of many of the Democrats, would probably have defeated Mr. Cleveland. That foolish, alliterative phrase of Burchard's, "Rum, Romanism, and Rebellion," which materially contributed to Blaine's defeat in 1884, had no weight with voters on second thoughts and mature reflection. Mr. Blaine in 1892 was probably, after all, the most popular man in the country, both with the industrial element and with the manufacturers, who constitute the backbone of the nation, and his plans for protection and reciprocity might have brought permanent prosperity to the United States. It is my opinion that he would have made a successful run, despite the popularity of his vigorous opponent.

This, however, was not to be, and the people, reflecting on the circumstances above narrated, naturally favored Grover Cleveland for a second term, believing that the same desire to guard the welfare of the country and promote its prosperity which marked his first term would still govern him, and that the same line of policy as had been exhibited in his best acts during the first term would actuate all his movements during the second. Minor delinquencies, such as Civil Service neglect, were forgotten or forgiven. In fact they faded out in the light of the superiority which he had manifested as a financier.

The surprise was astounding, therefore, when Mr. Cleveland

sprang upon the people the object lesson which brought about panic Number One. He acted on the principle that the best way to get a bad law repealed is to enforce its execution. Mr. Cleveland's strange and incomprehensible excuse for teaching this object lesson was that suffering among the people was absolutely necessary to cause them to bring sufficient pressure upon their representatives in Congress to impel the latter to vote for the repeal of the purchasing clause of the Sherman Silver Law of 1890, and this clause was repealed in November, 1893, during the extra session that had been called for that purpose.

To my mind, the chief error regarding this repeal was the inopportune time at which it was forced. The people were exceedingly sensitive about everything relating to the financial situation, and they thought all legislative interference with the currency foreboded panic. It is a fact well known to those who have been close observers of the history of finance that when any considerable number of people hold such views, they become virtual panic-makers. So it was in 1893. Mr. Cleveland should have dealt with the Sherman Act immediately after his inauguration. He deferred his action too long. The people had become apprehensive at the remembrance of the recent Baring panic, from the effect of which they were just beginning to recover. The year 1892, moreover, had been in a very large measure prosperous, for the reason that it was the first year since the McKinley Bill had been passed that the law had a chance of exhibiting its good effects above disturbing influences. The time therefore, I say, was very inopportune for the President to recommend legislation that, however good or innocent in itself, was likely to make people apprehensive. If all our people were thoughtful and reflective and could understand the nature of a law, the case would have been very different; but they are not so. While the act in question repealed the purchasing clause, it recommended to the government to make every effort to establish such a system of bimetallism as would maintain the equal value of every dollar coined or issued by the United States, in the markets, and in the payment of debts.

I append herewith the entire section, verbatim, by which the idea of the intent, spirit, and purpose of the law can be more fully understood : —

ACT OF NOVEMBER 1, 1893. AN ACT TO REPEAL A PART OF AN ACT APPROVED JULY 14, 1890, ENTITLED "AN ACT DIRECTING THE PURCHASE OF SILVER BULLION AND THE ISSUE OF TREASURY NOTES THEREON, AND FOR OTHER PURPOSES.

"*Be it enacted*, etc., That so much of the act approved July 14, 1890, entitled 'An act directing the purchase of silver bullion and issue of Treasury notes thereon, and for other purposes,' that directs the Secretary of the Treasury to purchase from time to time silver bullion to the aggregate amount of 4,500,000 ounces, or so much thereof as may be offered in each month at the market price thereof, not exceeding one dollar for $371\frac{25}{100}$ grains of pure silver, and to issue in payment for such purchases Treasury notes of the United States, be, and the same is, hereby repealed. And it is hereby declared to be the policy of the United States to continue the use of both gold and silver as standard money, and to coin both gold and silver into money of equal intrinsic and unchangeable value, such equality to be secured through international agreement, or by such safeguards of legislation as will insure the maintenance of the parity in value of the coins of the two metals, and the equal power of every dollar at all times in the markets and in the payment of debts. And it is hereby further declared that the effort of the government should be steadily directed to the establishment of such a safe system of bimetallism as will maintain at all times the equal power of every dollar coined or issued by the United States, in the markets and in the payment of debts."

This " equal power " of every dollar would be lost if owners of silver mines could have their wealth multiplied by two by simple fiat of the National Legislature, and no kind of class legislation could be worse, as it would make gifts of millions to monopolists and silver trusts by the votes of the poor people who are loudest against trusts and monopolies. The policy of the free-silverites would destroy all chances of bimetallism, for which the act invokes the aid of foreign governments.

After the repeal of the purchasing clause there was a run on the Treasury to exchange greenbacks for gold, and the public seemed to be seized with a spasmodic feeling that nothing in the shape of money was reliable except the yellow metal.

Object lesson Number Two consisted of the agitation over the Wilson Bill, and its final passage in such a deformed condition, however, that its paternal relative was totally unable to recognize his own offspring. Mr. Cleveland obstinately refused to be the godfather of the baby which had been so maltreated by a wicked and prejudiced Senate.

The bill had passed the House with easy success. The baby was a smiling cherub in the eyes of a large majority of Congress, and never uttered a squall until it reached the upper House, and the unfeeling senators began to pinch the poor thing. The silverites, and others in that honorable body, had the audacity to make 640 amendments to the bill, until it was like the Irishman's gun, regarding which the gunsmith said, when he was asked if he could mend it, that it wanted a new lock, stock, and barrel.

No wonder that Mr. Cleveland exclaimed, when the ugly changeling was presented to him, " It is an act of perfidy and dishonor." We can only imagine what Professor Wilson's feelings must have been when he beheld the metamorphosed production of his fine and profound intellect.

To say that the House was thunderstruck on the return of the bill, when they beheld its curious metempsychosis, would be putting it mildly. They soon discovered, however, it was either " that or nothin'," according to the Senate's mandate, and they mournfully accepted it.

It is almost needless to say that Mr. Cleveland did not sign this deformity and he was too indignant even to veto it. He let it go by the constitutional ten days' default, and it became a law in all the horrors of its " perfidiousness." No wonder, therefore, that Messrs. Cleveland and Carlisle were "short" on government expenses and "long" on bonds to procure gold. If the President had exercised his veto power, it would have been a good thing for the country, as in that event the McKinley Law would have continued in existence, and we probably would have had better times; but if better times had not ensued, the country's condition would have given the Democrats an excellent opportunity to attribute their luck to the McKinley Bill, instead of the Republicans being able, as things turned out, to set down all business troubles and calamities to the Wilson Bill.   Mr. Cleveland's conduct in regard to the bill, and the weak front shown by the House in swallowing it with the absurd amendments, will afford, it seems to me, a barrier for a long period against making free trade an issue in a presidential campaign.

Probably a new generation will have appeared on the scene, with little or no knowledge of, or interest in, the disasters of the last four Democratic years, before there can be any possible political recovery for that party, or before free-trade doctrines, as against protection for United States industries, can have any favorable support from the people.

In view of the facts herein stated and the references to the tariff bills, it is fitting to quote some official figures regarding the outcome of the two bills.

Total receipts under McKinley Law,
  October, 1890–1892 . . . . $759,456,825
Total expenditures under McKinley Law,
  October, 1890–1892 731,211,184
      Surplus $28,245,641

Total receipts under Wilson Law,
  September, 1894, to December, 1895 . . . . $373,790,648
Total expenditures under Wilson Law,
  September, 1894, to December, 1895 444,290,692
      Deficiency $70,500,044

The total deficiency in meeting government expenses up to November, 1895, exceeded $130,000,000.

If the Wilson Bill had passed the Senate as it left the House of Representatives, the deficiency in the revenue would have been still larger than it was in December, 1895 ; so the Administration should have been glad that the Senate disfigured the bill. The Wilson Law, moreover, caused the first deficiency that had occurred in the revenue since the close of the Civil War. Every year, from that time up to 1893, there had been a surplus and a consequent reduction of the national debt.

CHAPTER XVI.

EX–PRESIDENT CLEVELAND PERSONALLY CONSIDERED.

The theory of his potent personality and an attempt to reveal the secret of his success through this mysterious power and other potentialities. — Striking a balance between his praiseworthy acts and some of his mistakes. — How he is likely to be rated by the future historian and biographer. — His name stamped indelibly on the politics of his own times. — His unflinching advocacy of sound money. — He drew all shades of politics after him and was independent of party. — Why he drew so many heterogeneous elements. — Comparison with Macaulay's Machiavelli. — His prompt and popular action in suppressing the Chicago riots and causing the overthrow of Eugene V. Debs. — His advice to the Democratic party.

IF anybody should happen to draw the inference, from the strictures I have made elsewhere on the errors and shortcomings of ex-President Cleveland, that he was not possessed of several elements of greatness, it would be a grave error in judgment on the part of the reader.

Mr. Cleveland has shown himself to be a great and remarkable man in many respects, and this will in all probability be the estimate of posterity.

My chief reason for this belief is that the man's potent personality in a few things that were highly important has stamped itself indelibly on the politics of his own times. For instance, he stood up for sound money, and was one of the strongest advocates of the cause against the clamor for free-silver coinage, which at one time came near carrying with it a majority. Of course the victory would have been only temporary, if such general dementia had seized the people at large, because the sober second thought of the thinking minority would have triumphed eventually after the country had perhaps passed through the ordeal of a panic worse than all former panics condensed into one.   From a calamity of this character Mr. Cleveland was one of the most potent agencies in saving us.   He was unflinching in his courage in the maintenance of the gold standard, and in all probability his influence and his powerful attacks on the free-silver heresy made almost as many votes for McKinley as Mark Hanna did ; and this in spite of Mr. Cleveland's deep-seated aversion to Mr. McKinley's pet theory of protection for our industries.

Cleveland has been very popular at intervals during both terms of his administration, and the secret of his popularity has been rather a mystery to both friends and foes.

The supreme test of the popularity of a President and an administration is whether during the greater part of the period of power the country has been prosperous.   Beyond this test the public are no more inclined to listen to excuses or apologies than they are in the case of a general who has been vanquished in a series of battles by the enemy.   That charity which is said to cover a multitude of sins is rarely, if ever, exercised in instances like these.

When Mr. Cleveland took possession of the White House, March 4, 1893, the country was prosperous.   When he went out of office, March 4, 1897, the country was almost on the verge of bankruptcy, and the worst prolonged depression in business that the nation has ever experienced prevailed during the greater part of the time.   Had it not been for the agitation regarding free-trade theories, together with certain other Utopian schemes of reform, the good times which the country enjoyed during the last year of General Harrison's administration would in all probability have been continued indefinitely.

Now it seems to be the popular belief that when Mr. Cleveland ran for President in 1892, after having been defeated by General Harrison in 1888, he was the candidate of the Democratic party.   He was nominally and officially so, it would appear, but he was besides a popular candidate, and did not seem to own allegiance to any party.   His aim from the first was to catch the popular ear and to make the impression deep in the hearts of the people that he was their candidate irrespective of party. That portion of his devotion which pertained to party he seemed to regard only as a matter of form, a kind of principle of politeness, with the formality of which political society expected compliance as mere pantomime, without putting any soul into it or having any conscientious sensations about it. Both his letters of acceptance and his speech on taking the oath of office bear out his theory, and it was the perception by the people of this feeling on his part that in large measure drew to him so many heterogeneous elements and gave him such a large majority over President Harrison.

He drew from all shades of politics and factions to swell his immense majority, from the Populists and protectionists as well as from the free-traders, and herein is revealed a part of the mystery. Careful investigation by expert politicians and journalists after the election showed the fact that even protectionists voted for him, without being able to assign a reason other than that they wanted a change and desired to experiment. Farmers and others said so, while admitting that they had enjoyed greater prosperity during the two former years of the operation of the McKinley tariff than ever before. Such instances as these only tend to deepen the mystery, and throw us back to the reflection that Mr. Cleveland, amid the discussion of a great variety of topics, never ceased to vibrate one chord wherever he had the opportunity, namely, that he was the representative of the people, always their obedient servant and ready to do their will and perform their behests at all times. Whatever derelictions there might be from these professions, they did not seem to count with the multitude either before or after the election, at least for the first year of his second term.

There could be no stronger proof of great personality, and that certain hypnotic potencies are largely developed in Mr. Cleveland. It is a proof of the attributes of generalship. Nothing drew the soldiers of Napoleon closer to him than a temporary defeat. This was true in every instance until Waterloo, and notably so after Moscow. Mr. Cleveland will have no chance of experimenting on a Moscow or a Waterloo. He retired peacefully and in good order, not to a St. Helena, but to a Fontainebleau at Princeton, New Jersey, where he entered into the full enjoyment of domestic happiness.

Mr. Cleveland may employ some of his leisure hours in writing the inside history of his administration, but it is questionable if he himself can satisfactorily explain the many-sided traits of character which he displayed during the period of his toilsome and arduous experience in Washington. Macaulay in his review of Machiavelli says : —

"Two characters altogether dissimilar are united in him. They are not merely joined, but interwoven. They are the warp and woof of his mind, and their combination, like that of the variegated threads in shot silk, gives to the whole texture a glancing and ever changing appearance. The explanation might have been easy if he had been a very weak or very affected man. But he was evidently neither the one nor the other. His works prove, beyond all contradiction, that his understanding was strong, his taste pure, and his sense of the ridiculous exquisitely keen."

Now, this is very high praise from the great English essayist, critic, and historian, bestowed upon a man who has been universally execrated on account of his politics and diplomacy ; and it is curious how closely this particular characterization will apply to Mr. Cleveland, unlike the wily Italian as the downright and honest "Grover" is. Concerning one point of the comparison, however, — the last clause, "his sense of the ridiculous exquisitely keen," — I am in doubt. If it were on record that Mr. Cleveland had laughed heartily when the Wilson Bill was sent to him with the Senate amendments, then this fragment of Macaulay's description of the great Florentine statesman might apply with some modifications to him. He appears to have been many-sided, yet without much inconsistency, paradoxical as it may seem ; and possibly the multi-sided aspect of the man may have been more in appearance than in reality. It may have been the reflection of others, but, like St. Paul, he appeared at times to be "all things to all men." This was doubtless the effect of reflex action. Several political parties and factions, holding diverse opinions, each seemed to consider him as the one man who could best represent them.   Hence we perceive one secret of his large majority.   He proclaimed himself the candidate of the people, and the large majority took him at his word, regarding as minor matters in their political faith what formerly had been considered of the first importance.

The support which the bankers gave to Mr. Cleveland illustrates how men took him at his personal word.   Although he accepted the Democratic platform in its entirety, yet the bankers connected with the national banking system gave him a hearty support, despite the fact that he was bound to favor, so far as executive favor can go, the plank in the platform which recommended the abolition of the ten per cent. tax on the state banks, a step which, in all probability, would have exercised a demoralizing influence on our whole currency system.   Yet the bankers seemed to overlook this very important point, in view of the fact that he was sound on the question of the gold basis.   To that all other considerations were secondary.   Again, high tariff men who had hitherto seemed to pin their faith on Major McKinley's sleeve with the enthusiasm of Mussulman devotees to Mahomet, voted for Mr. Cleveland in spite of the fact that he denounced the tariff laws as " the vicious, inequitable, and illogical source of unnecessary taxation."   Even Populists, anarchists, and socialists gathered to his standard, notwithstanding his well-known antipathy to all enemies of a firmly established government by the will of the people on a conservative and permanent basis.

The attraction of such diverse elements can be accounted for only by the strength of his personality, and by the additional fact that there must have been something in him which inspired confidence.

When he saw his way clearly he was usually prompt in action, though some of his unaccountable delays were irritating to the people as well as injurious to public prosperity.   His remarkable quality of promptitude in action was manifested in a very laudable manner in the suppression of the railroad riots

at Chicago.   The country was then on the brink of a revolution.   Governor Altgeld of Illinois did not show any inclination to suppress the riots.   Adhering closely and technically to
the language of the Constitution, he did not see the necessity
of calling on the United States troops until the forces within
the State at his disposal were proved unequal to the task, and
he had apparently no desire even to utilize those forces.   In
fact, he appeared to be rather pleased with the uprising against
the capitalists, the movement being in accordance with his
views on national politics, and the rule of the rabble appearing to him as the proper means of establishing a paternal government.

In this extremity General Schofield, observing with the keen
eye of a practical leader in an emergency, that the passions
already engendered in the mob were gathering strength and
ferocity every hour, concluded that the incipient insurrection
might soon be fanned into a revolutionary flame and extend all
over the Union.   In fact, it appeared as if the country might
be threatened with something as direful as another civil war.
He therefore lost no time in consulting the Attorney-General,
Mr. Olney, to find out if there were no means of quelling the
riot by Federal authority without depending on Governor
Altgeld.   Mr. Olney soon discovered that the case involving
the Chicago riots was not confined to the State of Illinois, but
was an interstate affair of national concern, and that the Federal government had the right to interfere with the train-
wreckers for the purpose of protecting the United States mails.
Thus the ostensible plea of Governor Altgeld was set aside, and
the United States authorities held the fort.   President Cleveland, as commander-in-chief of the army, promptly gave
orders that Federal troops should be sent to Chicago for the
purpose of reducing to order and decent behavior all riotous
persons who should attempt to wreck railroad cars containing
United States mail.   The troops came and conquered, without the shedding of much blood, and the revolution was nipped
in the bud.   The labor unions all over the country, restless, and
tempted to a simultaneous rising by Eugene V. Debs, were

quieted by this display of force, and since then there has been no serious show of hostility against capital.

Had it not been for Mr. Cleveland's promptness on that occasion, it is hard to say how the trouble might have ended. If he had been a man of weak and vacillating purpose, the forces of disorder would doubtless have made rapid headway while he was coming to a decision ; but the emergency in question shows that he has a well-balanced mind, that he is quick to apprehend combinations of circumstances, real, probable, and possible, has the judgment and comprehension to devise plans to meet them, and the courage to execute the plans without hesitating or wavering.

These are a few of the qualities of a great general, but not all. The statesman and the general are seldom united in the same person, except in military geniuses, like Cæsar, Scipio, Marcus Aurelius, Justinian, Napoleon, and a few others. A large number of generals aspire to be considered statesmen of the highest type, but they are generally failures, like the Duke of Wellington, for instance.

In statesmanship, it must be candidly confessed, Mr. Cleveland was not as sagacious as some of the great occasions required. Yet some of his mistakes can probably be laid to the charge of these very attributes of generalship, one of which is to assail the enemy at every weak point and on every favorable opportunity, to be constantly on the lookout for defects in his armor, and to strike vigorously at those defects. Now the very thing that may be considered bravery of the highest type in a military officer may also be regarded as indiscretion in a statesman. The Venezuela panic message, for instance, mixed the expressions of a statesman with the brusqueness of a general of the army. If it had been carefully edited by a calm statesman, it would have been much better both for the personal comfort of the author and for the business interests of the country.

But Mr. Cleveland might not have permitted anybody to draw the blue pencil through the last paragraph of that message, in which the chief source of trouble lay. It is probable that Mr.

Olney did propose to do so, but was checked in the attempt. Mr. Cleveland has always been decidedly averse to relinquishing his individuality, and its bold assertion, more in action than words, perhaps, is one of the secrets of his success in bearing down opposition and succeeding against the onslaughts both of friends and enemies. Take the case of Tammany, for instance, in Cleveland's last campaign. This solid organization imagined that it held New York as in a safe for which nobody but the "boss" had the combination, and the state committee of seventy-two had instructions from that mighty mogul to arrange matters politically so that Mr. Cleveland would be excluded from the White House. Bourke Cockran, moreover, the official orator of Tammany, who has since done "works meet for repentance," denounced the man of destiny, bringing all the tricks of the orator most effective and telling with the average audience, to aid his purpose. Vituperation in its various forms was directed against the popular candidate, and satire, cynicism, and irony were hurled in reckless profusion at him. "Grover Cleveland," said the silver-tongued orator in a tone of withering sarcasm, "is the most popular man in the country every day in the year, except election day." This hit drew roaring applause, but it proved a terrible boomerang to Cockran on the 8th of November following that applause.

I have referred to Mr. Cleveland's habit, in whatever he said or wrote, of keeping in prominence the idea that the people were the first object of consideration, and that parties and their machines should be relegated to a secondary position or totally ignored. His method in this respect was pretty well illustrated in a speech at the Manhattan Club, a short time after his last election, a speech which also reveals what he himself considered largely as the secret of his success. He said : —

"The American people have become politically more thoughtful and more watchful than they were ten years ago. They are considering now, vastly more than they were then, political principles and party policies, in distinction from party manipulation and the distribution of rewards for partisan services and activities. In the present mood of the people neither the Democratic party nor any other party can gain and keep the support of the majority of our voters by merely promising or distributing personal spoils and favors from partisan supremacy.   They are thinking of principles and policies, and they will be satisfied with nothing short of the utmost good faith in the redemption of the pledges to serve them in their collective capacity by the inauguration of wise policies and giving to them honest government.   I would not have this otherwise, for I am willing that the Democratic party shall see that its only hope of successfully meeting the situation is by being absolutely and patriotically true to itself and its profession.   This is a sure guaranty of success, and I know of no other."

The last words of this sapient advice naturally recall the language of Shakespeare in the mouth of old Polonius in that famous advice to his son, who was just going out into the world :

> " This above all, — to thine own self be true ;
> And it must follow, as the night the day,
> Thou canst not then be false to any man."

CHAPTER XVII.

THE SIGNIFICANCE OF THE WILSON TARIFF LAW.

Intended to wipe out every vestige of Republican tariff legislation. — How
the law has proved a boomerang and deprived the Democrats of a
return to power for a long period. — How men accustomed only to
little places and little interests cannot be expected to deal with great
matters.

THE special purpose of the Wilson Bill was to wipe out
every enduring vestige in tariff legislation of the Republican party. That party had been in power for thirty-two years,
and now that the Democrats had got into office for the first
time since the war, they were anxious to make a record all
their own, with a view of installing themselves for a long period,
as the Republicans had done. The party was greatly elated.
It determined to make a clean sweep of the country, and to
that end it was necessary to come before the people with a
popular issue ; but the popularity of the issue chosen proved
delusive. The issue was free trade thinly disguised under the
cloak of " tariff for revenue only " ; and as soon as the Democratic party began to doctor the tariff, want of confidence in
the wisdom of the Administration began to make itself manifest, and this feeling increased as the presumable reform in
tariff went on. The people did not want it, never did want it
in this country, and never will want it in its entirety, although
we will naturally, as we become permanently a large creditor
nation, gravitate nearer and nearer to it.

The Wilson Tariff Law may prove a blessing in disguise,
however, as it has effectually barred the Democratic party
from raising the free-trade issue again for many years. Of
course it has been a very expensive experiment for the country,

having cost it, in panics, hundreds of millions of dollars, per-haps; but the history of the experiment will stand in our annals as a solemn warning to voters for all time to let free-trade theories alone if they want to see the country prosperous.

Pursuing their belligerent method of reasoning, then, the first aim of the Democrats was to get the McKinley Law out of the way. Major McKinley had been a conspicuous leader in the Republican party, and the law that bore his name was a popular measure and one calculated to bring prosperity in its wake, as was abundantly proved by results, until free-trade agitation blocked the path of prosperity. It would never do, reasoned the free-traders, to let any part of that law remain on the statute book as a menace to the towering ambition of Democrats and their ideas of sweeping reforms. It would spoil the Democratic issue, and throw discredit on that bait of cheap clothing offered to voters who would have no money to buy it under a free-trade régime. It was resolved, therefore, that free trade in the disguise of " tariff for revenue only " would prove an effective scheme to capture voters.

The eventual election of Major McKinley, however, was a sad blow to this fondly cherished hope. Instead of the Wilson Law being instrumental in consigning the name of McKinley to oblivion, as had been intended, it has been one of the chief instruments in making him a more marked personage than ever, and has helped materially to give him a chance of mak-ing a world-wide and durable reputation among the political benefactors of his day and generation.

As the Wilson Law was calculated to take away from the wage earner a considerable portion of what he had been accus-tomed to earn, in many instances from one third to one half, besides throwing hundreds of thousands out of employment, it did not matter to him whether the price of a coat was two, five, or ten dollars. He could get no money to buy it at any price. So that argument was soon demonstrated to be a cruel mockery to the wage earner, however plausible or conclusive it might seem from a theoretical and professional point of view.

It was no wonder that Mr. Cleveland was highly incensed

when he discovered that an obstinate Senate had altered that solemn production, which he had regarded as a sort of new Declaration of Independence, into a kind of serio-comic farce, and that the document, when presented to the President and compared with the original, afforded a fine illustration of the Napoleonic maxim, " it is but one step from the sublime to the ridiculous,"— the step on that occasion being from the House of Representatives to the maliciously humorous Senate.

Nevertheless, those 640 amendments inserted by the Senate, though they were loudly denounced at the time by the free-trade party as ruinous to the beneficent purposes of the bill as originally designed, turned out to be an unexpected blessing to the country. The Senate is entitled to the praise and admiration of the whole people on account of its masterly mutilation of that bill, for if the measure had passed in the shape that it left the House, it would have been fraught with even more financial mischief. The feeling of distrust and worry inflicted on the seventy million inhabitants of this country would have made them appear so careworn and broken down in health and spirit, as well as in pocket, that people who had not seen each other for several years would have found as much difficulty in mutual recognition, as Professor Wilson experienced in the identification of his own political progeny after the 640 amendments had been attached thereto.

But seriously, this, like many other fiascos, goes to show that if legislators want to be able to judge aright in national financial affairs, if they aim at broad-gauge legislation and wish to shed the shell inseparable from their existence in village communities, they must go to headquarters occasionally, and that is New York City. If they want to exercise clear judgment in regard to business, as commingled with their legislative functions and purposes in the interest of the whole people and in touch with the country at large, they must become imbued, verily saturated, with cosmopolitan ideas. After working themselves for a time into the belief — as by this faith they shall be saved — that financially at least New York is virtually the United States, in the same sense that London is England, and Paris is

France, they should return home and reflect studiously on their experience.

When this supposable trip to the metropolis is over, and a day or two of reflection is indulged in regarding the journey thus enjoyed, the eyes of the traveler will gradually open, and he will begin to wonder why he has been trifling his time away around his native town for half a lifetime with his eyes half shut. His ears also will have passed through a course of similar development, and his whole intellectual capacity will be endowed with vastly improved powers of absorption, reception, and retention. For the first week or so he will look upon his fellow townsmen with a feeling similar to that with which Captain Lemuel Gulliver regarded the Lilliputians, according to the account given by Dean Swift of that remarkable nation of midgets ; and after going through this preliminary process, the legislator will find himself much more capable of legislating in the interests of finance and business, and the measures which he may introduce or influence by his speeches and advice in committee, or on the floor, will take on a more statesmanlike character than those that he had assisted in passing prior to his metropolitan experience.

Moreover, he will become a missionary and make converts by the dozen of the stay-at-homes. He will have discovered that a month's travel is worth a year's reading, or a college or office education, for all the practical purposes of mental evolution ; and as soon as he gets through the next session he will come again and probably bring a few of his friends with him. He may finally settle down here and become a millionaire. There is no romancing about this ; I can quote historical and biographical examples within my own personal experience for the probabilities and possibilities which I am now considering.

People who have been born in small towns and interior places, and leave those haunts of boyhood in early youth, may return to them for social reminiscences or to renew the feelings of family ties, but they never go back there to get any information or knowledge to guide them as lawyers, statesmen, or financiers. The information which they must seek is not there to be obtained.   We never read of Daniel Webster, for instance, going back to Salisbury in New Hampshire to post himself for any of his great speeches; nor do we ever hear of Henry Clay having gone to Ashland, near Lexington, Kentucky, for that purpose; nor of John C. Calhoun returning to South Carolina.

The metropolitan community, for these and many other reasons, is the great center of attraction.   It draws within its irresistible influence people from all parts of the globe, as the loadstone mountain was said to have drawn Mahomet in his coffin.   But, unlike the case of Mahomet, the metropolis draws the people while they are very much alive, and the more vigorous they are the more easily it draws them.

It is not from the best of libraries that people learn most in the metropolis.   It is from the actual contact with such a large variety of people of many minds and opinions, and of many nations, that are constantly to be met there.   This has a quickening effect on the perceptive faculties that men who pass their existence in small towns never experience. " Iron sharpeneth iron," says Solomon; " so a man sharpeneth the countenance of his friend."   There is, perhaps, no place where this shrewd observation of the wise king of Israel is more vividly realized than in Wall Street.

Some men attempt to ignore this educational power and civilizing influence of large cities, but had it prevailed in the last Democratic Congress, there would have been, in truth, no Wilson Bill to menace our prosperity, no paralyzing amendments, and no regrets and sorrows and heartburns over what was and what could never be.

CHAPTER XVIII.

A BATCH OF LEGACIES.

Devised and bequeathed to the Republican party by the last will and testament of the last Democratic Congress. — The unfinished business of eight years of hard and anxious work in the White House. — Lincoln's views on the Constitution and the tariff.

THERE never has been another such large batch of legacies left by any retiring political party in the United States since the origin of the Republic as that devised by the Democratic party to its successors in office.

Not one of the various reforms which the President introduced and had toiled over many a day and night during eight years was satisfactorily consummated. All were left in such an inchoate condition that we might aptly refer to them as " unfinished business." If that archaic prejudice which stands in the way of a President's enjoying a third term did not exist, perhaps Mr. Cleveland might have been afforded an opportunity of seeing the fruits of his anxious thoughts and arduous labors, and the country might have been made permanently prosperous and happy by the result. Republics are proverbially ungrateful, however, and Mr. Cleveland found this to be true. Perhaps the numerous cautions and the sound advice which he has been in the habit of giving the Democratic party may bear fruit when that party gets into power again, and his reforms may be prosecuted, but probably not with the same vigor and enthusiasm with which they were begun. Future generations may produce men of as great vim and self-confidence as Mr. Cleveland, but it is doubtful.

Chief among the legacies, that of the tariff has been already dealt with by the McKinley administration, and the deficit in the revenue, which was a source of so much trouble to the Democrats, has been changed into a surplus.

It may not be out of place to note here that England and English manufacturers were even more disappointed than Mr. Cleveland that he was not chosen for a third term. He is one of the most popular Americans in Great Britain. Yes, many of the English regard Mr. Cleveland as a second Washington, despite the matter of the Venezuela boundary, thus proving that the bread-and-butter question appeals more strongly to the human heart with many people than does any feeling of patriotism. Free trade with this country would be one of the greatest instrumentalities possible for enriching England at our expense. It would make of us a semi-philanthropic treasury from which England could draw largely as long as we should be able to avert national bankruptcy. When this crisis should arrive, England might send over a receiver, wind the thing up, and establish most of her manufactures on this soil. This would have the merit of being a bloodless victory for the autocrats of cheap labor.

Of the other half dozen or so of reforms projected by Mr. Cleveland, none but the repeal of the purchasing clause of the Sherman Silver Law came to any definite result, and that, as I have shown elsewhere, was so ill-timed and otherwise mismanaged that it caused a disastrous panic. The abortive attempts made at these reforms were a fruitful auxiliary cause of our financial ills during the four years prior to Mr. McKinley's election.

With regard to Mr. Cleveland's personal interference in originating legislation, as in the case of the Sherman Bill, he seems to have disregarded two of his own maxims, namely, " Public office is a public trust," and " The duty of a President is simply executive." As I have formerly remarked, the rule of action as laid down in the Constitution regarding the extent to which the President may go in giving Congress " information of the state of the Union," and in " recommending for its consideration such measures as he shall judge necessary and expedient," may give rise to some nice distinctions, as may also the further power accorded to him by the same instrument " to convene both Houses or either of them on extraordinary occasions."

These points have been subjects of considerable comment by jurists, politicians, and statesmen ; but Abraham Lincoln, in one of his short, pithy, common-sense analyses, has probably thrown more light on the subject than the majority of those who have attempted it.   Mr. Lincoln, referring to this provision in the Constitution (Article II., 3, 1) and also to the tariff question, says : —

"By the Constitution, the Executive may recommend measures which he may think proper, and he may veto those which he thinks improper, and it is supposed that he may add to these certain indirect influences to affect the action of Congress. My political education strongly inclines me against a free use of any of these means by the Executive to control the legislation of the country. As a rule, I think it better that Congress should originate as well as perfect its measures without external bias. I therefore would rather recommend to every gentleman who knows that he is to be a member of the next Congress, to take an enlarged view and post himself thoroughly, so as to contribute his part to such an adjustment of the tariff as shall produce a sufficient revenue, and in its other bearings, so far as possible, be just and equal to all sections of the country and classes of the people."

If this wise advice of the martyr President had been always taken by his successors, what a boon it would have conferred on the country !   But it was not consonant with the disposition or cultivated habits of our late Executive to pay much heed to advice, either of ancient sages or modern legislators. When a legislator or expert financier, thinking he had a good thing to communicate to the presumable fountain of legislative wisdom, would call at the White House, President Cleveland would receive him cordially, listen to his statement, and then make a brief reply, at the conclusion of which he would mentally move the previous question, cutting off all debate while he preserved an attitude of politeness toward his visitor, who in most instances soon grew weary of the one-sided conversation, and was gracefully bowed out by the secretary, who doubtless congratulated his chief that another "crank" had been summarily disposed of.

The attempt to run the government on theories, as substitutes for practical measures, proved, and always will prove, a signal failure. Hence the people thought that it was safer to return to the old practical method that had worked so well, generally, for thirty-two years.

One of the remarkable features of the attempted legislation of the late Democratic administration was the ill-considered and crude character of the greater number of the measures formulated. They showed evidence of being mentally undigested, and exhibited a deficiency in breadth of view and comprehensiveness. Take, for example, the Income Tax Bill, which was killed by the United States Supreme Court. That measure provided for throwing more than half the burden on the State of New York, and pretty nearly all that half on New York City. This was pleasing enough to the Southern and Northwestern people, and of course made the bill very popular in those sections.

Such crudeness and narrowness appeared in many legislative measures during the last Democratic administration. It was so with the currency question, and also when the administration essayed to settle international complications by applying to these the ordinary methods of running party politics. The idea of the fitness of things seemed frequently lost sight of, and often discord instead of harmony ruled in administration affairs.

CHAPTER XIX.

TARIFF FOR PROSPERITY ONLY.

The invaders of our home markets repulsed. — Foreign manufacturers and the products of their pauper labor not in demand. — Definitions of revenue tariff and protective tariff. — The latter fairly provided for in the Dingley Bill, and wool restored to the farmers. — Home markets in preference to foreign. — How McKinley humorously caught the clothier member for Boston on the cheap clothing argument. — Home capital and home labor will get a chance for development, and the time of prosperity has come. — Practical outcome of the protection and free-trade doctrines considered. — The testimony on this subject of two eminent witnesses, James Buchanan and Grover Cleveland.

THE most important measure of a Republican Congress was the Tariff Bill. This, despite the strongest possible free-trade opposition, was passed almost on the lines of the former McKinley Bill, which during the brief period of its existence gave such bright promise of permanent prosperity.

The salutary effect of the late tariff legislation has been demonstrated most conspicuously in the unparalleled showing of our foreign trade, which I shall review in the following chapter. Another good result of the tariff law is that a sufficient revenue, if economically administered, seems to be assured to the government, and that "endless chain," which had a constant tendency to deplete the treasury gold reserve, and which gave such trouble to the last Democratic administration, has vanished. The Treasury at the end of the fiscal year had a gold surplus of $188,000,000; the largest, I believe, during the past eight years.

There can be no doubt about the legitimacy and propriety of this taxation, for the Constitution of the United States says in the Eighth Section of the First Article : " Congress shall have power to lay and collect taxes, duties, imposts, and excises to pay the debts and provide for the common defense and general welfare of the United States . . . also to regulate commerce with foreign nations." This authority, being the highest law of the land, places the power of Congress to " collect taxes, duties, and imposts " beyond doubt.

The question may then arise : If Congress has power to impose taxes other than those for " revenue only," has the lawmaking machinery the power to lay taxes, through tariff laws, for the protection of American industries and labor? Most decidedly it has, for it is expressly stated in the section quoted that these taxes are to " provide for the common defense and general welfare of the United States." There is no provision for defense more urgently required than that against the invasion of the needy manufacturers of Europe, with their pauper-labor goods and merchandise, for the purpose of capturing our markets, breaking up our manufactories, and reducing our great army of artisans and laborers to their own status.

If the free-trade party in this country should get the upper hand, the invasion suggested would be worse than that of the Goths, Huns, and Vandals who overran western Europe and eventually brought about the fall of the Roman Empire.

If anybody should consider this opinion as to the possible invasion exaggerated, I should simply give him an object lesson in geography. Europe has an army, most of it hungry and desperate, of 312,000,000 to be drawn upon for the purpose of that invasion, with the forces of Asia, more hungry still, consisting of a reserve of 800,000,000. If 100,000,000 of the latter were imported — a number that would hardly be missed — Americans would have a hard time of it, and this, or something like it, is the inevitable prospect if ever the free-traders should get a chance of running this country on the lines indicated in the original Wilson Tariff Bill. If these immigrants did not appear here in physical form, the fruits of their labor would, and that would be worse.

This contingency, I think, however, is now remote. The people have had a rude awakening from the soft lethargy into which they had been lulled by those who promised to lead them to the Elysian fields of permanent prosperity, where, by virtue of European cheap clothing and a list of luxuries put before their hungry gaze (which they had no money to buy), they might pass the remainder of their days in rest, quietude, and happiness. That dream has passed away, I hope forever; and the people are able to look back and perceive how they were misled and cajoled out of their votes to create a condition of things that had brought the country, but for its wonderful internal strength and unlimited resources, to the very verge of bankruptcy. Four years more of that régime would probably have left the reserve corps of the invaders very little except land to plunder on their arrival. The free-trade leaders, with their foreign myrmidons, seemed determined on making a clean sweep of everything available, and bringing ruin upon all that the protective system had been instrumental in building up since the close of the war.

True, their late chief has not relinquished hope nor ceased trying to inspire the small remnant of his adherents to maintain the fight in the future. He left office exhorting his followers to "continue the struggle" against "mad protection," to "challenge boldly to open warfare the enemies of free trade, and guard against treachery and half-heartedness in the camp." This was the language which he had used a few years before to Mr. Catchings, a Congressional friend of his, and these were the sentiments with which he still seemed to be inspired on his departure from the White House, despite the signal defeat of all the factions by whom he had been elected.

His former forces, however, met their defeat in November, 1896, and the McKinley administration, despite the war with Spain in the meantime, has brought prosperity to the nation, as shown in the unprecedented balance of trade in our favor. On the subject of this balance of trade, as exhibited in the report of the Bureau of Statistics, a separate chapter will show the prosperous results of the recent tariff law as opposed to the free-trade idea.

The subject of tariff taxes, or duties, divides itself into two parts. One is a tariff for revenue only, and the other is a tariff for both revenue and the protection of labor and native industries. Failure to recognize this distinction has led to grave and numerous errors, one of which is that all articles, both home and foreign, which are on the tariff list, cost consumers the price of the article as estimated by the manufacturer or producer, to which is added the amount of the tariff. This seems at first sight to be very plausible reasoning, but it is quite erroneous, applying only to the foreign productions which are not also produced on this side, or not in sufficient quantity to supply demand. The consumer "pays the freight" in that case, but the articles that are produced exclusively on the other side are in a very small minority and are becoming daily smaller. This is one reason why there is such deep anxiety there for a share, and that the lion's share, if possible, of our markets. When a foreigner tells you that this desire arises purely out of international love and amity for the United States and a strong desire to patronize our country without any ulterior motive, you should take his statement *cum grano salis*, — and sometimes the dose of salt must be a very big one. There must be a selfish motive in all trade, outside the ranks of socialists, and they are unselfish only theoretically.

As Mr. McKinley has given the best definition of these two kinds of tariff, let us allow him the floor on that subject. In the course of a speech he says, regarding a revenue tariff: —

"This brings us face to face with the two opposing systems, that of a revenue as distinguished from a protective tariff, and upon their respective merits they must stand or fall. Now, what are they? First, what is a revenue tariff? Upon what principle does it rest? It is a tariff or tax placed upon such articles of foreign production imported here as will produce the largest revenue with the smallest tax; or, as Robert J. Walker, late Secretary of the Treasury and author of the tariff of 1846, from whom the advocates of the measure draw their inspiration, put it: —

"'The only true maxim is that which experience demonstrates will bring in each case the largest revenue at the lowest rate of duty, and that no duty be imposed upon any article above the lowest rate which will yield the largest amount of revenue. The revenue (said Mr. Walker) from *ad valorem* duties last year (1845) exceeded that realized from the specific duties, although the average of the *ad valorem* duties was only 23.57 per cent. and the average of the specific duties 41.30 per cent., presenting another strong proof that the lower duties increase the revenue.'

" To secure larger revenue from lower duties necessitates largely increased importations, and if these compete with domestic products the latter must be diminished or find other and distant, and I may say impossible, markets or get out of the way altogether. A genuine revenue tariff imposes no tax upon foreign importations the like of which are not produced at home; or, if produced at home, in quantities not capable of supplying the home consumption, in which case it may be truthfully said the tax is added to the foreign cost and is paid by the consumer.

" A revenue tariff seeks out those articles which domestic production cannot supply, or only inadequately supply, and which the wants of our people demand, and imposes the duty upon them, and permits as far as possible the competing foreign product to be imported free of duty. This principle is made conspicuous in the bill under consideration; for example, wool, a competing foreign product, which our own flock-masters can fully supply for domestic wants, is put upon the free list, while sugar, with a home product of only one eleventh of the home consumption, is left dutiable."

Mr. McKinley defines a protective tariff as follows : —

" What is a protective tariff ? It is a tariff upon foreign imports so adjusted as to secure the necessary revenue, and judiciously imposed upon those foreign products the like of which are produced at home or the like of which we are capable of producing at home. It imposes the duty upon the competing foreign product; it makes it bear the burden or duty, and, as far as possible, luxuries only excepted, permits the non-competing foreign product to come in free of duty. Articles of common use, comfort, and necessity which we cannot produce here it sends to the people untaxed and free from custom-house exactions. Tea, coffee, spices, and drugs are such articles, and under our system are upon the free list. It says to our foreign competitor, if you want to bring your merchandise here, your farm products here, your coal and iron ore, your wool, your salt, your pottery, your glass, your cottons and woolens, and sell alongside of our producers in our markets, we will make your product bear a duty; in effect, pay for the privilege of doing it. Our kind of a tariff makes the competing foreign article carry the burden, draw the load, supply the revenue; and in performing this essential office it encourages at the same time our own industries and protects our own people in their chosen employments. That is the mission and purpose of a protective tariff. That is what we mean to maintain, and any measure which will destroy it we shall firmly resist, and if beaten on this floor we will appeal from your decision to the people, before whom parties and policies must at last be tried. We have free trade among ourselves throughout thirty-eight states and the territories and among sixty millions of people. Absolute freedom of exchange within our own borders and among our own citizens is the law of the Republic. Reasonable taxation and re- straint upon those without is the dictate of enlightened patriotism and the doctrine of the Republican party."

Free-traders, both foreign and domestic, seem to assume that the human race is one happy family, and that each nation should share its peculiar advantages and surplus production with every other nation. They appear to think this is the natural right of the latter, but they do not extend this style of reasoning to other concerns of life. They do not seem to see that our markets are a part of our natural rights which have been built up by the people, just as much as a piece of property belonging to any one is his peculiar right; or, to make the illustration clearer, as much as a share or number of shares of stock in a corporation is the property of the person who purchases or obtains them for some valuable consideration. No one of common sense and discretion would think of asking that person for a part of those securities without paying for them; and the United States citizen has just as vital and solid interest in the markets which he and perhaps some of his forefathers have assisted to build up, while the free-trade foreigners with the aid of our own free- traders were trying hard to pull them down, as the holder in the supposed case has in his corporation securities. The only difference is that the law of the land does not always recognize property in general markets, yet the claim of the citizen is as equitable from the standpoint of natural justice in the one case as in the other, and that is one of the strongest reasons why we want a statute law that will recognize our equitable claim.

If it is asked why the consumer does not pay the full amount of the tariff, it is easy to point out that the sharp competition, both foreign and domestic, has a tendency to keep prices down, while in the case of the non-protected article, there is no competition, and the seller as a matter of course takes full advantage of the demand. The consumer and foreign producer pay the tariff between them.

The doctrine of the Cobden Club is just the reverse of our tariff principle. Their rule is to tax no foreign product whose like is a home product. Our protective principle is to tax every product whose like is a home product, and to put those we do not produce on the free list. It is very well for a nation to take the Cobden attitude when it is not self-supporting in the prime necessities of life, and when it is to its great advantage to have all the ports of the world open to it; but even England does not carry out the Cobden free-trade idea *in toto*.

The *ad valorem* system has been done away with as far as possible in the new Dingley Tariff Bill, and the specific system has been adopted wherever it was practicable. The *ad valorem* system is based upon value, the other upon quantity. The one is based upon the foreign valuation, difficult of ascertainment and resting in the judgment of experts, whose interests are usually on the side of undervaluation; the other rests upon quantity, fixed and well-known the world over, always determinable and always uniform. The one is assessed by the yard-stick, the ton, and the pound weight of commerce, and the other is assessed by the foreign valuation fixed by the foreign importer or his agent in New York or elsewhere, fixed by the producer, fixed by anybody, at any price, to escape the payment of full duties. The valuation under the *ad valorem* system is not even uniform throughout the United States, for the valuations fixed upon imported goods at the port of Boston are often different from the valuations fixed on the same class of goods arriving in New York, Philadelphia, San Francisco, or Charleston.

So we do not have and cannot have a uniform value, for the value is subject always to the cupidity or dishonesty of the foreign importer or producer. It is a system that has been condemned by all the leading nations of the world, for the reason that there can be no honest administration of the revenue laws so long as the value is fixed thousands of miles away from the point of production and impossible of verification at home. Henry Clay said fifty years ago : "Let me fix the value of the foreign merchandise, and I do not care what your duty is."

The "home market" is another object of disapproval on the part of the free-trader. He wants it abolished, and this with the knowledge that it absorbs more than nine tenths of our own products. He wants us to go outside and hunt for new markets, in competition with nations who can procure labor for as much per week, and in some instances per month, as we pay by the day. How would the country get along without the home market of New England, for instance? The New England states purchase about $200,000,000 worth annually of products from the northwest, middle, and Pacific sections. It would be foolish to give up such a profitable market as this to go in search of another in some foreign country. Yet that is virtually what free-traders ask us to do, although we have competition to face, no matter which way we turn. Even in our great staple, wheat, competition is becoming exceedingly sharp. India, for example, which about a dozen years ago shipped only about 50,000 bushels, is now shipping more than 50,000,000 annually ; and India can put wheat down in the markets of Europe, counting both cost of production and carriage, about as cheaply as we can transport it to the markets abroad, without calculating the cost of production. Of course that country is now handicapped in exports through the recent famine, but this is only temporarily. Just think of it, the transportation of wheat is as heavy an item to our farmers as the whole cost of raising and transportation is to the farmers of India ! This would seem impossible, but a prominent member of the House of Representatives, Mr. Dunn, is responsible for the figures; and, if they are correct, competition in wheat is certainly out of the question.

I learn from another source that agricultural wages in India range from $20 to $25 a year. This would be but a moderate rate per month for a farm laborer in the United States, where the average, I believe, is about $25. Yet we find some free-traders who seem to be under the delusion that wages are as high abroad as they are here. Mr. William Barbour, of the Flax Spinning Company, Paterson, New Jersey, who has also a flax mill at Lisburn, Ireland — the number of hands in the Irish mill being 2900 and in the New Jersey mill 1400 — says that the total pay roll is pretty nearly the same in both establishments, which makes the wages here more than double. The German laborer gets from 47 to 70 cents per day, and for skilled labor 80 to 92 cents. In England the wages paid for agricultural labor is about $12.65 per month. In British India the wages of men is 6 cents per day, and $1\frac{1}{2}$ cents for women. In Kurnel the highest permanent wages are 50 cents per month. In Bombay and Madras laborers are paid from 6 to 12 cents per day.

So these are some of the rates against which we should have to seek new markets for our grain if the free-trade doctrine should prevail.

When the free-trader is driven from most of his strongholds in argument, he takes refuge in that of cheap clothing. A laughable incident occurred a few years ago in Congress illustrating this point. Major McKinley played the comedy part with serious effect, and an honorable member of the House, who was also the head of a prominent clothing establishment in Boston, furnished the chief butt for the ridicule, in company with Mr. Mills of Texas. Major McKinley was arguing that the subject of cheaper clothing so much talked about was not broad enough for a national issue, and that there was more talk than reality about it. This was the whole scene as reported verbatim in the *Congressional Record*. Major McKinley was saying: —

"I represent a district comprising some 200,000 people, a large majority of the voters in the district being workingmen. I have represented them for a good many years, and I have never had a complaint from one of them, that their clothes were too high. Have you? [Applause.] Has any gentleman on this floor met any such complaint in his district?

"MR. MORSE (of Massachusetts). They did not buy them of me.

"MR. MCKINLEY. No! Let us see; if they had bought of the gentleman from Massachusetts it would have made no difference, and there could have been no complaint. Let us examine the matter.

"[Mr. McKinley here produced a bundle containing a suit of clothes, which he opened and displayed amidst great laughter and applause.]

"Come, now, will the gentleman from Massachusetts know his own goods? [Renewed laughter.] We recall that the chairman of the Committee on Ways and Means [Mr. Mills of Texas] talked about the laboring man who worked for ten days at a dollar a day, and then went with his ten dollars' wages to buy a suit of clothes. It is the old story. It is found in the works of Adam Smith. [Laughter and applause.] I have heard it in this House for ten years past. It has served many a free-trader. It is the old story, I repeat, of the man who gets a dollar a day for his wages, and having worked for the ten days goes to buy his suit of clothes. He believes he can buy it for just $10; but "the robber manufacturers" have been to Congress, and have got 100 per cent. put upon the goods in the shape of a tariff, and the suit of clothes he finds cannot be bought for $10, but he is asked $20 for it, and so he has got to go back to ten days more of sweat, ten days more of toil, ten days more of wear and tear of muscle and brain to earn the $10 to purchase the suit of clothes. Then the chairman gravely asks, Are not these ten days entirely annihilated?

"Now, a gentleman who read that speech or heard it was so touched by the pathetic story that he looked into it and sent me a suit of clothes identical with that described by the gentleman from Texas, and he sends me also the bill for it, and here is the entire suit, "robber tariffs and taxes and all" have been added, and the retail cost is what? Just $10. [Laughter and applause.] So the poor fellow does not have to go back to work ten days more to get that suit of clothes. He takes the suit with him and pays for it just $10. [Applause.]

"But in order that there might be no mistake about it, knowing the honor and honesty of the gentleman from Massachusetts [Mr. Morse], he went to his store and bought the suit. [Laughter and cheers.] I hold in my hand the bill.

"Mr. Struble (of Iowa).   Read it.
"Mr. McKinley (reading) : —

"'Boston, May 4, 1888.

"'J. D. Williams, bought of Leopold Morse & Co.; Men's, Youths', and Boys' clothing; 131 to 137 Washington street, corner of Brattle.   To one suit of woolen clothes, $10.   Paid.'

"[Renewed laughter and applause.]

"I never knew of a gentleman engaged in this business who sold his clothes without a profit. [Laughter.]   And there is the same $10 suit described by the gentleman from Texas that can be bought in the city of Boston, can be bought in Philadelphia, in New York, in Chicago, in Pittsburg, anywhere throughout the country at $10 retail the whole suit, coat, trousers, and vest, and at 40 per cent. less than it could have been bought for in 1860 under your low tariff and low wages of that period.   [Great applause.]   It is a pity to destroy the sad picture of the gentleman from Texas which was to be used in the campaign, but the truth must be told.   But do you know that if it was not for protection you would pay a great deal more for these clothes?"

The bewildering inconsistency of some of the items in the Wilson Law bordered on the sublime of effrontery.   For instance, while it taxed the farmer on almost everything he has to buy, it put one of his best paying staples, wool, on the free list, thus at the same time depriving the country of the means of making good cheap home-made clothing, turning the market over to the foreigner, and also depriving the people of cheap mutton.   Cheap mutton is a great boon, especially when the "Beef Trust" raises prices.   Mutton at such times has usually been advanced in price only very slightly as compared with other provisions.

The restoration of wool to the farmer is another good point in the Dingley Bill, which is substantially a restoration of the McKinley statute, and it has thus far been largely instrumental in reviving a state of business and industrial prosperity such as that enjoyed under the free operation of the McKinley Law, especially during the last year of the Harrison administration.

It was rather amusing to witness the ostensible surprise (for it would be an insult to their judgment to call it real) of certain of the free-trade and low-tariff newspapers at the high tariff of the Dingley Bill. Certain of these exponents of public opinion pretended that they imagined the changes, if any, were going to be on the lines of the Wilson-Gorman Law. Now this is a confession that these organs know less than the rank and file of the voters whom they propose to instruct. Did not a large majority of the latter state emphatically, at the polls, that they had had enough of the Wilson Bill and all similar enactments? and by the same silent expression did they not demand the higher tariff that would protect labor and the industries upon which labor has to depend for sustenance? It was the plain duty of Congress to proceed, as the servants of the sovereign voters, to formulate this expression of the latter into a bill, which they did, and for the same reason it became the executive duty of the President to sign that bill, making it a law, if it were to his mind in harmony with the will of the people who elected both him and Congress to do this work.

Some of these very newspapers referred to strongly advocated the election of the McKinley ticket, knowing that in the platform of the Republican party there was a plank promising " the most ample protection for wool, the product of the great industry of sheep raising, as well as for the finished woolens of the mill "; and then the same newspapers turned around, because the Republican Congressmen proposed, very unlike free-trade politicians, to fulfil their promises as laid down in the platform on which they were elected. The only question about the wool schedule was the real meaning of " most ample protection " in the platform. Though the phrase is somewhat vague, perhaps designedly so, yet it is manifest that it cannot mean any less protection by the Dingley Law than that afforded by the McKinley Law. The people wanted it, and they were bound to have it.

With all the free-trade complaints about high-tariff taxation, the foreigners have managed, even under the Dingley Law, to send us as much stuff of the kind easily produced here as would give profitable employment to half a million of men on this side. From these data, it can be faintly imagined what the condition of enforced idleness would be to a few millions of our wage earners under a full free-trade enactment, with the contraction of and loss to capital which that would imply.

In order to prove that this state of things is no fancy picture, that my inferences are reasonable, and that the unfortunate history of distress and business stagnation is liable to repeat itself under either free-trade or very low-tariff principles, I herewith present the opinions and testimony of two of the most reliable witnesses on this subject, namely, Grover Cleveland and James Buchanan.

In Buchanan's message of December, 1857, a year after his election and thirty-six years before the election of Mr. Cleveland, the following language was used : —

"The earth has yielded her fruits abundantly; our great staples command high prices, and up till within a brief period our mineral, manufacturing, and mechanical occupations have largely partaken of the general prosperity.   We have possessed all the elements of material wealth in rich abundance, yet notwithstanding these advantages, our country in its monetary interests is at present in a deplorable condition.

"In the midst of unsurpassed plenty we find our manufactures suspended, our public works retarded, our private enterprises abandoned, and thousands of useful laborers thrown out of employment and reduced to want.   Under these circumstances a loan may be required before the close of your present session, but this, although deeply to be regretted, would prove to be only a slight misfortune when compared with the suffering and distress prevailing among our people."

In President Cleveland's message of August, 1893, ten months after his election, this emphatic language descriptive of the business and industrial situation was used : —

"With plenteous crops, with abundant promise of remunerative production and manufacture, with unusual invitation to safe investment, and with satisfactory assurance to business enterprise, suddenly financial distrust and fear have sprung up on every side.

"Numerous moneyed institutions have suspended, because abundant assets were not immediately available to meet the demands of frightened depositors.   Surviving corporations and individuals are content to keep in hand the money they are usually anxious to loan, and those engaged in legitimate business are surprised to find that securities they offer for loans, though heretofore satisfactory, are no longer accepted.

"Values supposed to be fixed are fast becoming conjectural, and loss and failure have involved every branch of business."

The periods at which these similar conditions are described in similar terms were thirty-six years apart, but in each instance the free-trade mania was the ruling passion of the leaders of the party in power.

Who can resist the inference that these similarly deplorable conditions of the country, so graphically described by both Presidents, originated to a large extent in the free-trade heresy?

CHAPTER XX.

OUR FOREIGN TRADE AND FREE TRADE.

The immense showing of our foreign trade for the fiscal year ending June 30, 1898. — Our balance of trade far ahead of that of other years and twice the amount of any previous record. — This has been achieved under a protective tariff which free-traders thought was going to ruin the country. — How it tallies with the free-trade doctrine of the Cobden Club and that of its representatives in this country. — The immense increase in the exports of our manufactured goods. — Our wealth increases as our imports diminish and as our exports increase. — We saved in 1898, by the much maligned protective tariff, an amount of money greater by half a billion than the national debt at the close of the Civil War. — The greatest profitable import to us was gold, of which we had a balance of $105,000,000 for the year.

IF anything were wanting to illustrate the great advantages of protective tariff legislation over that for "revenue only," — which failed sadly in affording sufficient revenue, — the history of the United States commerce for the fiscal year ending June 30, 1898, would amply supply that evidence.

The exports of merchandise for this period amounted to $1,231,311,868. This exceeded the exports of the previous fiscal year by $180,318,312, and the exports of 1892 by $201,-000,000. The excess of exports over imports, or the balance of trade in our favor, amounted to $615,259,024, or more than twice the amount ever before recorded in our commercial history.

In the fiscal year in question we sold about two dollars' worth for every dollar's worth we bought, and our growing prosperity is manifested very clearly through this operation. According to the ideas of free-traders of the Cobden Club, such a balance in our favor would indicate that the country was on the way to national ruin ; but it is difficult to understand this theory, so far as we are concerned, when the contrary reasoning gives us such a large balance on the other side of the ocean, and makes us to this extent a creditor nation. Such a financial position can hardly be regarded as a sign of national decay. Our wealth increases as our imports diminish, which is in direct contravention of the arithmetic of the Cobden Club. The total imports for the fiscal year amount to only $616,052,844, against $764,730,412 for the previous year. Our merchandise imports were the smallest since 1885. They fell $148,677,568 short of the aggregate for 1897, and $250,000,000 below that of 1893.

It has been computed by expert statisticians, one of whom is Bradstreet's, that the centennial year of 1876 was the turning-point when the balance began in our favor. Prior to that time, during eighty-five years from 1791, the balance had been generally against us, the aggregate excess of imports over exports for the period having amounted to no less than $2,215,404,610. During the twenty-three years since the centennial year the aggregate excess of exports over imports had been $3,191,268,300, or an amount greater by $510,620,431 than our national debt at the close of the Civil War, in 1865.

It is worthy of note that during the latter period, which shows such a large balance in our favor, the advocates of a protective tariff have been always gaining ground, with the exception of an occasional repulse from which they soon recovered, until they achieved a final triumph in the passage of the Dingley Bill.

If free-traders had had their own way during the past twenty-three years, this immense balance of more than $3,000,000,000, about three fourths as much as all the gold above ground at present, and more than one fourth as much as the money of every description now existing, instead of having been spent in this country, would have gone to be spent in other countries, thus enriching them at our expense. If we had only had protection enough to retain those two odd billions which we lost through free trade in the first period of eighty-five years, we would now have, by actual trade calculation, about half the amount of all the money in the world.

Though the fiscal year ending June 30, 1898, was the most prosperous in the history of our commerce, and of our financial relations with other nations, the proportion of our agricultural exports was not so large as in some former years. They were only 71 per cent. of the total, whereas in 1894 they were 72; in 1893 they were 74; in 1892 they were 78; in 1881 they were 82; and in 1880 they exceeded 83. The exports of our manufactured goods, however, far more than made up the deficiency. They amounted to almost the unprecedented sum of $300,000,000, whereas they never before this time rose to more than $100,000,000.

The increase in the total exports of merchandise for the previous ten years amounts to nearly 100 per cent.; and yet some people, and among them many who were born here, pretend to think that this country has been decreasing in prosperity, and that it has seen its best days.

These exports of our manufactures, under a protective tariff, have been made to all parts of the globe, thus showing that, in order to extend our markets for manufactured articles, a free-trade policy on the part of our government is not absolutely necessary. The free-trade assumption has never been so practically answered as by the figures above quoted.

It will be remembered that after the passage of the Dingley Bill there was some disquieting talk in free-trade circles regarding the way our trade was going to be menaced by retaliation instead of reciprocity, especially by Germany, France, and Great Britain. The first, however, showed her spirit of retaliation in a friendly and appreciative manner by increasing her bill of goods from $50,000,000 in 1897 to $150,000,000 in 1898; the second by increasing hers from $40,000,000 to $100,000,000; and the third, our greatest competitor, by increasing hers from $362,000,000 to $540,000,000. Even Darkest Africa made an increase from $3,000,000 to $17,000,000. Japan increased her order from $4,000,000 to $21,000,000, and China her quota from $4,500,000 to $10,000,000, while Austro-Hungary, which had taken only $500,000, in 1897–98 raised her demand to $5,000,000. Belgium rose from $10,000,000 to $47,000,000, Denmark from $3,000,000 to $12,000,000, and the Netherlands jumped from $16,000,000 to $65,000,000.

There is nothing more agreeable in reviewing the list of these increases than to reflect upon the curious action of Great Britain, who had been preparing to wreak her retaliative vengeance upon us, on account of the tariff laws. Instead of pursuing this inimical policy, she turned around, and, in a truly Christian spirit, even before the sun had gone down upon her wrath, nearly doubled her former large order. Such enemies in commerce are our truest friends.

Another large item of prosperity is shown in the commercial status of gold. The excess of imports in that precious article came within $51,000 of being $100,000,000, and if we count $5,000,000 of gold ore, an addition of $105,000,000 will appear to our balance of trade credit. When to this amount $60,000,000 from our gold mines is added, we need have no dread of gold shipments, which have so frequently been the scare of the stock market, and have often created a nervous feeling in financial circles generally.

Now, we may safely arrive at the conclusion that in order to increase our prosperity further our importations may be limited very considerably. The most important of these is gold, and the others are classified in that part of the tariff schedule which includes all articles of necessity which we do not manufacture ourselves, most of which are on the free list.

The wealthy are also free to enjoy the foreign luxuries that they may fancy by paying the tariff, though that is in every instance so much loss to our own country. There is no law against bestowing benefits and free gifts personally upon foreigners, and this may be looked upon to some extent as reciprocity. We owe some of our great institutions of learning to the free gifts of foreigners, but though we may owe them much, yet we would be overpaying our indebtedness to make a present of our industries to them, the greatest source of our wealth and increasing prosperity.

It is superfluous to multiply arguments on the national wisdom of the policy of protection. The foregoing figures, demonstrating our great prosperity as the result of that policy are sufficient, and this report of our foreign trade by the Bureau of Statistics amply justifies the policy of a tariff for the protection of our industries, artisans, and laborers, as well as for government revenue, and not for revenue only.

Statistics of our foreign trade in the fiscal year ending June 30, 1899, show a favorable balance of trade, not so large as in the former year, but still very considerable. In compensation for the large increase in our imports of merchandise, our exports of manufactured articles show an increase of $50,000,000 We may also study how raw material contributes to this end, and compare the commercial standing of other nations of the world with our own ; we may also reflect upon our last decade's surplus prosperity, our great pelagic expansion and its wonderful possibilities, our commercial relations to other nations, and what those nations think of us in these respects.

The addendum to this chapter will bring up the statistical position of our foreign trade to the end of the fiscal year ending June 30, 1899. The comparative exports and imports for the two years can be seen at a glance, thus : —

For twelve months ended June 30 : —

Merchandise —	1899	1898
Imports — Free of duty	$300,251,333	$291,414,175
Dutiable	396,826,055	324,635,479
Total	$697,077,388	$616,049,654
Exports — Domestic	$1,204,370,305	$1,210,291,913
Foreign	23,073,120	21,190,417
Total	$1,227,443,425	$1,231,482,330
Excess of exports	530,366,037	615,432,676
Gold —		
Imports	$88,954,603	$120,391,674
Exports	37,522,086	15,406,391
Excess of imports	$51,432,517	$104,985,283

Silver —	1899	1898
Imports	$30,696,878	$30,027,781
Exports	56,318,855	55,105,239
Excess of exports	$25,621,977	$24,077,458
Merchandise — Month, June.		
Imports — Free of duty	$25,881,331	$22,820,436
Dutiable . . .	35,804,877	28,344,795
Total	$61,686,208	$51,165,231
Exports — Domestic	$94,828,732	$93,012,297
Foreign	1,995,413	1,966,426
Total	$96,824,145	$94,978,723
Excess of exports	35,137,937	43,813,492
Gold —		
Imports	$3,105,686	$3,330,612
Exports	20,908,327	375,529
Excess of imports		$2,955,083
Excess of exports	$17,802,641	
Silver —		
Imports	$1,917,215	$2,028,803
Exports	3,843,099	4,156,650
Excess of exports	$1,925,884	$2,127,847

These figures are compiled by the Bureau of Statistics at Washington. The first, and most attractive item, perhaps, in this table is our balance of trade or excess of exports over imports. It is still large, namely, $530,366,037, though fully $85,000,000 less than it was the previous year, our imports being $81,000,000 more.

There are items which partly compensate for this large increase in our imports of merchandise. Our exports of manu-factured articles, which are considered separately (and not yet returned), will show an increase of probably $50,000,000 over those of 1898. Moreover, the increase in our imports is largely of raw material and goods that we do not produce except on a small scale. Our profits through the raw material are real-ized in the finished articles which we manufacture from this material, and export. Our decrease in crop exports, therefore,

is considerably offset by our increase in the exports of manufactured articles.

It is worthy of note that, in the calculation of this question
of foreign trade, we have the advantage of most other nations
in our large possession of raw material to be worked up, as
well as the material which furnishes the power for such working. Germany, for example, one of the most enterprising of
our manufacturing competitors, has to import very large quantities of her raw material and a considerable part of her
coal.

If, in this comparison of the increase of our manufactures
with those of other nations, we should take ten years instead of
two, the increase for that period would probably exceed 100
per cent., perhaps 110 or more. The problem of our foreign
trade would become still more interesting, and would place us
in a position where, by a kind of inevitable destiny, we should
become the general absorber of all the surplus business in the
world, and that without any extraordinary ambition or aspirations on our part to attain the distinguished honor, but by
necessity of our position.

Meanwhile we are now actually doing, through the medium
of a protective tariff, paradoxical as it may seem, what our
free-trade friends have long been insisting that we should do
under their tutelage, — capturing the world's markets in defiance of cheaper labor throughout the rest of the globe. Those
ancient centers of commercial power would have stood aghast
at the idea of such an achievement. Who knows but that in
the future we may become not only the center of financial
power and attraction, but the peaceful arbitrator of political
and universal harmony among the nations, when peace conventions shall take rank as historic curiosities in the annals
of a fully developed Republic of the World?

In the language of Tennyson : —

"Not in vain the distance beacons. Forward, forward let us range.
Let the great world spin forever down the ringing grooves of change.
Thro' the shadow of the globe we sweep into the younger day ;
Better fifty years of Europe than a cycle of Cathay."

Let us improve, if possible, in our prosaic way on the Tennysonian sentiment, by taking for the periodic times of our evolution, ten years each of America, instead of fifty years of Europe or a cycle of China.

The result of this retrospect of a decade shows, as I have just stated, that our increase in foreign trade has exceeded 100 per cent. How has it been during the same period with other great commercial nations? We will take the greatest of these, the British, for the purpose of comparison. Let us hear what Lord Farrar has to say upon the subject. At a recent meeting of the British Iron Trade Association, this eminent authority, speaking on the famous subject of the " open door " in commerce, said : —

" The gist of the case put before me is that, while the exports of the iron and steel manufactures of Great Britain are still very large, and indeed larger than those of any other country, their proportion to similar industries in other countries, especially Belgium, Germany, and the United States, is much less than it was ; that there is a large and increasing import of foreign iron and steel into the United Kingdom, and that foreign countries are rivaling us in neutral markets. From these facts it is suggested that this important branch of our industry may be in danger from foreign competition ; and it is whispered, rather than suggested, that we may have to depart from the policy of the ' open door ' and exclude foreign iron and steel goods by different duties."

Now, while this is a thoughtful expression of a most intelligent representative of one of the most favored nations in commerce, some of our free-trade journals are attempting to prove that a nation becomes wealthier in proportion to the continued increase of its imports as compared with its exports.

Let us see what that great authority of John Bull, the *London Iron and Coal Trades' Review*, has to say on the subject.

" In 1876 Great Britain was exporting to the United States from 500,000 to 1,000,000 tons of iron and steel annually, and probably the last thing that troubled our manufacturers at that time was the reflection that the United States could ever manufacture those commodities so cheaply as to be able to compete against themselves in Europe markets.   But the times change.   We have lived to see the day when it is not the getting into American markets, but the keeping of Americans out of our own, that is the chief source of anxiety."

Now, amid a host of general conclusions that might be drawn from the premises and considerations herein enumerated, several are clearly evident ; one is that our country, at the end of the century, exhibits the greatest developments in all history, and, again, that our own progress has been a thousand times greater in all respects than that of any other nation either ancient or modern.   Who can venture to predict what our millennium will be?

It is true, this comparison savors of self-glorification, but it seems thoroughly warranted by events, as well as by what little we can divine of future prospects.

CHAPTER XXI.

RETROSPECTS AND PROSPECTS.

Certain comments and predictions about free-trade legislation and an answer to charges of pessimism. — Analysis of past legislation in its practical outcome, and the prospective hopes of the operation of the measure now gone into effect.

STATEMENTS have been made by certain of my critics that I have been pessimistic on questions in which free-trade theories were concerned.

Such an opinion does not do me full justice. On the contrary, I have been optimistic regarding future prosperity. I have, for instance, been of opinion that the country, though seriously handicapped by free-trade theories embodied in law, might yet rise superior to them and grasp prosperity, though of course not to the same extent as under a judicious measure, affording protection to our industries and to the wages of labor.

I am on record as having given free expression to such opinions on various occasions. I have professed only the capacity of reasoning regarding the future from observation of the past and present; a power which most people of ordinary intellect and education may possess in a greater or less degree, according to the closeness and accuracy of their observations.

Napoleon said, "labor is genius," and it was a familiar aphorism of the old Latin writers that labor could conquer and surmount all obstacles. These are expressions of a solid truth in an exaggerated form, and simply serve to remind us of the inherent power of industry both mental and physical, at the same time affording us encouragement under apparent defeat, and showing us the fatuity of relinquishing hope under the most discouraging circumstances. Most of this world's progress is dependent upon hope. Impelled by laudable feelings of this nature, I wrote the following article, for instance, in January, 1894, at the request of the proprietor of the *New York World* : —

"You ask my opinion as to the prospects of business for 1894. You could not have put a question about which I should be less disposed to be prophetic. There is not much difficulty, perhaps, in making a diagnosis of the present condition of the patient, but if you ask me what is to be the course of his recovery, I must in return ask you, What are going to be the factors acting upon his enfeebled system during the process of convalescence?

"We all know that the trade, the industry, and the finances of the country were, last summer and autumn, prostrated to a degree beyond all former experiences. But just what that portends as to the progress and the date of recovery is not to be determined off-hand. We are not to regard the panic of 1893 as one of the ordinary kind. It was not caused by industrial over-production, nor by financial inflation, such as comes, for instance, out of over-issues of securities for new railroads or other new enterprises ; nor was it caused by over speculation and an excessive inflation of prices ; nor by war, nor by sympathy with great European political complications. None of these ordinary causes of panic had anything to do with the great crisis of last year. The entire business of the country in all its departments of production, trading, financing, and credit was, as a rule, in a perfectly sound, conservative, and fairly profitable condition when the tidal wave struck us. It started and it progressed to its culmination under a sudden fright, lest the excess of silver introduced into our currency system might cause a run on the Treasury gold and compel a general suspension of gold payments, the fear being instigated by a sudden and very large export of gold. This blow at the credit of the government became, in its rebound, a still greater blow at the general credit system of the country at large. Lending at banks was suspended, and business had to be conducted on a cash basis, while sudden liquidation became universal, and failures were consequently unprecedented in number.

"There was here surely havoc enough; never so much, never so cruel. But there is a most radical difference between a panic coming upon sound conditions and one precipitated by intrinsic rottenness; all the difference that there is between an accident to a man in vigorous health and to one weakened by constitutional disease. In one case, nature helps by a self-curative process ; in the other, diseased organic conditions aggravate the mischief caused by the accident. For this reason, I look for a much more rapid recovery from the effects of the purely monetary causes of the panic than has followed our previous great crises ; and, of course, the more so as the source of the silver alarm has been removed by Congress, and public opinion has shown its resolute soundness on that question.

"By this time, we should have witnessed a much larger measure of recovery than has actually appeared, had it not been for the intervention of a new disturbance of confidence arising from the introduction of measures for revolutionizing the commercial policy of the country. Without caring here to express my views either for or against the policy of the Administration in that matter, it is not to be denied that virtually our entire manufacturing industries earnestly regard the proposed large reductions of duty as vitally threatening their business, which is a most potential factor bearing on confidence, regarding which there can be no question that the interval of transition from the old conditions to the new could not be attended with anything short of widespread suspension of both manufacturing and trade ; and, as a matter of fact, it is estimated by competent authorities that the retail business of the country is now curtailed to the extent of from 15 to 20 per cent. of its usual volume, while in most branches of manufacturing the contraction is double that proportion.

"That is the condition of affairs now patent to everybody's eyes. It is so alarming that many cool-headed men even are scared out of all exercise of cool judgment, and ninety men out of every hundred are more or less hopelessly pessimistic about the future. I confess that I am unable to go to the full length of these forebodings. As a young country of marvelous wealth and unequaled powers of recuperation, we are capable of a rapidity of convalescence that can be matched by no other nation. As a largely self-dependent country, we are little exposed to suffer in sympathy with the causes that have prostrated the European commercial states and their colonial dependencies and trade connections. Europe is vitally dependent upon us ; we can afford to be comparatively independent of Europe. In the next place, we have none of the débris of dry rot to get rid of. The equipments of our industries are fresh, complete, up to the most modern improvements, and only delayed by the getting up of steam, while capital is waiting in immense idle hoards to apply the impelling power, and the banks are prepared to afford as much support to business as they were giving on the eve of the unsuspected panic. These certainly are not the sort of conditions that are ordinarily found at this early stage after an ordinary panic; and for this, among other reasons, I do not expect recovery in this case to follow the pace of former tardy recoveries.

"The most stubborn obstacle that now remains to be overcome is the suspension of business until the new tariff duties take effect. Here, also, I think the real probabilities are underestimated in the present gloomy public mood. We have already used up our stocks of merchandise to the verge of absolute exhaustion; our imports are declining to such an extent that the December arrivals of dry goods at New York were only one third of those of a year ago. With supplies in this condition, and with the current output of manufactures falling behind the requirements of consumption, it is not difficult to see that our closed factories must reopen long before the new tariff goes into operation; and, with the reduction in the prices of raw materials and the general concessions in wages that are taking place, there is no apparent reason why moderate profits should not be made upon an early resumption of operations. In proportion as work is resumed, labor will be better employed; and the better employment of labor will extend the market for goods. Under these conditions, the way seems clear to a gradual revival of business and a steady sliding into a healthier and more active condition of affairs. Any mere mood of feeling proves to be a transient sentiment among an active commercial people, and, in this case, we will soon recover our courage and cease to view the situation 'through a glass darkly.' By the close of 1894, I expect to witness a degree of recovery far beyond what most of us now dare to predict. To that extent, I am willing to become a prophet."

Now, this process of reasoning was based on a comparison of the past with the present, and the conclusions were drawn on premises that left out the surprises which never can be foreseen. Such results might have been as foreshadowed, even in the face of the semi-free-trade measure, had it not been for fresh agitation at the wrong time on the silver question in connection with the Sherman Act.

Nobody can now dispute my right to reason on the practical consequences of the Wilson Law after it has cost the nation a positive deficiency debt of $200,000,000 ; to say nothing of the far greater loss in trade and commerce and the various national industries, together with the untold sufferings borne by the armies of idle laborers, the depressed and bankrupt condition of our farmers ; and last, though not least, the business of Wall Street reduced to a state of stagnation never experienced prior to that time. I refer to the time between the passage of that measure and the inauguration of Mr. McKinley, and for a month or two after the latter event, while free-trade consequences were still at work and ably assisted in their depressing effect by obstructionists in the United States Senate.

CHAPTER XXII.

THE TRANS–MISSOURI CASE.

A ruinous decision of the Supreme Court of the United States. — Destructive influence on values and a blow to general business. — A pool law wanted that will ensure railroad and business prosperity.

THERE has been no other subject, perhaps, in the industrial world or in finance and economics for a long period, on which there has been a greater variety of opinions than on the decision of the United States Supreme Court in the case of the Trans-Missouri Freight Association, on the 22d of March, 1897. Nor has there been any other decision in a long time which took by complete surprise so many judges, lawyers, financiers, railroad managers, and newspaper men.

It is my opinion that this famous decision has done more injury in the disturbance of values and the wrecking of fortunes than any half dozen judicial decisions that have ever been rendered in this country. It came, too, in the very worst possible time, just when the country was making the hardest struggle for recuperation.

This Trans-Missouri Association, composed of eighteen railroads beyond the Missouri River, as its name indicates, and covering territory between that eastern boundary and the Rocky Mountains, had entered into an agreement, the real purport of which was to maintain rates up to a living standard on the "live and let live" principle for all, and so as to prevent any of the properties from being driven into bankruptcy by what is known in railroad circles as "cut-throat competition."

Looking at the matter from a common-sense point of view, there seems to the ordinary mind, unbiased by any predilections, nothing unfair in a proposition of this kind. It was merely an arrangement for mutual defense, the bond of mutuality being assurance that the weaker brethren would not or could not readily shirk the maintenance of the principle of the Association upon which its efficiency, vitality, success, and very existence depended, namely, that of inseparable union for one and the same purpose — protection to all.

The essential motive was to maintain reasonable rates, and the object of the association is stated clearly by itself in the following language, " For the purpose of mutual protection by establishing and maintaining reasonable rates, rules, and regulations on all freight traffic, both through and local."

The particulars of the agreement, which are described in detail, relating to management and disposition of freight throughout the territory of the Association, are of no special interest.

In 1890 there was a law passed of which John Sherman, then United States Senator from Ohio, was the father. This law was directed against trusts that were organized in restraint of trade and against public policy. The act was termed "An Act to protect Trade and Commerce against Unlawful Restraints and Monopolies." The first short section describes, in brief, all that is material in the act, for the purpose of understanding its design. It reads as follows : —

" Every contract or combination, in the form of trust or otherwise, or conspiracy, in restraint of trade or commerce among the several states, or with foreign nations, is hereby declared to be illegal. Every person who shall make any such contract or engage in any such combination or conspiracy shall be deemed guilty of a misdemeanor, and, on conviction thereof, shall be punished by fine not exceeding five thousand dollars, or by imprisonment not exceeding one year, or by both said punishments in the discretion of the courts."

Now, the point to be proved in this case is that the Association in question had been guilty of the offense against which the act is directed, namely, " conspiracy in restraint of trade," and arguments of great length were used for the purpose of proving this allegation. The opinion was written by Justice Wheeler H. Peckham and consisted of about 25,000 words. Some of the arguments are strong, but some of them are far-fetched, and, to the minds of the able minority of four judges of the Supreme Court, were far from being conclusive regarding the guilt of the defendants.

If the Sherman Anti-Trust Law and its latest interpretation by a bare majority of one in the Supreme Court are to stand, it is difficult to see how any business where more than one is concerned on either side, can be transacted legally. Almost any transaction can, by strict literal interpretation of the words of the statute and the nature of the case, be construed as im-plying " conspiracy and restraint of trade."

It seems to me that the effect of the Joint Traffic Associa-tions is to hold up the weak roads, whereas the decision of the Supreme Court is to drive them into bankruptcy, which will enable the strong roads to acquire them on their own terms. This will make poor corporations poorer and rich corporations richer. If railroads are to be compelled to surrender to the decision of the United States Supreme Court, then consolida-tion of roads will be the inevitable result, and before the close of the next decade we may witness in this country four or five great systems of railroads, instead of, as at present, several hundreds of them. Already strong evidences of this appear in the New York Central and Pennsylvania acquisitions. Neither the Supreme Court nor Congress can interfere with one road leasing itself to another, nor preventing one road from buying another ; therefore, instead of discouraging consolidation of roads, which should be the case for the general good of the country, the Sherman Anti-Trust Law, under the Supreme Court decision, will drive them into a confederation comprised of few.

This process would certainly be in " restraint of trade," and would so far restrain the smaller roads as to wipe them out of existence, making the monopolistic circle of management more and more circumscribed at every freezing-out operation, until the supreme managerial power would be in the hands of a few companies or possibly only one.   This would be, as it appears to me, a very dangerous power, not only in restraint of trade, but in restraint of government as well.   It might soon become powerful enough to dictate terms to government.   Then what after that?   Probably a railroad oligarchy to supersede the Republic, rendered possible by the manner in which the highest court of the nation had been forced to interpret an unwise statute which throttled the freedom of contract and broke up the government for, of, and by the people.

The decision, however, settles the question in the meantime regarding any combination or agreement among railroad companies to prevent ruinous rate-cutting where the facts are so clearly on record that they are capable of proof; and it would never do to invent or devise mere schemes of evasion of the law, for this would be a false and fraudulent method of doing business.   The companies, however, can act individually and independently, and if they would only observe the amenities of good society toward one another, things might go very well practically.

If the Joint Traffic Association, for instance, should be compelled to disband under the decision of the United States Supreme Court, why could not the members of that association form themselves into a social club, where they could meet and confer with each other ?   It would certainly tend to preserve a harmonious feeling amongst them, and most likely result in uniformity of action in the conduct of their business.   They could talk over the rate question among themselves and easily arrive at conclusions.   One of the number could then establish on his road the rates talked of, and all the others would have the right to adopt similar ones voluntarily.   Such action could not be considered as a combination or an agreement in restraint of trade and commerce.   It is a well-known fact that most of the important diplomatic matters in the relations between civilized nations are talked over and virtually arranged at the social board, which is about the same method as that proposed above for the railroad managers to meet the present unfortunate predicament in which they are placed.

Though the opinion of the majority of the court observes in many of its paragraphs an apparently strict adherence to the letter of the law, it may, perhaps, neglect the spirit to a certain extent. The law, in its essence, is the very thing that the court asserts its infraction to be. It is in restraint of trade and against public policy. The only reliable relief, therefore, is to be found in its repeal. All plans that may be invented to help tide over the trouble will prove nothing but temporary makeshifts, and will be likely to involve the experimenter in further difficulties.

Returning to the decision, it will be seen that the chief point of disagreement between the majority and the minority reports is that the majority adheres to an extremely literal construction, unmindful of the scriptural admonition that " the letter killeth, but the spirit giveth life " ; while the minority dwells on the spirit and the supposable intention of the law ; for nobody who knows the man can conceive of the possibility of John Sherman framing a measure that would drive people, possessed of the most honest intentions, out of business, and help to throw into chaos that financial fabric which he has spent many of the best years of his life in helping to construct.

This view the minority more fully elucidates by the following strictures on the forced construction of the majority : —

" But, admitting arguendo the correctness of the proposition by which it is sought to include every contract, however reasonable, within the inhibition of the law, the statute, considered as a whole, shows, I think, the error of the construction placed upon it. Its title is ' An act to protect trade and commerce against unlawful restraints and monopolies.' The word 'unlawful' clearly distinguishes between contracts in restraint of trade which are lawful and those which are not.

" The plain intention of the law was to protect the liberty of contract and the freedom of trade. Will this intention not be frustrated by a construction which, if it does not destroy, at least gravely impairs both the liberty of the individual to contract and the freedom of trade ? If the rule of reason no longer determines the right of the individual to contract, or secures the validity of contracts upon which trade depends and results, what becomes of the liberty of the citizen or the freedom of trade ? Secured no longer by the law of reason, all these rights become subject, when questioned, to the mere caprice of judicial authority.

"Thus, a law in favor of freedom of contract, it seems to me, is so interpreted as to gravely impair that freedom. Progress, and not reaction, was the purpose of the act of Congress. The construction now given the act disregards the whole current of judicial authority, and tests the right to contract by the conceptions of that right entertained at the time of the year books, instead of by the light of reason and the necessity of modern society. To do this violates, as I see it, the plainest conception of public policy, for, as said by Sir G. Jessel, Master of the Rolls, in Printing Company *vs*. Sampson, 'If there is one thing which more than another public policy requires it is that men of full age and competent understanding shall have the uttermost liberty of contracting, and their contracts, when entered into freely and voluntarily, shall be held sacred, and shall be enforced by courts of justice.'

"The remedy intended to be accomplished by the act of Congress was to shield against the danger of contract or combination by the few against the interest of the many and to the detriment of freedom. The construction now given, I think, strikes down the interest of the many to the advantage and benefit of the few. It has been held in a case involving a combination among workingmen that such combinations are embraced in the act of Congress in question, and this view was not doubted by this court."

But the destructive and inequitable tendency of the act is probably most clearly discerned in the light thrown upon it by Judge White's opinion on its far-reaching influence on labor combinations : —

"The interpretation of the statute, therefore, which holds that reasonable agreements are within its purview, makes it embrace every peaceable organization or combination of the laborer to benefit his condition either by obtaining an increase of wages or diminution of the hours of labor.

"Combinations among labor for this purpose were treated as illegal under the construction of the law which included reasonable contracts within the doctrine of the invalidity of contract or combinations in restraint of trade, and they were only held not to be embraced within that doctrine either by statutory exemption therefrom or by the progress which made reason the controlling factor on the subject.

"It follows that the construction which reads the rule of reason out of the statute embraces within its inhibition every contract or combination by which workingmen seek peaceably to better their condition. It is, therefore, as I see it, absolutely true to say that the construction now adopted, which works out such results, not only frustrates the plain purpose intended to be accomplished by Congress, but also makes the statute tend to an end never contemplated, and against the accomplishment of which its provisions were enacted.

"To my mind, the judicial declaration that carriers cannot agree among themselves for the purpose of aiding in the enforcement of the provisions of the Interstate Commerce Law will strike a blow at the beneficial results of that act, and will have a direct tendency to produce the preferences and discriminations which it was one of the main objects of the act to frustrate."

As an instance of some of the fallacies and inconsistencies of the reasoning on the part of the majority, the following from the majority report is very pertinent : —

"In business or trading combinations, they [meaning the conspirators aforesaid] may even temporarily or perhaps permanently reduce the price of the article traded in or manufactured, by reducing the expense inseparable from the running of many different companies for the same purpose. Trade or commerce under these circumstances may, nevertheless, be badly and unfortunately restrained by driving out of business the small dealers and worthy men whose lives have been spent therein, and who might be unable to readjust themselves to their altered surroundings. Mere reduction in the price of the commodity dealt in might be dearly paid for by the ruin of such a class, and the absorption or control over one commodity by an all-powerful combination of capital."

This language is noteworthy, for the pathetic sympathy it indicates is even more remarkable when the source from which it emanates is thoroughly appreciated. Shocking as it may seem at the first blush, these Supreme Court judges have all been guilty of the offense which they here seem to deplore. They have either established or been prominent members of large law firms open to the charge of the same kind of " conspiracy and restraint of trade" aforesaid, and without any compunction, so far as the public know, until exhibited in this opinion. They have, to use their own language, " driven out of business [the law business, however] worthy men whose lives have been spent therein, and who might have been unable to readjust themselves to their altered surroundings," were it not for the law trusts. To such disaster have these hard-working, educated, honest lawyers been brought eventually through the restraint of trade and the unlawful conspiracy practiced by the large law firms. Yet this is not the worst of it, as regards the case of the law firms compared with other monopolies and trusts. The latter have the merit of reducing the price of the commodity dealt in, which Judge Peckham declares " might be dearly paid for " by the ruin of the class producing the commodity. But who ever heard of a large law firm reducing the price of its advice and services? If it did, its brethren of the bar would in all probability apply for a writ *de lunatico inquirendo* for the purpose of testing its sanity, or the Bar Association would be induced to introduce a bill in Congress for the maintenance of " reasonable costs."

In contradistinction to the majority of opinion it seems, on a fair reading of the Interstate Commerce Act, without being too closely technical, that Congress must have had in mind the idea of protecting reasonable rates when that measure was passed. The first section of the act reads as follows : —

" All charges for any service rendered, or to be rendered, in the transportation of passengers or property as aforesaid, or in connection therewith, or for the receiving, delivering, storage or handling of such property, shall be reasonable and just, and every unjust and unreasonable charge for such service is prohibited and declared to be unlawful."

This would seem to recognize the principle of maintaining reasonable rates, and the terms are evidently employed emphatically in conspicuous contrast to " unjust and unreasonable " rates, which are declared to be unlawful.

One of the worst features connected with the Sherman Anti-Trust Act has been its uncertainty, coupled with the possibly unwitting deception that has been practised in its administration. The law had not only reposed quietly for six years without its mischievous or fatal tendency being discovered, and without giving any intimation of the coming explosion, but it had lulled the people, and especially the railroad companies, into a feeling of perfect security through the several decisions of the United States District Court and Circuit Court of Appeals. In every instance the pooling clause and the agreement to sustain reasonable rates had been sustained until the Trans-Missouri case arose. A series of decisions by these inferior courts, therefore, had induced the parties concerned to believe that contracts, like that of the Trans-Missouri Freight Association, were perfectly legal, until the surprise came from the highest court of appeal. These circumstances all tended to intensify the demoralization to business interests when the certainty was revealed.

CHAPTER XXIII.

THE LAWS RELATING TO TRUSTS, CORPORATIONS, AND RAILROADS.

A better administration of these laws needed. — Safeguards of corporations, and a comparison of ours with those of foreign countries. — The railroad situation and the Supreme Court decision. — Views on the subject. — The pooling question and business interests. — A new law to regulate railroad rates and to define a violation of railroad law indispensable.

IN so far as the laws on the statute book are sufficient to deal with any abuse that corporations or trusts may be guilty of, the question resolves itself into one of execution or of enforcing the law ; and upon the necessity of this in relation to all business concerns in the management and profits of which more than one person is interested, I have always insisted that the terms of the charters of corporations should be fully complied with, and that means of a public official character should be resorted to for the purpose of compelling such compliance.

In some foreign nations matters relating to corporations seem to have better safeguards thrown around them than here. France, Germany and Belgium are all noteworthy in this respect, and England also could impart to us some useful lessons learned in the school of hard experience since the South Sea Bubble and the Mississippi Scheme. The rule regarding paid-up capital is more strictly adhered to abroad, and, in this respect and other matters of administration, New York State lags behind several other states, notably Massachusetts. I see that since the famous court decision in the Trans-Missouri case treated in the preceding chapter much emphasis has been laid on this vital point of administration ; and Mr. V. H. Lockwood and the

Hon. Perry Belmont, both very close reasoners on this subject, have dissected and laid bare the insidious defects of the administration of existing laws in a way that should commend itself to all lovers of justice and equity.

Mr. Belmont in his very elaborate and pithy essay of twenty-five pages in the *North American Review* for April, 1897, dwelt at some length on the conflict of opinion in the United States Supreme Court arising out of state laws regarding railroads and other corporations ; and he finally arrived at the conclusion that congressional legislation is absolutely necessary to settle the pending trouble.

The precedents which Mr. Belmont cites are somewhat unique as well as important in this discussion, and I regret that space will not permit a full quotation, but I insert two paragraphs which illustrate his sharp, legal, and strictly logical method of drawing conclusions : —

> "Although the court has, by the narrow majority of one, decided that the law of 1890 covers common carriers, and has adjudged the comprehensiveness of the word 'every' before the word 'contract,' yet the published conflicting opinions have exhibited such evidence of exhaustive debate in the consultation, if not of animated feeling, between the judicial disputants that there seems little hope of a change of vote on reargument, and another consultation — the members of the court divided *on a question of law*, not of fact.   Therefore the question now at issue is one for Congress.
>
> "There are two new and important considerations confronting the country.   On a first superficial view it is not easy to discover why it should be that if railway directors are really competent — if, as the law demands, they really direct in prescribing rates ; if they do not abandon the work and illegally delegate it to freight agents — the railway corporations cannot achieve, without formal agreements with each other, the thing they have heretofore done by agreements now condemned by the court.
>
> "The other consideration is that if it shall now be seen that organized private capital is not, by its boards of directors acting in corporations, capable of reasonably and safely conducting interstate railway transportation, aided by such help in administration as an energetic Interstate Commerce Commission can give, then socialism

will be heard in an attempt to show that only organized political government can do the work, as it now does in so many European countries, and as the Populists insist must be done in the United States, by government ownership of railways, telegraphs, telephones, and other agencies in public use."

It is not amiss to call attention here to the operations of these great combinations of capital, the development of which seems to have become inseparable from modern business methods, and which are in common parlance erroneously designated as " trusts."

To state the case in plain and simple terms, the object sought to be attained is to put various interests belonging to different parties together so as to form a large concern represented by stock capital without personal liability, having in view a reduction in expenses, greater efficiency, production on a larger scale, and the realization of greater profits without advancing the price. When a number of small individual plants are thus united for a common object, under efficient official management, the expenses are materially cut down. With the increased capital which this method admits, better machinery is secured, with better results in meeting foreign competition, which adds largely to this country's exports. In this way this country has, during the past ten years, increased to an immense extent its ability to compete successfully with Great Britain and other European countries.

Now, the great and underlying principle that has put it in our power during the last decade to make such an unprecedented advance in a department of commerce from which we were generally supposed to have been almost excluded, is that of the much maligned combination of capital. Without such means as we possess (despite much ignorant hostility) of aggregating capital, there could have been no such progress as statistics clearly demonstrate.

People who take a narrow view of the subject say that the system throws men out of employment. To my mind it is evident that there must have been far more money spent in wages when the manufactured exports were $182,000,000 than when they were only $78,000,000 ten years previously. More than double the value of material by nearly $300,000,000 worth, certainly could not be moved by a less number of men. It probably required more than half as many more, namely 50 per cent. ; and during this period labor itself has increased only 25 per cent., thus leaving the workman better off than before the combinations began to make much progress in the improvement of machinery.

It seems unnecessary to go over much more of the ground in detail, as this example very clearly and amply illustrates the principle.

Can anybody imagine that the railroads could employ an army of 800,000 workmen at good wages and that $\frac{1}{100}$ part of a cent per ton per mile would make the difference between dividend and no dividend to certain prosperous roads, if the principle of combination were not worked extensively in the railroad industry? As similar arguments apply to other industries with equal cogency, I consider it unnecessary to multiply examples, as any one can do so for himself simply by opening his eyes, looking over the industrial field past and present, coolly reflecting on the situation, and without permitting political prejudice or newspaper sensationalism to cloud his reason or distort his common sense. One of the results inseparable from combinations, no matter how selfish the promoters may be, is that they make everything which they produce cheaper to the consumer than it possibly could be without their existence ; and the larger the combination, as a rule, the better and the cheaper is the consumer served. It is only during the brief transition period of the change from the separate concerns to the combine that wage earners suffer. After that they are better off and labor is more fully employed, usually at higher wages. Many of the smaller concerns that go into the combines and obtain very profitable remuneration for their properties would otherwise become bankrupt.

The fact that a reduction in the price of a manufactured article invariably stimulates consumption needs no more demonstration than that the inflexible law of supply and demand disposes of any fear as to arbitrary advances in price.

The chief good achieved by the so-called " trusts " consists in the power and facilities which they possess of making almost everything of use and desirability cheaper to the consumer than it could possibly be by any other means. During the last two decades the staple articles of commerce in general have been reduced to the consumer from 15 to 50 per cent. If the trust were an octopus, as has often been unthinkingly asserted, these large profits, instead of being divided among consumers, would be appropriated by the trust.

The most important contributors to this great desideratum on behalf of the consumers have been the railroad corporations, frequently regarded as each a trust in itself. And here it is appropriate to remark that these corporations, as a rule, above all others least deserve to have any odium attached to them, for it has chiefly been through them that products of every kind have fallen so much in price, largely in consequence of the reduction in freight rates from 3 cents per ton in 1870 to about .805 at the present time.

If the railroad corporation or trust were an octopus it would have held this important item of nearly two cents a ton within its greedy tentacles, thus realizing many hundreds of millions during the thirty years in question, and a very large amount in the years between the former period and the invention of the locomotive.

One of the most difficult things connected with the whole abstruse and vexed question of trusts is the definition of the term. So far as anything approaching a clear idea of a trust can be gleaned from the Sherman Act of 1890, which has given so much rise to controversy, it may be defined, according to the author of the bill, as " a contract in restraint of trade between the different States."

The application of this definition gave rise to a good deal of dissatisfaction and controversy at the time of the decision of the United States Supreme Court in the case of the Trans-Missouri Traffic Association. The knotty point assumed in this matter, as in that of the Chicago warehouse affair, was that every business forming a part of interstate commerce and affected with public interest should be subject to the legislation and control of Congress.

To show how poor a chance the general public has of understanding the rendition of this Sherman Act, the division of opinions of the Supreme Court in that case will amply illustrate the point in question. There were two issues before the Court, one being as to whether the Sherman Anti-Trust Law applied to railways, and the other related to the nature of agreements in restraint of trade, partial as well as general.

The Court was divided, the decision being rendered by the casting vote of Chief Justice Fuller, who, with four others — Justices Harlan, Brewer, Brown, and Peckham — held that the statute applied to railroads and included every agreement in restraint of trade which might be entered into by any company, corporation, or person. The opinion, which was about half as long as the latest novel or law book, was written by Justice Peckham. The minority opinion, in which four of the nine Justices coincided, dissented from the majority on both issues. They held that common carriers, being already under the regulation of the Interstate Commerce Law, were not within the purview and were not to be held within the operation aimed against trusts. They maintained that the statute can be rightly construed as applying only to general and unreasonable contracts in restraint of trade, and not to reasonable contracts only partially having that effect. They also held that to extend its operations to all contracts and agreements indiscriminately would not only be destructive of the freedom of contract and of trade, but against the whole current of judicial authority. The opinion goes on to say: "The plain intention of the law was to protect the liberty of contract and the freedom of trade. Will this intention not be frustrated by a construction which, if it does not destroy, at least gravely impairs both the liberty of the individual to contract and the freedom of trade? If the rule of reason no longer determines the right of the individual to contract, or secures the validity of contracts upon which

trade depends and results, what becomes of the liberty of the
citizen or the freedom of trade? Secured no longer by the law
of reason, all these rights become subject, when questioned, to
the mere caprice of judicial authority. Thus, a law in favor of
freedom of contract is so interpreted as gravely to impair that
freedom. Progress and not reaction was the purpose of the
act of Congress. The construction now given to the act disregards the whole current of judicial authority. The remedy
intended to be accomplished by the act of Congress was to
shield against the danger of contract or combination of the few
against the interest of the many and to the detriment of freedom. The construction now given strikes down the interest
of the many to the advantage and benefit of the few."

The following comments were entirely to the purpose : —

" The interpretation of the statute, which holds that reasonable agreements are within its purview, makes it embrace every
peaceable organization or combination of the laborer to benefit
his condition, either by obtaining an increase of wages or a
diminution of the hours of labor. It is, therefore, absolutely
true to say that the construction now adopted which works out
such results not only frustrates the plain purpose intended to
be accomplished by Congress, but also makes the statute tend
to an end never contemplated and against the accomplishment
of which its provisions were enacted."

In the light of practical events it will be observed that the
Sherman Law has a very plausible but at the same time a very
seductive and deceptive reading. The pretence is that it is
directed against " unlawful restraints of trade," while it really
intermeddles with agreements of a lawful character indispensable to the equitable distribution of profits among the members
of a company or corporation. The execution of the law thus
imposes hardships and suffering of the most tyrannical character upon innocent people, as illustrated in the Trans-Missouri
case, by the interpretation of the law by which it is made a
crime for people united in the same kind of business to have
a fair division of their honest and equitable profits. A large
amount of those profits is distributed among the people at

large for the various necessaries of life, through grocers, bakers, clothiers, landlords etc.   Thus we see that a trust or combine of this description, instead of being an octopus or greedy monopoly, assumes the character of a most beneficent agent of distribution in every walk of life.

Arbitrary laws, after the manner and spirit of the Sherman Act, are calculated to rob people of their vested rights, and are clearly in violation of that clause of the Fifth Amendment to the Constitution which states that " No person shall be deprived of property without due process of law, nor shall private property be taken for public use without just compensation."

The practical effect of this wrong was clearly set forth in the famous Nebraska Maximum Freight Rate case, in which it was shown that the reduction effected in freight rates by the legislature amounted to about thirty per cent. of the entire rate as fixed by the company upon an equitable paying basis.   The case was brought into the United States Supreme Court to test the validity of the law passed by the Nebraska Legislature of 1893, prescribing the maximum freight rate within the State of Nebraska.   It has been estimated that if the law of Nebraska were carried out in this instance, its execution would amount to a practical confiscation of the railroads in that State.

It would seem to be a most desirable thing, calculated to disarm prejudice and at the same time to conserve public right, that the several States should unite in passing laws requiring these great industrial combinations to submit periodical statements of their financial condition and operation.   Such legislation should be in the line of that governing the railroad corporations ; and in the case of corporations transacting business in several States, supervision could be very properly lodged with the present Interstate Commerce Commission by enactment of a national law.   The industrials cannot expect to gain full public confidence until they furnish reliable annual or semi-annual reports of their operations and conditions.   In view of the enormous powers and advantages which they hold, the public has a right to this information ; and legislation against the trusts could take no wiser or more effective form than an enforced publicity. By such means the public would be protected against monopolistic abuses, investors would be saved from fraud, and the industrials themselves would gain through commanding the confidence which many of them now lack.

One thing, which seems to me very defective about legislation in regard to trusts and corporations, is that we are left very much in the dark as to what acts constitute a violation of the law. This part of the statutes is so indefinite that the judiciary has quite too wide a range afforded it for definition; and this defect becomes especially marked when a judge without practical business and financial knowledge attempts to adjudicate upon a case, for a clear understanding of which such an equipment is indispensable. Knowledge of this character should be better represented on the Supreme Bench, and it is not so difficult to procure at the present time as it has been in the past, for many lawyers now get a fair business and commercial education, and certain members of the United States Bar all over the country have in the last few years organized themselves into a special association for the promotion of the study and practice of commercial law. I believe many of the best lawyers will agree with me when I say that this educational defect was clearly visible in the majority opinion of the Supreme Court in the Trans-Missouri case, and I say it without any disposition to detract from the great ability of the learned members of that court.

This kind of training is seen to advantage wherever it is brought into the settlement of questions involving a combination of law and business calculations. The point was recently illustrated in an interview of a daily newspaper with the Hon. Chauncey M. Depew, in which he spoke of a case where free railroad competition had sway, and a merchant in a small town who gave all his business to one road on exclusive terms was enabled through a special rate to monopolize the business of that town and freeze out the other merchants in the same line. If pooling had been permitted under proper surveillance and regulation, this action in restraint of trade could not have happened, and a lawyer who was expert in commercial matters could have warned the victims of the impending danger.

The want of a rule to follow in defining what is an act involving this so-called crime of "restraint of trade" was conspicuously illustrated in the abortive attempt of the Lexow Committee to discover illegality in the organization and workings of certain corporations. In its report it floundered around in a very ridiculous fashion, aiming fruitlessly at some definite charge to prefer.

Some organization akin to the Massachusetts Commission, now so generally referred to in the periodicals, might be a good medium for helping to enforce the law in cases of alleged delinquency, and for defining more clearly what a violation of the law is, so that a person or a company could know when an illegal act had been committed; for these are things of which everybody but the Supreme Court appears to be ignorant. The District Court and Circuit Court of Appeals are equally in the dark with all who may have anything to do with the question, and who may be liable to be involved in the commission of an indefinite and undefined crime punishable by fine of $5000 and a year's imprisonment.

There are sufficiently urgent reasons why Congress should intervene in a matter of such paramount importance and take a short cut toward ending the danger by the adoption of a law or resolution to the effect that the Sherman Anti-Trust Law shall not apply to the railroads. This would at once end the troubles arising out of the decisions of the Supreme Court in the Trans-Missouri case, and prevent any such difficulties in the future; while the question of devising new legal regulations authorizing pooling, revising the relations between the roads and the Interstate Commission, and for holding destructive competition in check, could be easily left over for more mature consideration. The question is a great, complicated, and difficult one; and its final solution by legislative enactments can be reached only by calm and more or less protracted deliberation.

Upon the whole, it is reasonable to expect that the more exciting phases of this question have been passed. Time is now ripe for readjustment.

CHAPTER XXIV.

CURRENCY LEGISLATION.

Beneficent effect of the New Currency Law. — Our improved credit shown by our new two per cent. bonds at a premium. — Gold now our unequivocal standard of value. — Baneful effects of previous uncertainty as to our standard. — Advantage to trade and to money-movement of the extension of national banks. — Good effect of the gold enactment on the value of American securities abroad. — The surprising and dazzling era of business prosperity into which the world is entering.

BY far the most important and most beneficial act of financial legislation since the resumption of specie payment has been accomplished by the recent passage of the so-called New Currency Bill. Its provisions are calculated to prove of great aid in maintaining the even tenor of prosperity, through a stability of the bases of credit, and hence, of necessity, a stability of credit itself. No country, be its resources never so vast, can develop these resources even through domestic commerce, without the underlying guaranty of a perfectly sound financial system upon which credit may be established, and without which latter trade languishes. Credit is the life of the individual, of commerce, and of the country. Therefore, I say that in placing the national financial system upon an absolute gold basis, the Fifty-sixth Congress has placed to its own credit, and that of the entire administration, a very great sum of national prosperity, to be enjoyed by them and by the country at large for many years to come.

The first and immediate result has been seen in our ability to refund a considerable portion of the national debt at a two per cent. interest-bearing note, thereby effecting a saving of many millions a year in interest. Moreover, these two per cent. bonds command a premium in the markets of the world, placing the credit of the government of the United States in the first rank.

Our unequivocal standard of value is now that of all the great civilized nations. To be sure, so far as the actuality went, our wise Secretaries of the Treasury have always practically maintained our finances upon a gold basis; but heretofore there have always been the elements of uncertainty and apprehension, the possibility of different and erroneous interpretations of the duties of the Secretary of Treasury. Now, our declaration of faith, as put on the statute books in the year of grace 1900, leaves no longer any ground for distrust.

It will be well remembered how, in times past, upon the least indication of financial agitation, gold has been withdrawn from this country in enormous quantities. In another chapter I have already referred to the disastrous effects which were brought about in very large measure by the depletion of the Treasury's stock of gold, this tremendous drain being the direct result of the fear that, through the pernicious effects of the nonsensical and unsound 16 to 1 silver agitation, we were drifting more or less rapidly, but none the less surely, to a silver basis. The reason for such great apprehension of danger is not far to seek. Our securities had been held in enormous volume by Europe, which had paid us for them in gold, investing its money in good faith as to its security. The inevitable result of a threat, however remote, that when it came to taking back these securities by either purchase or redemption, we would pay for them in depreciated silver, was an outpouring upon us in vast quantities of the stocks and bonds. The accompanying panic and its direful train of disasters before temporary legislative relief came, are matters which have been fully treated elsewhere in these pages.

But we may cheerfully turn away from such contemplation, in the assurance of being safeguarded from any further danger from that source. American securities may now be held in foreign countries, without any misgivings as to their repayment in the best money of the world. And herein lies a great promoting factor in stability. The movements of gold will be left free to the natural influence of supply and demand. The current will simply flow where money may be most needed at the time, or where it may command the best interest rate. Consequently, hoarding of the yellow metal is a thing of the past. Gold is the most timid commodity in the world, but now, when it seems reasonably sure it will not be driven out of the country by an overwhelming deluge of degraded money, it will not hide away in strong boxes and vaults, but will come forward to give its invaluable assistance in the regulation and adjustment of the exchanges inseparable from business.

The extension of the limit of bank circulation to the par value of government bonds held in Washington as security, is a wise provision of the bill under discussion. While emphasizing the excellent credit we enjoy as a nation, it permits a considerable increase in the volume of money in circulation, really necessary, and at the same time perfectly safe in its nature, being a natural and gradual expansion and not an inflation of the currency.

I look favorably as well upon the provision for the founding of national banks upon smaller capitalization than hitherto required. I think that one result of this will be the establishment of a large number of these institutions in a profitable field of action, namely, at smaller points throughout the great cotton and grain-growing districts. The relief that this would afford the large money centers of the country is needed. The periods of crop movement are invariably periods of disturbance and stringency in the money markets. If banking facilities are brought nearer to these vast agricultural sections, and more widely distributed through them, a very great measure of the burden of crop movements will be lifted from the banking institutions of the East. Here again we observe another element tending toward the stability of trade. Our legislators have wisely refrained from interference with the greenback legal tenders, which are a necessity from the best economic point of view.

Taking the Currency Bill all in all, therefore, we, as a nation, have good cause for self-congratulation. Our credit, based upon a sure foundation, is the best in the world. Confidence is an established institution in this country, and whoever may assail it should receive short shrift from every thinking man, be he capitalist or day laborer.

There has been a very considerable discussion of this currency question within the past few years, but more especially during the last presidential campaign. The people have become educated to a marked degree in the rudimentary principles of a sound monetary system, and it hardly seems likely at this juncture that this knowledge will permit any other course on their part than a continuance in power of the great political party through whose instrumentality so much of substantial benefit to the country has been achieved.

The effect of the placing of this country on a permanent gold basis by national enactment, has not yet been fully appreciated in Wall Street, as it has been amongst the great financiers and capitalists of London. American securities have a backing now for intrinsic worth such as they have never had before, through the status which the adoption of the gold standard has given them, of which there can be no revocation. The attention of the world will be called to American securities more forcibly than ever before, from this time forth, making them more sought after for permanent holding. Now that the misgivings as to the future of our money have been settled, the important factor of a large commercial balance in our favor will prevent the return of such misgivings. Our present large railroad earnings will inevitably encourage the making of future investments on a large scale in this country, at the termination of the South African war.

The present wonderful showing made by American railway and industrial corporations is only a foreshadowing of the immense activity to come. The entire world is entering upon an era of commercial progression and prosperity that will far surpass all existing records. National conquests will in time be made by the weapons of commerce rather than by those of war. The great increase in the gold product of the world is the moving power, and the faster the precious metal is brought up from the bowels of the earth, the greater will be the impetus of business ventures and developments. The future will be brilliant in inventions and discoveries, and in the advancement of gigantic business enterprises, without limit as to sphere. We are to witness a race of mankind for supremacy in the world's markets. The " open door " will be the policy of all the great powers. The completion of the trans-Siberian railway points to the development of the heretofore almost unknown resources of Russia. Upon the ending of the Transvaal War we shall see a tremendous sweep of civilization into Africa, which means the opening up of its well-nigh fabulous resources. Who can gainsay that the results will be marvelous? There is not a corner of the globe where they will not be felt. These are the prevailing conditions in this closing year of a wonderful century. The prospect for the century to come is indeed a dazzling one.

CHAPTER XXV.

PROPHETIC VIEWS ON SILVER.

A review of the subject prior to the great presidential campaign which resulted in the maintenance of the gold standard. — Bryan's great coup at the Chicago Convention in 1896, which he carried by the power of plagiarism from the old play of "Jack Cade." — The deadly parallel of the two comedians. — A decent respect for old plays to be encouraged. — The theory of an international agreement discussed, and the theory of national free coinage of silver shown to be erroneous and fraught with national danger. — The effect upon international trade would be disastrous. — A plan proposed for an international currency that would greatly facilitate business operations in all channels of trade and commerce, and vastly aid the progress of prosperity in this country. — What is left of the silver issue to-day.

SENATOR STEWART is reputed to be the principal author of the bill which is said to have demonetized silver, by providing for the coinage of the trade dollar which Mr. Stewart imagined would create an immense foreign demand for silver in China, Japan, and India. It did not, however, and Senator Stewart has been unhappy ever since for being chiefly instrumental in the passage of that bill, and has tried very hard to fasten the responsibility for it upon the wicked and avaricious gold monometallists.

This piece of legislation in 1873–74 opened the door for further action on the part of Congress, and accordingly that honorable body, on July 22, 1876, framed a measure in the shape of a joint resolution of both Houses, limiting the coinage of the trade dollar to export demand, and repealing its legal tender quality in the United States. It never was demonetized, except in this sense and until the time here stated, which was three years after the alleged " crime of 1873."

Provision was made by the act of February 19, 1887, to receive the trade dollar, " if not defaced, mutilated, or stamped," at the office of the Treasurer or any Assistant Treasurer of the United States, in exchange for a like amount, dollar for dollar, of standard silver dollars, or of subsidiary coin of the United States, to be melted and recoined. There were 35,965,924 of the trade dollars coined in all, but I have no account of the number returned to the Treasury ; and I should state that these trade dollars were not counted in the silver purchased by provision of the Bland and Sherman Acts.

This is the history, in brief, of what is indignantly called the " crime of 1873 " by the silverites, but which was not consummated until 1876, and for which eminent silverites were themselves mainly responsible, being accessory to the " crime " both before and after the fact. The " crime " was really a free-coinage act and remained so until 1876, so there was no intermission authorized by law in the free coinage of silver from the establishment of the mint in 1792 until 1876 ; and from the former period up to 1873, an interval of eighty-one years, under this free-coinage law, there were only 8,000,000 silver dollars coined in the United States. It must be admitted that during this time the silver dollars of several other nations, notably those of Mexico and Spain, were freely circulated in the United States ; but there is no means of procuring statistics as to the volume of the foreign currency.

It is said, though history is not very clear about it, that by order of President Jefferson silver coinage was discontinued for many years ; but Jefferson never had any authority to issue such a mandate, and, if it ever was issued, it was a dead letter. The total number of silver dollars coined up to December, 1893, the Limited Coinage Act having been in existence from the passage of the Bland Bill in 1878, was 427,304,000. So, if it is volume of money that is required, it would appear that the restricted coinage of silver is better adapted to reach that end than free coinage.

In the same connection, and as a vital part of this subject, it is necessary to refer to the lady who, while an employée in the Treasury, wrote a book in which she charged Ernest Seyd of London, an agent of the Rothschilds, of having been in this country at the time the " crime of 1873 " was committed, and that he touched the " itching palms " of some of the assassins of free silver with a liberal amount of Rothschild's gold.   It is well authenticated that Mr. Seyd was in London at the time and had not been in this country for more than a dozen years prior to the agitation over the silver question, and there are letters of his on record advising certain statesmen on this side not to think of demonetizing silver.   Seyd was an uncompromising bimetallist, and an able writer and author on the subject. Yet, with all this evidence easily procurable, the silverite orators took as their text the error in that lady's book and were particularly noisy on the strength of it, and they will, I have no doubt, do so again.   That author is dead, I believe.   She wrote simply from hearsay evidence.

Let us now go to Chicago and pay our respects to Mr. Bryan and a few of his political friends.   As I have already intimated, the doleful state of the country arising from the Cleveland panics had caused the people to look around for a change in the Executive as well as in the party of which he was the chosen chief; and thus Mr. Bryan and his colleagues were enabled to capture the Democratic machine at Chicago in 1896. The fiery eloquence of the " Boy Orator," coupled with the revolutionary enthusiasm of a number of his followers, took the convention by storm, when the machine politicians were off their guard.   It was a kind of historic repetition of a scene in English politics, of which Disraeli said in his epigrammatic way that Sir Robert Peel and his party caught the Whigs bathing and stole their clothes.

But the " smartest " thing that Bryan did at Chicago was at the close of his peroration, when he delivered with intense fervor and deep emotion, as if it were the inspiration of the moment, a portion of the metaphorical speech of an English low comedian in the old play of " Jack Cade, or The Bondman of Kent," which drew vociferous applause at Chicago, almost as loud as that from the " gods " in Drury Lane and Sadler's Wells, generations ago.

I quote verbatim from both the modern and the ancient actor, and leave the inference to the reader in the discovery of resemblance. I quote the last paragraph of Bryan's peroration in full, so that his masterly art can be the better appreciated. After making the modest claim that the issue of 1896 was the issue of 1776, he concluded as follows : —

"Therefore we care not upon what lines the battle is fought. If they say bimetallism is good, but that we cannot have it till some nation helps us, we reply that instead of having a gold standard because England has, we shall restore bimetallism, and then let England have bimetallism because the United States has. (Applause.) If they dare to come out in the open and defend the gold standard as a good thing, we shall fight them to the uttermost, having behind us the producing masses of this nation and the world. Having behind us the commercial interests and the laboring interests, and all the toiling masses, we shall answer their demands for a gold standard by saying to them : ' *You shall not press down upon the brow of labor this crown of thorns. You shall not crucify mankind upon a cross of gold.*' "

The words in italics are dovetailed in the end of that peroration like a piece of mosaic, and do great credit to Mr. Bryan's editorial capacity. Uttered with dramatic effect, they were madly and unanimously cheered, the convention went wild, and nothing could restrain it until it nominated the orator by unanimous acclamation. It was difficult to succeed in obtaining even a complimentary mention for other prominent members of the party. The convention had no ears for any name but that of Bryan.

Now let us examine the "crown of thorns" and "mammon's cross " in " Jack Cade." The dramatist puts the following language into the mouth of the hero of the comedy, just as Bryan made himself the hero of the serio-comic drama at Chicago : —

"Upon the brow of toil thou shalt not place the crown of thorns, and the bondman of the soil shall not be crucified upon mammon's cross."

The resemblance is too striking to have been the result, as

sometimes happens, of two men of similar modes of thought, thinking alike and using similar language. The only material changes made by the modern speaker are that he uses the word " gold " instead of " mammon," and the word " mankind " instead of the words " bondman of the soil." The construction of the clause in which the words " crown of thorns " occur is simply changed by transposition, but the plagiarism is manifest.

One moral to be drawn from this is, — Never despise an old play. It may make your fortune. Wherever you see one on a second-hand book stall, pick it up and drop your five cents for it, even if it should be the price of your car-fare home. It may not enable you to reach the presidential chair, but the old play, if it contains a good stock of epigrams, may obtain for you a lecturing engagement for a year at $1000 a lecture.

I do not take any credit to myself for being somewhat prophetic on the result of the silver agitation as it happened in the change of national administration in November, 1896, for I believe the consequence was easily foreseen by all persons familiar with the general principles of finance and currency and unbiased by political affiliations. It may not be uninteresting, however, to those of my readers who followed up the great discussion on that subject, to know what I thought about the matter at the period prior to the time when the disputations had arisen to fever heat. In September, 1892, I wrote the following, which was published in *The Independent* : —

" The outworking of the world's pregnant silver problem is rapidly nearing the phase of finality. All nations are agreed as to the transcendent importance of the question, and that assent finds a fitting expression in the prospective assembling of representatives of the leading governments to consider whether any concerted means can be devised to stay the drift toward the common demonetization of the white metal. Nothing short of an international treatment can effectually deal with the question ; and if the conference to assemble next month closes without devising radical remedial measures, the rehabilitation of silver may be abandoned as a hopeless case, and a currency revolution the world over may prove to be the result.

" Any expedient short of a compact between a majority of the leading nations to coin, upon a common valuation and without restriction,

all silver brought to their mints, must fail to accomplish anything
beyond a paltry and transient alleviation of the depreciation of
silver bullion. It would be premature to prophesy, in advance of
the conference, whether any such radical conclusion will issue from
its deliberations. It appears, however, entirely safe to assume that
neither England nor Germany will commit themselves to free
coinage; and the chances of any hopeful results, therefore, narrow
down to the possibilities of the old Latin Union nations combining
with the United States and British India to maintain the unrestricted
coinage of silver, either on the basis of the present valuation of 15½
to 1, or upon some lower valuation. It would not be easy to overestimate the force and influence of such a combination; and considering the extreme gravity of the alternative course of allowing
silver to drift without any regulating force, many practical observers
are likely to regard such an expedient as well deserving an earnest
trial. So deeply, however, has confidence in the possible stability of
silver been shaken, and so impressed are European statesmen with
the expediency of evading all the risks attending silver money by putting their respective countries upon the exclusive gold basis, that
there is little probability that a limited international agreement of this
nature may be realized.

"With so much uncertainty about the outcome of the forth-
coming conference, it may not be deemed premature to consider
what course should be taken in the event of a barren issue of its
deliberations. Few practical financiers would be disposed to encourage further tinkering and delay. With very good reason it
would be argued that, if the dangers attending the present position
of silver are not sufficient to alarm Europe into undertaking its
treatment in earnest, it is hopeless to dream that the great powers
will at some future time come to appreciate the necessity for action.
The failure of the conference would most probably be followed by a
further depreciation of silver. That debasement might but too easily
produce world-wide despair of the metal being retained in use for
any function beyond that of a subsidiary currency; and it is not difficult to foresee what would be the result of such a surrender of hope.
The disposition to discard silver would become almost universal.
The metal that, under wiser counsels, might have been restored to
coördinancy with gold, would be thrown upon the market while governments, banks, and individuals were shunning it; and what, under
such conditions, might be the extent of its further depreciation?

"In such a crisis, the United States could have but one safe alternative. To continue the coinage of silver would be the wildest

insanity.   Fortunately our stock of the nobler metal is large enough
to enable us to put our currency system upon the simple gold basis,
and that should be our first and instant duty.   Our silver should be
withdrawn as fast as the public convenience might permit, and its
place filled by correspondingly augmented issues of bank notes ; but,
so long as our silver was kept in circulation, it should be held equal
to gold in the payment of debts.   Any policy short of this would
expose us to the loss of our gold and to consequent drifting into
an exclusively silver currency.   For in the contingency supposed,
every European nation, and most probably India also, would seek to
protect itself by accumulating the yellow metal.

" However impossible it might be to get gold enough to put the
world at large upon the gold basis, yet every nation would not the
less become a competitor for that metal, and all sorts of means
would be employed to deplete our large stock and to control our
current production.   Moreover, it is never to be forgotten that we
stand exposed to such a drain beyond all other countries, from the
circumstance of our immense foreign indebtedness.   Probably two
billions of our securities are held in Great Britain and on the Continent ; and to allow room for any doubt of our ability to pay those
obligations in gold or its equivalent, would be to invite a return of
these foreign-held stocks and bonds to an extent sufficient to transfer to Europe the bulk of our supply of gold.

" It is impossible to exaggerate the great gravity of this factor in
the situation.   It is not easy to say what is impossible in the way
of financial disaster when the sensitive fears of a large mass of
investors are aroused.   Our past trifling with silver — though but
a transient incident of debased politics — has proved sufficient to
bring home some $150,000,000 of securities, thereby causing an
export of over $100,000,000 of gold which otherwise would have
been kept in the country.   What, then, might be expected if we
showed any inclination toward a policy that seemed to threaten
the payment of hundreds of millions of our foreign debts in silver
instead of gold ?   In view of this danger, it is to the last degree
imperative that, in the event of the failure of the conference to provide for international free coinage, the most prompt and positive
steps should be taken to afford universal assurance that the United
States would discard silver, conserve gold, and adopt the single
gold standard.   That being done, we could have nothing serious
to fear from the failure of the conference ; but any course short of
that would invite the most serious forms of financial disaster.

" The situation created by the position of silver very directly suggests the question whether something cannot be done toward economizing the use of gold in international intercourse. The extensive use of that metal in the settlement of foreign balances is an anomalous waste of the utility of the most potent force of finance. It has no justification in necessity; it is a useless relic of a bygone age. The internal exchanges of the several nations are settled without the intervention of money, and why should the same kind of economy be impracticable in the adjustment of international balances? The nation that is debtor this month is creditor next, and we send millions of gold to England to pay our debts maturing in September, when the same cash may have to be re-shipped in October to settle England's debts to the United States. As the whole commerce between the two nations is conducted by means of credits, why should it be difficult to adjust these oscillating balances of trade through the use of a suitable form of credit instrument? Gold settlement is so obviously needless, so costly and so deranging to the world's money markets, that the only question to be seriously considered is, — What form of instrument would be best adapted to supersede cash settlements?

"In other references to this matter, I have suggested that the leading governments might issue a bond bearing a low rate of interest and possessing qualities specifically adapting it for international transfer. If it should be found impracticable to induce national governments to undertake such an arrangement, or if it were objected that political contingencies would make the value of a government obligation fluctuating and uncertain, is there any valid obstacle to the issue of a suitable credit under other entirely safe and feasible auspices? Every financial center of the world has its clearing house, or national bank, or community of resourceful bankers, any of which contains the raw material from which this international currency might be formed. In some countries one of these forms of organization might be found most available, and in others another. In England, France, and Germany, it would probably be found most feasible to invest the respective national banks with the needful powers of issue, whilst in the United States, the New York Clearing House might be induced to perform the function under due authorization. The issuers should occupy a status that would enable them to command confidence under all possible contingencies, and should be required to deposit unquestionable guaranties against the issues. The notes should bear a low rate of interest and be payable on demand upon the makers. The issuer would receive cash for the notes, which would constitute an important banking resource the use of which would enable the issuer to pay the interest carried on the notes. This interest-bearing quality would prevent the notes from being immediately sent home for redemption; and thus, at all the centers of foreign finance, there would always be an accumulation of this international currency issued in the various nations; and that fund would be available in lieu of so much gold for the settlement of interstate balances."

Again, in September of 1898, I wrote the following : —

"Some unwelcome surprise is felt at the silver issue again raising its head in Western politics. The politicians of that section feel impelled to take up the old fad in the absence of other policies that would attract public interest. The money conference recently held at Omaha showed by the composition and the spirit of its speakers that there is still enough of the old free-coinage spirit among the politicians to keep up a certain amount of agitation; and this is unfortunate in view of the distrust which the past excitement has created in European investment circles.

"It is well that this foreign jealousy about our money standard is so vigilant, for it is precisely at that point that any attempt to force the adoption of free coinage would meet its first check. We may prostitute the force of law by compelling our own citizens to accept an unstable or depreciated form of money, but we can apply no such compulsion to foreign countries. For all that we buy from them, they would demand settlement in gold; and if we should drive our gold out of the country, then our settlements must be made in silver, not at its fictitious face value, but at its true bullion value. On the other hand, our exports would be paid for not in gold, but in silver at its current rate of depreciation. No country so situated can successfully compete in foreign commerce with nations which pay and receive payments in the most stable form of money.

"To meet this pregnant fact with the empty assertion that we can afford to assume a position of independence of foreign commerce is merely to substitute braggadocio and falsehood where honest argument fails. Even before this revolution could get under headway it would be self-overthrown. Before the mania had run its course for one month the consequences would be upon us in all their force. And what then? Would the country supinely permit the ruin to run its unchecked course and wait for the worst possible culminations of disaster? Not for a moment. There are some follies so monstrous as to be impossible even at the hands of madmen. There is always a limit somewhere to the freaks of political lunacy; and, in this case, the strait-jacket would be put in use before the precipice was reached. The men who control finance would see the consequences before the consummation of the act, and a clear prospect of the enactment of a free-coinage law would produce anticipatory effects which would either prevent the passage of the law or bring about its repeal quickly upon its enactment.

"Men who scientifically and practically understand the destructiveness of this scheme, and the effects which the approach of its consummation must have upon public feeling, have no fear about the agitation beyond the possibility of its bringing us near to the verge of an appalling catastrophe. They are satisfied beyond question that, if free coinage could be enacted at all, its duration would be but momentary. This view is now so generally understood that the silver mania affects but a small minority, consisting largely of fanatics."

CHAPTER XXVI.

PRESIDENT McKINLEY'S POLICY AND THE NATION'S FUTURE.

A résumé of the policy of the present administration as outlined in the inaugural address of the President, speaking for himself and his party. — The keynote of his policy is, first, sufficient revenue to run the government. — Afterward, a commission on the currency question. — The wisdom of McKinley's policy in putting revenue and tariff reform before the currency. — Revision, but not revolution, of the tariff. — The government to remain in the banking business, but the currency to be taken out of politics and remodeled without reducing the volume. — Industrial interests and the rights of labor to be guarded against foreign invasion.

ALTHOUGH President McKinley's inaugural address was published long since, it contains much valuable material and profound thought, that, more fully elucidated by the progress of events, will be highly interesting for many years to come. In this chapter, therefore, I propose to make a brief résumé of the policy of the President as outlined in his inaugural address, especially his financial policy.

That address was unique in the manner in which it got down to the most important business without any preliminaries. The President first described the business situation, as he found it, in the most succinct terms. After a few introductory remarks, he said : —

"The responsibilities of the high trust to which I have been called — always of grave importance — are augmented by the prevailing business conditions, entailing idleness upon willing labor and loss to useful enterprises.

"The country is suffering from industrial disturbances, from which speedy relief must be had.

"Our financial system needs some revision ; our money is all good now, but its value must not further be threatened. It should all be put upon an enduring basis, not subject to easy attack, nor its stability to doubt or dispute.

"Our currency should continue under the supervision of the government. The several forms of our paper money offer, in my judgment, a constant embarrassment to the government, and a safe balance in the Treasury is absolutely indispensable. Therefore I believe it necessary to devise a system which, without diminishing the circulation medium or offering a premium for its contraction, will present a remedy for these arrangements which, temporary in their nature, might well in the years of our prosperity have been displaced by wiser provisions.

"With adequate revenue secured, but not until then, we can enter upon such changes in our finance, laws as will, while insuring safety and volume to our money, no longer impose upon the government the necessity of maintaining so large a gold reserve, with its attendant and inevitable temptations to speculation. Most of our financial laws are the outgrowth of experience and trial, and should not be amended without investigation and demonstration of the wisdom of the proposed changes. We must be both 'sure we are right' and 'make haste slowly.'"

When adequate revenue was once secured, many of the financial difficulties, out of which there seemed no easy way during the previous two or three years, found their own solution. For instance, the necessity for bond sales to replenish the gold reserve no longer existed. This was an inevitable result which the former administration could never see and which the McKinley administration demonstrated with ease; nor was it entitled to very much credit for its discernment, except as compared with its predecessor.

"Our money is all good now, but its value must not be further threatened," said the President. These words are very significant, especially in their application to those who have been proposing reforms since the inauguration which would strike at the very root of Mr. McKinley's wise recommendation. This "value" to which he refers would certainly be further "threatened" by retiring the greenbacks and the Treasury notes, and thus converting a non-interest-bearing debt of $500,000,000 into an interest-bearing one.

"It has been our practice," said the President, "to retire, not to increase, outstanding obligations." This, certainly, though mild in form, was a very strong rebuke in its essence to those who were diametrically and avowedly opposed to these views. Of course it is all right for cabinet officers to cherish their own independent opinions, but if they try to enforce them when they are not in harmony with the views of the majority of the cabinet or of the President, I think it has a decided tendency to cause discord.

The whole plan of providing a sufficient revenue, and at the same time laying the true foundation of national prosperity, is ably condensed in the following remarks of the President : —

"The government should not be permitted to run behind or increase its debt in times like the present.

"Suitably to provide against this is the mandate of duty, the certain and easy remedy for most of our financial difficulties. A deficiency is inevitable so long as the expenditures of the government exceed its receipts. It can be met only by loans or an increased revenue.

"While a large annual surplus of revenue may invite waste and extravagance, inadequate revenue creates distrust and undermines public and private credit.

"Neither should be encouraged. Between more loans and more revenue there ought to be but one opinion. We should have more revenue, and that without delay, hindrance, or postponement.

"A surplus in the Treasury created by loans is not a permanent or safe reliance. It will suffice while it lasts, but it cannot last long while the outlays of the government are greater than its receipts, as has been the case during the past two years. Nor must it be forgotten that, however much such loans may temporarily relieve the situation, the government is still indebted for the amount of the surplus thus accrued, which it must ultimately pay, while its ability to pay is not strengthened but weakened by a continued deficit.

"Loans are imperative in great emergencies to preserve the government or its credit, but a failure to supply needed revenue in time of peace for the maintenance of either has no justification.

"The best way for the government to maintain its credit is to pay as it goes (not by resorting to loans, but by keeping out of debt), through an adequate income secured by a system of taxation, external or internal, or both.

"It is the settled policy of the government, pursued from the beginning and practised by all parties and administrations, to raise the bulk of our revenue from taxes upon foreign productions entering the United States for sale and consumption, and avoiding for the most part every form of direct taxation, except in time of war.

"The country is clearly opposed to any needless additions to the subjects of internal taxation, and is committed by its latest popular utterance to the system of tariff taxation. There can be no misunderstanding, either, about the principle upon which this tariff taxation shall be levied. Nothing has ever been made plainer at a general election than that the controlling principle in the raising of revenue from duties on imports is zealous care for American interests and American labor. The people have declared that such legislation should be had as will give ample protection and encouragement to the industries and the development of our country.

"It is therefore earnestly hoped and expected that Congress will, at the earliest practicable moment, enact revenue legislation that shall be fair, reasonable, conservative, and just, and which, while supplying sufficient revenue for public purposes, will still be generally beneficial and helpful to every section and every enterprise of the people. To this policy we are all, of whatever party, firmly bound by the voice of the people, — a power vastly more potential than the expression of any political platform.

"The paramount duty of Congress is to stop deficiencies by the restoration of that protective legislation which has always been the firmest prop of the Treasury. The passage of such a law or laws would strengthen the credit of the government, both at home and abroad, and go far toward stopping the drain upon the gold reserve held for the redemption of our currency, which has been heavy and well-nigh constant for several years."

The President was exceedingly circumspect in these recommendations. He very adroitly anticipated and forestalled the critics who were keeping ostentatious and pretentious watch over Uncle Sam's purse.

In this instance he drew the line between these two extremes of a large surplus and a deficiency which have proved the Scylla and Charybdis of some other administrations. It has been a feast or a famine with some of them : either too much money, or else an embarrassment that menaced the country with a burden of debt and the payment of a big interest bill for many years to come. President McKinley can strike very hard without being offensive, and he has a peculiar knack of conveying a profound meaning in what seem to be the most unstudied expressions, as when he said, for instance, "A surplus created by loans is not a safe reliance."

The last sentence of the above quotation from the inaugural address is unique in that it so combines the two indispensable points in legislation, "revenue" and the "tariff," as to show clearly without argument that they cannot be considered apart. It completely forestalls in a very simple style some of the favorite arguments of the free-traders, and shuts off by way of anticipations a flood of opposition oratory long since prepared to burst forth on the first favorable occasion.

Events since this very comprehensive inaugural address was delivered have fully justified the wisdom and foresight which are implied in its sage advice. While many financiers and professors of economics were working hard over currency schemes, the advice of the President to "go slow" was both timely and prudent, and the admonition is as good to-day as it was then. His counsel concerning the most judicious methods of going about the question of currency reform is worthy of the most profound consideration of all who are interested in this subject; and it should be carefully studied by those who imagine that they have made the only true discovery in the department, before they rashly run into print with the publication of their views. He says : —

"If, therefore, Congress in its wisdom shall deem it expedient to create a commission to take under early consideration the revision of our coinage, banking, and currency laws, and give them that exhaustive, careful, and dispassionate examination that their importance demands, I shall cordially concur in such action.

"If such power is vested in the President, it is my purpose to appoint a commission of prominent, well-informed citizens of different parties, who will command public confidence both on account of their ability and special fitness for the work. Business experience and public training may thus be combined, and the patriotic zeal of the friends of the country be so directed that such a report will be made as to receive the support of all parties, and our finances cease to be the subject of mere partisan contention. The experiment is, at all events, worth a trial, and in my opinion it can but prove beneficial to the entire country.

"The question of international bimetallism will have early and earnest attention.

"It will be my constant endeavor to secure it by coöperation with the other great commercial powers of the world. Until that condition is realized when the parity between our gold and silver money springs from, and is supported by, the relative value of the two metals, the value of the silver already coined, and of that which may hereafter be coined, must be kept constantly at par with gold by every resource at our command.

"The credit of the government, the integrity of its currency, and the inviolability of its obligations must be preserved. This was the commanding verdict of the people, and it will not be unheeded."

The latter part of this advice about keeping the value of silver at par with gold until bimetallism on international principles shall be realized, fell foul of several well-matured schemes in both the Republican and Democratic ranks to get silver out of circulation as suddenly as possible, both sides failing to see that the success of such a policy would give the free silverites the greatest triumph they have yet had, and would be a bad blow at the gold standard.

Such a serious and sudden contraction of the currency, without something no more expensive than silver to supply its place, might readily cause one of the greatest panics in history, and enable the free silverites to say that their theory of the expansion of the currency volume would have prevented all this; the fact being, however, that free coinage of silver would probably have brought about an even worse calamity. The President's comments, therefore, on this phase of the subject, were not only timely but full of financial wisdom, and showed the extensive range of financial vision with which he is endowed. No doubt he had in his mind the ordeal of business embarrassment through which Germany passed during the few years succeeding her demonetization of silver, although she had the immense store of gold furnished by the French war indemnity to rely upon.

The following points on reciprocity and the power of Congress in restoring prosperity show the President's keen appreciation of the then existing emergencies, as well as the means of relief : —

"In revision of the tariff, special attention should be paid to the reënactment and extension of the reciprocity principle of the law of 1890, under which so great a stimulus was given to foreign trade.

"It will take some time to restore the prosperity of former years, but we can resolutely turn our faces in that direction, and aid its return by friendly legislation. The restoration of confidence and the revival of business depend more largely upon the prompt, energetic, and intelligent action of Congress than upon any other single agency affecting the situation."

The "reciprocity principle" was suppressed by mere partisan feeling, but it is hoped that we shall yet benefit largely by its revival.

At the conclusion of the inaugural address the President dilated further on the necessity of the special session, and corrected some popular errors concerning its purpose and influence. He said : —

"I do not sympathize with the sentiment that Congress in session is dangerous to our general business interests. Its members are the agents of the people, and their presence at the seat of government in the execution of the sovereign will should not operate as an injury but a benefit. There could be no better time to put the government upon a sound financial and economic basis than now.

"The people have only recently voted that this should be done, and nothing is more binding upon the agents of their will than the obligation of immediate action. It has always seemed to me that the postponement of the meeting of Congress until more than a year after it has been chosen, deprived Congress too often of the inspiration of the popular will, and the country of the corresponding benefits.

"It is evident, therefore, that to postpone action in the presence of so great a necessity would be unwise on the part of the Executive, because unjust to the interests of the people. Our actions now will be freer from mere partisan consideration than if the question of tariff revision was postponed until the regular session of Congress.

"We are nearly two years from a congressional election, and politics cannot so greatly distract us as if such contest was immediately pending. We can approach the problem calmly and patriotically, without fearing its effect upon an early election."

The peroration of this address is so fine, patriotic, and conciliatory in tone and sentiment, that I consider it worthy of being given in full.

"In conclusion, I congratulate the country upon the fraternal spirit of the people and the manifestations of good will everywhere so apparent. The recent election not only most fortunately demonstrated the obliteration of sectional or geographical lines, but to some extent also the prejudices which for years have distracted our councils and marred our true greatness as a nation.

"The triumph of the people, whose verdict is carried into effect to-day, is not the triumph of one section, nor wholly of one party, but of all sections and all the people. The North and the South no longer divide on the old lines, but upon principles and politics; and in this fact surely every lover of the country can find cause for true felicitation.

"Let us rejoice in and cultivate this spirit; it is ennobling, and will be both a gain and blessing to our beloved country. It will be my constant aim to do nothing, and permit nothing to be done, that will arrest or disturb this growing sentiment of unity and coöperation, this revival of esteem and affiliation which now animates so many thousands in both the old antagonistic sections; but I shall cheerfully do everything possible to promote and increase it.

"Let me again repeat the words of the oath administered by the Chief Justice, which, in their respective spheres, so far as applicable, I would have all my countrymen observe: 'I will faithfully execute the office of President of the United States, and will, to the best of my ability, preserve, protect, and defend the Constitution of the United States.'

"This is the obligation I have reverently taken before the Lord Most High. To keep it will be my single purpose, my constant prayer, and I shall confidently rely upon the forbearance and assistance of the people in the discharge of my solemn responsibilities.'"

It is interesting to reflect how vividly these sentiments of the oneness of all sections were illustrated during the war with Spain.

Apropos of Mr. McKinley's reference to reciprocity, it is presumed by the free-trade element in politics that if got down to a free-trade level it would greatly encourage and stimulate other nations to purchase our goods, produce, and manufactures ; or, in other words, that it would "extend our foreign markets," as the ordinary free-trade phraseology has it. There is no good reason, resting upon business principles, to expect any such result. Nations, like individuals, buy in the cheapest market and sell in the dearest, the latter being the chief reason why England is anxious to obtain control of our markets for her goods. The people of other nations will not buy anything for friendship's sake from us that they can get cheaper elsewhere ; and certainly we do not put any tariff on the goods that we send abroad, though free-traders talk as if we did. We sell at rates that will enable us to compete with foreign manufacturers, if we can produce the article cheap enough to come down to that scale. If we cannot, we have to do the best we can with our home market; and if, as free-traders hold, our home market is already overcrowded, it will certainly not stop the native glut if we give away a large portion of what is too small for ourselves to British manufacturers and to investors, speculators, and adventurers in British and foreign goods.

The people who talk free trade seem to forget, when they tell us about the money we save in buying foreign goods, that the home-made goods afford about one third or more of the working population of this country the means of earning a living, through the prudent and skillful investment, by our own manufacturers, of money which would on free-trade principles go abroad. It may be objected that the manufacturers on this side take the lion's share of the profits. We may grant that ; but do not the British manufacturers and manufacturers of other nations do the same? They are certainly not philanthropists in business. Besides, they do not possess the merit of leaving half as much residue for wages as the American manufacturers do. To put the case even as strongly as the most rabid social-ist would do, namely, that it is "robbery," then it is robbery on both sides of the Atlantic ; and, if we are forced to a choice between two robbers, is it not better to choose the one that will give us enough of the plunder to feed and clothe us de-cently, than to permit ourselves to be victimized by the other, who will reduce us to starvation and rob our own "robber" manufacturers besides? I, for one, should certainly prefer to be "robbed" by our native monopolists, who generally keep the money in the country where I have a chance of getting some of it, even though it be not a fair share, than to throw myself and the fruits of my labor recklessly into the hands of foreign pirates, who spend it in Europe where we never have a ghost of a chance of getting back a solitary cent. If this argument is not clear and conclusive, common sense must be a very scarce commodity, and therefore an article of great value, according to the political economists.

One of the strong charges of the free-traders is that the former McKinley Law prevented importation in order to give the American market to "trusts and combines." Suppose, it will be granted for the sake of argument, that they were Ameri-can trusts and combines, not British or foreign? This is simply the same argument, and the same answer applies to it. The McKinley Law was "A bill to reduce taxation, and for other purposes." Paradoxical as it may seem, it was more of a free-trade bill in one sense of the term than was the Wilson measure as the latter finally passed, which put only 48 per cent. of all our importations of merchandise on the free list, while the McKinley Law let in 60 per cent. of the whole list free of duty. There was this important distinction, how-ever, with regard to the quality and class of the goods : The McKinley Law admitted as few articles as possible that came in competition with our manufacturers, artisans, farmers, mechan-ics, and laborers, while the goods which the Wilson measure admitted came largely in direct competition with all these. These five special classes of our industrial system have had the object lesson which enables them to draw conclusions from their own respective standpoints; and they expressed their views very forcibly, more in actions than words, by the election of President McKinley by an overwhelming majority, and by the return of positive working majorities in both houses of Congress, in which the majorities four years previously were so decidedly in favor of something akin to free trade that the Democrats were predicting the enjoyment of half a century of unassailable power in office. But the people again proved that they themselves are the disposing power. It required this object lesson to teach the would-be reformers the great object lesson that was to be the forerunner of national prosperity.

And now what has become of all the free-traders, with their panaceas and specifics for all financial ills? If they are dead, have they no successors among their many admirers of the past? Seldom has there been in politics such a large conversion of a big majority into a vanishing minority.

It is important to note the fact that President McKinley favored revision, but not revolution of the tariff, and a remodeling of the currency without diminishing its volume. He did not propose " taking the government out of the banking business" either; but he did propose taking the currency revision out of politics by placing it in the hands of a commission composed of up-to-date business men, irrespective of party politics. "Taking the government out of the banking business," "The endless chain," "The greenbacks must go," and other phrases of that kind should now be considered as having gone down with the general wreck. One of the best and most reassuring utterances of President McKinley in his inaugural address is this sentence : "The value of silver already coined or to be coined must be kept at par with gold by every resource at our command. The credit of the government and the integrity of its obligations must be preserved." If Mr. Cleveland had made a similar statement in his inaugural address four years before, this country might have been saved from the disastrous panics which took place during his term.

I think, in conclusion, that a word of friendly counsel which

I have already suggested, might not be out of place, as far as the present Secretary of the Treasury is concerned. Mr. Gage favors taking up the greenbacks, thereby relieving the government from the responsibility of sustaining gold payments and putting that obligation upon the national banks. He admits that it would result in a contraction of the currency which would depress values generally, but he says the situation would adjust itself through that process, as values would go down sufficiently low to induce foreign buying, which would make gold flow this way, so supplementing the currency thus contracted. To bring about a condition of depression such as Mr. Gage suggests, for the purpose of making bargains in our securities and products for the benefit of foreigners, would be resented by the people injured thereby in every State. The very thing that reduced securities and commodities to panic prices would revive the silver mania, on the belief of the need of more money, and would justify foreign capitalists in believing that this country was surely going to drift to a silver basis. If once they believed that, they would not buy our securities, however low in price ; but, on the contrary, the lower they sold, the more Europe would liquidate what they held. That was the experience during the last silver dementia. The taking up of greenbacks by the government would of course save the United States Treasury from being exposed to the suspension of gold payments ; but it would be at the expense of the national banks, as it would take from them the money which they now hold for their reserves and for the redemption of their notes. The banks in times of severe depression and distrust would then be almost sure to suspend gold payments ; besides, as soon as the government went out of the legal tender currency business, the national banks would immediately begin to contract their circulation rather than be exposed sooner or later to a default in payment when gold should be demanded for their notes. A severe depression in business, such as Mr. Gage proposes, would surely elect some such man as William Jennings Bryan as President of the United States in 1900. We had better "bear the ills we have than fly to others that we know not of."

PART III.

WALL STREET AND SOCIAL PROBLEMS.

CHAPTER XXVII.

THE MASSES AND THE CLASSES.

No room for jealousy where political equality, by virtue of the Declaration of Independence and of the Constitution, exists. — Sectional hostilities and class animosities should not be fostered, but suppressed. — Erroneous logic of those who want to get rich quickly. — The evil influence of communism and socialism on the body politic. — Geographical discriminations to be repudiated. — George Washington's opinion on the subject. — The question of the distribution of wealth and its rapid progress in the division of large fortunes. — If monopolies rule, whose fault is it ? — Accumulation of capital in the hands of a few, and how the socialistic remedy would work. — Advice to those who want to get rich rapidly. — Victims of soaring ambition. — How the Gould and Vanderbilt estates are distributed effectually without the aid of the socialists.

IT is peculiarly deplorable that class distinctions should exist in this country. The whole idea is semi-barbarous in its character and unworthy of a people professing advanced civilization. It is a feeling, moreover, that a man should be ashamed to acknowledge on cool reflection, for the reason that it detracts from his own dignity as an American citizen, and deprives him in part, especially in the eyes of foreigners, of that character which is one of his greatest marks of distinction wherever he may travel.

Then, too, the spirit of jealousy displayed against the East in many of the new States in the far West, because of the disparity in wealth which exists, is simply absurd. The people who cherish that animosity forget the fact that the Eastern people have had over a hundred years' start in the accumulation of wealth. The remoter new States occupy a position similar to that which young men just commencing life hold toward old men who have made their fortunes. Such starters in life should not become dissatisfied because they have to cope with powerful competitors. In assuming this attitude, they do not take into account that the older men have given three score or more years of hard work to the accumulation of wealth, and that they have the same opportunities to accomplish all that the older ones have done, providing they apply themselves to the effort with equal diligence. With the equality of opportunities in this country that most men possess, why should there be any feeling of envy simply because one part of the country has had a hundred or more years' start over others, and has become rich in comparison? England was rich, through the accretions of many centuries, before the United States came into existence. Did the people of the United States feel animosity toward the English people because they had the start of them in money-making by many generations? Take all the great fortunes in this country at the present time, — they were founded by men on the common level of all the people and without any money backing. This applies to the Astors, the Vanderbilts, the Goelets, the Mills, the Huntingtons, the Pullmans, the Rockefellers, the Carnegies, the Havemeyers, and nearly all our other very rich men. What has been accomplished by them can be accomplished by others in the future, and there will be just as good opportunities to make money in the coming generation as there have been in the past.

There is no law of primogeniture or entail in this country by which the eldest son is preferred and falls heir to the whole estate, as in England and some other countries. Here, when the head of the family dies without making a will, the property, after his debts are paid, is divided equally among his children, or among the next of kin, in the event of direct issue failing. If he makes a will, he cannot do exactly as he pleases. He cannot tie up his property longer than for the life of the survivor of two lives in existence at the time of making his will.

The necessity for this restriction in the law of wills arose out of the case of the will of Mr. Thellusson, a London merchant, who lived a hundred years ago, and was possessed of a morbidly vain desire to have some one of his name very wealthy in the distant future. He died worth half a million sterling, leaving three sons and three daughters to whom he bequeathed nothing, and his property, according to the will, was to accumulate for a century. As he died in 1797, the Thellusson heir came recently into an estate which exceeds $500,000,000.

Absurd as Mr. Thellusson's will was, the trusts which it created were held valid by the Court of Chancery, and the decree was affirmed in the House of Lords.

Commenting on this case Chancellor Kent says, —

"This is the most extraordinary instance on record of calculating and unfeeling pride and vanity in a testator, disregarding the ease and comfort of his immediate descendants for the miserable satisfaction of enjoying in anticipation the wealth and aggrandizement of a distant posterity."

The case gave occasion to the Statute of 39 and 40, George III., Chap. 98, prohibiting thereafter any person, by deed or will, from settling or devising real or personal property for the purpose of accumulation beyond a limited period; and it was upon this act that the New York Act, New York Revised Statutes I., Chap. 773, was founded, relating to the restriction by will of future accumulations, — a principle which holds good with slight modifications throughout the United States. It will thus be seen that real estate cannot be kept out of the channels of commerce longer than the ordinary existence of a generation, and it may be set free much sooner, as life is uncertain.

Now, reflecting further on these malcontents who want to get wealthy by hops and bounds without going through the hard preliminary struggle in most cases absolutely necessary to attain the goal of this ambition, I should like to ask some young and avaricious upstarts, who are probably trying hard to make both ends meet on salaries ranging from ten to twenty-five dollars a week, if they would exchange places with some of those old and wealthy veterans who have borne the brunt of life's battle up to

the present time. Would they resign their youth and the prospects of the enjoyment incident thereto, and assume the infirm-
ities of old age and the decay that indicates proximity to the
grave, for all the wealth the aged millionaires possess?

A common observation very often used thoughtlessly, when
a rich man happens to be the subject of discussion, is, " I
wish I had his money." It seldom strikes the person who
utters the wish that there is any dishonesty implied in the
expression of this desire, but there is, whether the person who
utters it may think so or not. The idea of stealing may be
very far from that person's mind, but the remark will often
bear the interpretation that the " wish is father to the thought "
of theft, provided security from punishment were guaranteed.
This is all wrong in a well-regulated, highly civilized, and law-
abiding community.

Another loose observation of an analogous character is very
common, especially among politicians. When people are discussing the subject of suddenly acquired wealth by a certain
individual who had been poor prior to his advent in politics as
a leader, perhaps some one will inquire, " Where did he get
it ? " This will draw out further remarks as to the only possible way in which he could get it, and some one will indignantly
denounce such a corrupt state of affairs ; but immediately
another thoughtful individual will speak up boldly in behalf of
the accused and say, " I don't blame him if he was clever
enough to do it." A number of others will very likely chime in
with the last speaker, and Tom, Dick, or Harry, or whoever the
fortunate politician may be, is at length probably absolved by
the majority of that coterie who candidly acknowledge that
they would take the risks of going to state prison, if they only
got the chance, for the sake of the " boodle " in question.

People of this description must have formed the subject of
the poetic thoughts of " rare Ben Jonson " when he wrote the
following : —

> " He that for love of goodness hateth ill
>   Is more crown-worthy still
> Than he who for sin's penalty forbears, —
>   His heart sins, though he fears."

As this style of poetry is too lofty in tone to reach the recep-
tive faculties of the class under consideration, I shall quote
another couplet, not by Ben Jonson, however, but better suited
to their capacity and more to the point as a solemn warning : —

> " He that takes what isn't his'n,
>   When he's caught should go to prison."

Regarding the evils of sectional jealousy and kindred feelings, Washington said : —

"In contemplating the causes which may disturb our nation, it
occurs as a matter of serious concern that any ground should have
been furnished for characterizing parties by geographical discriminations, — Northern and Southern, Atlantic and Western, — whence
designing men may endeavor to excite a belief that there is a real
difference of local interests and views. One of the expedients of
party to acquire influence, within particular districts, is to misrepre-
sent the opinions and aims of other districts. You cannot shield
yourselves too much against the jealousies and heartburnings which
spring from these misrepresentations. They tend to render alien
to each other those who ought to be bound together by fraternal
affection."

Distinctions are frequently made between " the masses and
the classes," — words which have a fine sound when placed in
juxtaposition, and have an attractive look in headlines, but
they do not exist as solid facts in the contrast intended. They
do not in reality imply any definite meaning. There are no
classes in this country as opposed to the masses, and we are all
one mass, at least all citizens are, and that mass is composed
of an aggregate of sovereign citizens of this great Republic.
The name " sovereign " excludes the very idea of having anything above it. It occupies the highest possible place of political eminence.

As regards distinctions, these may be acknowledged in mental, moral, and social qualifications, but not in the political status
of the citizens of the United States. We are all equal before
the law just in the same sense that we are " created equal,"
according to the language in the preamble of the Declaration

of Independence. This idea alone should bury in unfathomable oblivion every thought of class, as well as of money and geographical distinctions, and we should heartily adopt the motto " Each for all and all for each," and glory in the idea of one united people. Negligence of this advice was the chief cause of the Civil War.

Now, I am strongly of opinion that the spirit of socialism and communism, twin relics of barbarism, have had a great deal to do in recent times with the feeling of jealousy, class distinction, and dread of the money power which we see so frequently exhibited, and which if not checked may prove deleterious to the industrial and social interests of this country. There is no true grievance for which the citizens have not ample redress through the ballot box ; and when they complain that they are trampled upon by monopolies, trusts, and political bosses, the answer is, It is your own fault. The people who have votes are a hundred times stronger than all these other forces banded together, with all the money that such a powerful aggregate could command. They are competent and fully equipped to defeat the whole army of trusts, monopolies, and selfish millionaires, with the communists and anarchists at their back, if we could possibly imagine such a heterogeneous combination ; for the latter elements of this supposed confederacy have no votes, as a rule, and the wealthy members only occasionally make use of their privilege of voting.

Surely, this accumulation of capital is not an unmixed evil. But for capital the respectable laboring men, and even those disorganized nondescripts without classification, would be far worse off than they are. Labor is impotent without capital, and it will never be able to acquire capital so long as it listens to the disorganizers and breeders of perpetual discord.

I should like to say a few more words to our Western brethren, especially the young and aspiring ones, on the subject of trying to grasp wealth too rapidly. The attempt to do so, in ninety-nine cases out of a hundred, ends in signal failure. Durable wealth can be acquired, as a rule, only by the method of slow and steady accretions, after the manner of constructing a coral reef.   Of course there are eminent exceptions, but these are either rare instances of genius, where all ordinary rules are largely dispensed with, or of what may be regarded, for want of a better explanation, as good luck.   Those who leave the regular path with such hopes will be almost sure to be disappointed, for geniuses in finance are very uncommon, and a turn of good luck may not come except at very long intervals.

But young men need not despair under the impression that the chances to become wealthy are all gone.   They are as good as ever.   Of course competition is sharper, but the facilities for meeting it are better, and those who keep pace with the times and improve their faculties, just as the old men had to do in their time, have brilliant prospects in store.   If the end is harder to attain, the means are better suited to the end ; and we have the experience of all the ages to draw upon, either for the purpose of enabling us to improve on the past, or by weighing the mistakes of others to help us to avoid similar ones in the future, and to keep clear of the rocks and shoals upon which former victims of soaring ambition were wrecked.   History and biography are the great charts by which we must steer our course — the philosophy that teaches by example.   The trouble in the use of these instruments is that we do not benefit as much as we might by the experience of others until we apply it to our own personal action, and then it may be too late. Each must work in his own way and according to the gifts with which he is endowed ; and he must proceed rationally, thoughtfully, and with premeditation.   " Give thy thoughts no tongue, nor any unproportioned thought its act," says Polonius to his son in *Hamlet.*   Commodore Vanderbilt clothed the same idea in language almost as terse, though less grammatical. " Never let nobody know what ye're goin' to do till ye do it," was one of the Commodore's pet maxims, and he often acted upon it, to the great discomfiture of his enemies and competitors, and to the building up of the Vanderbilt millions.

The main objection of communists, and others of the same bent, to present conditions is on the score of the unequal distribution of wealth.   I think there could be no better object lesson on this subject than that which the Vanderbilt millions afford. They have within a generation been transferred from a single owner to probably nearly a hundred possessors, either actually or in immediate prospect. There has been no tying up there. So it was with Jay Gould's hoards. They are rapidly coming under the same law of distribution, and even Paris is enjoying a part of his hard-earned gathering, when the accumulator of it all has been but a few years dead. Other parts are being divided up among workmen in various industries, while certain amounts are expended in the encouragement of art, music, and the drama. Within a few years those hundred odd millions have been wrested by the hand of death from the original owner, from the one monopolistic hand and put into the hands of dozens of liberal distributers, who are sowing them broadcast. The communists themselves could hardly do the work faster.

If Gould himself left nothing to charity, his elder daughter is making up for that omission by devoting a large portion of her life work and a liberal amount of her fortune to that purpose. So "there's a divinity that shapes our ends." Gould "builded better than he knew," — for the world and for the communists also.

If Commodore Vanderbilt was not a patron of letters, having no taste therefor, it must not be forgotten that he did a great thing for the Southern University by his bequest to that institution ; and other Vanderbilt charities, such as the Clinic, must be taken into account in this important question of distribution.

This natural method of division of property, unhampered by primogeniture, is far ahead in principle and in equity of anything that the world has ever seen. Certain socialists eulogize the Mosaic law of distribution, but according to that code the division and reversion took place only every fifty years, in the year of jubilee. Under the existing methods, which are constantly in operation, half a dozen apportionments may take place in the half century, and the diffusion is much better and more equitable. Certain theorists have suggested that the division to fill the aching void should be made during the mortal existence of the monopolists and bondholders; but the result of the experiment made in this direction by Mr. Andrew Carnegie would seem to have cast a damper on the benevolent sentiments of such philanthropists.   Mr. Carnegie has been one of the best abused men in the country since he made arrangements to spend millions for the mental and moral improvement of the people.   Public ingratitude is a great enemy to benevolence, and frequently closes the door against it.

CHAPTER XXVIII.

A QUESTION OF GOOD CITIZENSHIP.

How do wealthy men compare with others as good citizens ? — Conditions
that antagonize good citizenship. — The character and influence of the
money hoarder and the absentee analyzed. — Decline in the rate of
interest and of faith in the security of property among the most important
questions of the day.

SOME time ago a discussion went the rounds of the press
on the subject of " good citizenship."

Special and pointed reference was made to the distinctly
wealthy citizen, to the man who had become conspicuous in the
eyes of the public as being classed among the millionaires ; and
the opinion seemed to be held by not a few that wealth has a
tendency to impair a man's usefulness as a citizen. In fact,
some people are disposed to think that a rich man cannot be
a good citizen, any more than he can enter the kingdom of
Heaven.

For the latter opinion we have the highest scriptural authority,
but in neither case would it be justice to the opinion to interpret the language literally. The Nazarene simply meant that
the man who made a god of his riches could not enter the kingdom of Heaven, for surely no one can imagine that Christ would
have excluded from Heaven such men as we see in our times
and in this nation spending millions in charity with their own
hands, and make provision for having millions more spent in
the same laudable cause after their death.

I am now thinking of such men as John Rockefeller, who has
already spent ten or twelve millions, and Andrew Carnegie, who
has spent probably an equal amount ; both of whom propose
to spend many more. In the same honorable catalogue I may

include the Vanderbilts and many others. If I should go into the list of the deceased, even of those who have died within my own recollection, their names and the amounts of their bequests alone would extend this chapter far beyond the limits allotted to it. The extent and number of the charities of the late Cornelius Vanderbilt will probably never be known.

Surely, Jesus of Nazareth never meant that the souls of these benevolent individuals should wallow eternally in despair, because they had been the mere instruments of collecting large fortunes, the greater portion of these fortunes being distributed where they would relieve the sufferings of humanity, and assist a large number of the community to avail themselves of a higher state of mental development than they had been provided with means to reach, merely by the accident of birth.

Peter Cooper's gifts and bequests afford vivid illustrations of this point. Who can imagine for a moment that Saint Peter would be commissioned by the Most High to send to perdition his philanthropic namesake because the modern Peter had the prudence, industry, and economy to gather the wealth that put the institute which goes by the grand old man's name on such a financial footing as to teach thousands to earn their living in intellectual pursuits who otherwise would never have enjoyed the means of raising themselves above the level of the ordinary unskilled day laborer?

Whatever the meaning of the mysterious Man of Nazareth might have been, common sense rejects the brimstone theory in its application to such a man as Peter Cooper, for instance, though he was not what was regarded in his day as an orthodox Christian. But, like another eminent man in his school of faith, " to do good was his religion," though unlike the other he did not claim " the world as his country," although in every sense it was. Peter Cooper was peculiarly and characteristically an American of the old school, and the truest type of genuine American manhood.

I think it requires, or, at least, should require no further argument to show that the strictly orthodox interpretation as applied to a man like Peter Cooper is unutterably absurd and can be entertained only by unreasoning fanatics.

I regard the opinion of the reprobation of rich men, simply because they are rich, as the rankest heterodoxy against the science of common sense and the best interests of the social condition as at present constituted with the family as its unit, in contradistinction to socialism and a paternal government. The wealth accumulators, I contend, are, as a rule, the best citizens. In fact, they are the citizens, above all others, who make it possible under our present system to attain the highest enjoyment and development, physical, moral, and spiritual, of which mankind thus far is capable.

How far these wealth accumulators are mere automatons, working through the media of apparent selfishness, is a question with which modern philosophers are just beginning to grapple ; but the point that I wish to make clear is that the wealth producers and accumulators, with but few exceptions, are the hardest worked slaves in existence and have on the whole the least enjoyment, as the world estimates enjoyment, out of the wealth which, in common parlance, they are said to create.

Of all writers on political economy, John Ruskin puts this condition of the wealth-creator, so-called, in the truest and most vivid, though in somewhat a ludicrous, light. He takes the position that the error in the popular view is the confusion of guardianship with possession, the real state of men of property being, too commonly, that of curators or managers, not possessors, of wealth.

Of the man of wealth viewed in this light, Ruskin says : —

" He cannot live in two houses at once. A few bales of silk and wool will suffice for the fabric of all the clothes he can ever wear, and a few books will probably hold all the furniture good for his brain. Beyond these, in the best of our but narrow capacities, we have but the power of administering, or maladministering, wealth. And with multitudes of rich men, administration degenerates into curatorship. They merely hold their property in charge as trustees for the benefit of some person or persons to whom it is to be delivered upon their death, and the position explained in clear terms would hardly seem a covetable one."

And again : —

"What would be the probable feelings of a youth, on his entrance into life, to whom the career hoped for was proposed in such terms as these: 'You must work unremittingly and with your utmost intelligence during all your available years. You will thus accumulate wealth to a large amount, but you must touch none of it, beyond what is needful for your support. Whatever sums you gain beyond those required for your decent and moderate maintenance, and whatever beautiful things you may obtain possession of, shall be properly taken care of by servants, for whose maintenance you will be charged, and whom you will have the trouble of superintending, and on your deathbed you shall have the power of determining to whom the accumulated property shall belong, or to what purposes it shall be applied'?"

And yet again : —

" The labor of life under such conditions would probably be neither zealous nor cheerful, yet the only difference between this position and that of the ordinary capitalist is the power which the latter supposes himself to possess, and which is attributed to him by others, of spending his money at any moment. This pleasure taken in the imagination of power to part with that with which we have no intention of parting, is one of the most curious though commonest forms of the eidolon or phantasm of wealth."

Now, if Ruskin's picture is a true-to-life portrait, and I am inclined to think it is, in spite of what to some people might seem its humorous exaggeration, then there can be no true reason why the wealthiest man should excite envy. In fact, the more wealthy the less enviable is he, as the burden of his mere trusteeship is the heavier.

As a general rule, and not forgetting the few conspicuous exceptions, the man who is wealthy is naturally led to be a good citizen, even if he is the most selfish of individuals. His desire to increase his wealth is a potent cause of its distribution, in which operation it must assist those who assist in its circulation, and benefit every man and woman through whose hands it passes as the medium of exchange for the necessities and luxuries of life.

There is a glaring and morbid exception to this rule. That is in the case of the man who hoards his money, thus keeping it out of circulation, and thereby depriving both himself and others of the profits and increase that it is capable of bestowing when prudently invested. Such men violate the law of their being as mediums of distribution. Happily they are rare, for the faculty of acquisitiveness is stronger, after all, than the mania for hoarding, and generally overcomes the morbid fear of losing what they have in the risk of augmenting it. This passion for hoarding strikes at the root of national prosperity by retarding the growth of wealth, which is usually the consequence of investment; and it is the duty of every citizen, in fact, it is one of the tests of good citizenship, for the successful man to share his prosperity with the people among whom he has achieved it.

It is undoubtedly true that wealth brings new temptations, but in making money most men so broaden and occupy their minds that they are better fitted for withstanding those temptations.

As far as national wealth is concerned, and looking at the subject from a patriotic point of view, — which is absolutely necessary in discussing the question of citizenship, unless a man claims to be a citizen of the world, — the chronic absentee is a bad citizen. He is no better for the United States than the English landowners are for Ireland, and he stands in a similar relation to his fellow-citizens as those rack-rent landlords do to their tenantry. Each draws a portion of the life blood out of his respective country to spend it in luxuries abroad.

The question arises then, Is a man justified in playing universal philanthropist at the expense of his compatriots? Should the latter be required to contribute to support the elegant leisure of a person who has ignored them as fellow-citizens? I know there is no law at present against it, but it seems to me from a moral standpoint that there should be set limits to the extent to which it should be tolerated. If a man virtually de-citizenizes himself, should he be permitted to retain all the rights and property benefits of good citizens whose constant aim and efforts have been in the direction of the best interests of the country?

It seems to me that equity, at least, should require an extra tax for this discriminating indulgence. We have passed laws against the immigration of people who come here simply with the intention of earning all the money they can in a certain time and of going home to spend it there, without any intention of assimilating with our people, or assisting to build up the nation in return for benefits received. Are they any worse than these habitual absentees? Hardly so bad, I should say, as they do not owe their origin and birth to this country. Their procedure, though selfish, is not unnatural.

There is a third influence at work which is antagonistic to the increase of wealth in this country, and that is the constant tendency for some years past to lower the rate of interest for money. To discuss this subject in all its bearings and in the numerous variety of its causes would require an entire chapter ; but one thing is evident in our social and political conditions, and that is that " populism " is undermining the very sources from which higher rates of interest were formerly drawn by becoming a potent instrument in rendering the status of society less secure. It threatens the stability of property, on which all security is founded ; and if once a feeling of insecurity should begin to spread, it would give rise to a transfer of capital to other scenes, where social and political conditions were less liable to change, and where it would incur less risk from the fluctuations of property values and incomes. There is nothing regarding which people are so sensitive as variations in the income upon which they are obliged to rely for the purpose of supporting a certain prescribed social status. Anything calculated to disturb this equilibrium makes them nervous and exacting as to the nature of the security for their capital and its income.

The growing populism of the Democratic party in this

country calls, therefore, for the most profound thought of our wisest statesmen, and the adaptation of the best measures to avert its evil influences. To establish the unquestionable security of property and income is one of the most important questions of the day for the statesman to solve. And the certain means of maintaining that security without liability to disturbance or loss of confidence therein, is a question which all good citizens are bound to consider with the deepest solemnity. It goes to the root of our very existence as the great Republic.

CHAPTER XXIX.

LABOR UNIONS AND ARBITRATION.

Even if there should be nothing to arbitrate, the arbitration will satisfy public opinion. — Strikes should be a last resort only against unbearable grievances. — The public are victims of the quarrels which they are innocent of provoking. — How arbitration works in Stock Exchange affairs. — Coöperation the true method of escaping the despotism of " bosses " and improving the condition of labor.

THE first part of the following paper on the subject of " Labor and Arbitration " was written at the request of the late Henry C. Bowen, editor of *The Independent,* several years ago ; and as similar conditions still exist in the field of labor, and similar troubles constantly arise between employer and employé, the observations and comments herein are as applicable to the present as they were to the past.

" It seems to me that in all differences of opinion on the question of wages or remuneration for labor, between employer and employed, arbitration should be tried in the first instance for all it is worth. There may be nothing to arbitrate, but no matter for that ; it will satisfy public opinion, and, in my opinion, is the best medium for throwing oil on the troubled waters.

" If it were a rule recognized by both employers and employed to exhaust all the possibilities of arbitration with becoming patience and mutual forbearance, before ordering a strike or lockout, I believe there would not be half the number of either that have been experienced during the last few years. The United States Strike Commission, in its reports on the Chicago strikes, briefly propounded two courses of action which it recommended to the American Railway Union, and which if followed out to their ultimate consequences would, I believe, be instrumental in preventing more than half the ordinary troubles :—

" '*First :* — To take a position against all strikes, except as a last resort for unbearable grievances, and to seek the more rational methods of concilation and arbitration. To this object the power of public opinion would lend aid to an extent not now appreciated.

" '*Second :* — Conservative leadership, legal status, and the education of members (of trades, unions) in governmental matters, with the principle in view that in this country nothing can accomplish permanent protection and final redress of wrongs for labor as an entirety except conservative progress, lawful conduct, and wise laws enacted and sustained by the public opinion of its rulers — the people.'

" Prior to the accomplishment of all that these two comprehensive paragraphs embrace, more than one campaign of education will be necessary. In fact it will require years of steady and persevering educational drill to arrive at the ideal of this commission ; but it is the only sure road to success, and though it will involve much weary plodding, the goal once attained, the fatigue and hardship endured will be amply rewarded.

" Wherever this method of arbitration has had a fair trial, it has worked like a charm. The Stock Exchange affords one of the best examples of its talismanic power. Misunderstandings are settled by this association without expense, sometimes in a few minutes or a few hours, that would drag their weary length along from one to two or three years, at great expense and incalculable vexation, if they were taken into a court of law. I am therefore in favor of arbitration, not only in labor disputes, but in others where criminal proceedings are not an absolute necessity.

" If all labor unions were the same in practice as most of them are in theory, they would be among the most beneficent institutions of the country. In proof of this I will quote a sentence or two from the constitution of one of them : —

" ' The order, while pledged to conservative methods, will protect the humblest of its members in every right he can justly claim, but no intemperate demand or unreasonable propositions will be entertained. Corporations will not be permitted to treat the organization better than the organization will treat them. A high sense of honor must be the animating spirit, and even-handed justice the end sought to be obtained, that the service may be incalculably improved and that the necessity for strike and lockout, boycott and black list, alike disastrous to employer and employed, and a perpetual menace to the welfare of the public, will forever disappear.'

" These are noble sentiments, clothed in appropriate words and earnestly meant ; but it is noteworthy that in the same constitution there is not a word to be found imposing punishment or any kind of discipline for infringement or violation of these sentiments by the members themselves. This the commission very properly designates 'a grievous omission,' and unfortunately, such omissions are frequent, and will be so until a more thorough education in the science of economics shall correct them.

" I am now called upon to answer the question, — Should associations of employers organize to meet the demands made by the labor unions? It is difficult to answer this question in full without many qualifications, but it would seem, if any considerable number of labor associations are united, that, unless the employers are also similarly united, the principle of arbitration could not be placed on an equitable basis or have a fair trial. In the case of managers of railroads there is a special difficulty about this. They are not authorized, it seems, by their charters, to form corporations or associations to fix rates for services and wages. Such privileges, it appears, must emanate from the same power that granted the charters.

" The most important question connected with unions and strikes, however, was developed in its most glaring monstrosity in the Brooklyn trolley strike. There the poor public were for weeks the innocent victims of the quarrel which they had no hand in provoking, and were exposed to exhausting fatigue and the inclemency of the weather, from which, no doubt, many died, while there were several outbreaks of riot and consequent bloodshed. Such distress, disgrace, and violence might have been averted by timely arbitration.

"The term 'compulsory arbitration' is frequently used, but that seems to be a misnomer, as compulsion and arbitration are contradictions in terms ; but the blame for refusal to arbitrate should be placed and punished in some manner.

"In conclusion I would say, without partiality to either employer or employed, never say 'there is nothing to arbitrate,' until the committee appointed for that purpose shall render its decision."

Since the events to which the foregoing observations refer, I think great progress has been made toward a mutual understanding between employer and employed on the subjects of labor and wages, but much yet remains to be done.

There is a manifest disposition on the part of wage earners to become more of an organized power in politics and to free themselves from the thraldom of the political " bosses." The greater headway they make in this kind of reform, the nearer will they be to the goal of their main purpose, which is to settle the question of wages upon an equitable basis, by virtue of which the capitalist may not oppress the wage earner by push- ing him as near to the starvation point as possible ; nor, on the contrary, may the wage earner insist upon remuneration which would reduce the capital below the point of living profits with sufficient surplus to preserve intact the capital from which the wage fund emanates, and without which wages and employment would be impossible, and bankruptcy the eventual fate of the capitalist.

I know this is a very difficult point to settle, as was amply demonstrated in the Carnegie strike and other troubles of a similar character, each side holding different opinions on a sub- ject that should be easily demonstrated by the simple rules of arithmetic. The great trouble is that the representatives of both labor and capital are prone to regard the matter too much from their own respective points of view. Neither party seems to have the capacity to imagine itself in the other's place, and when it does sometimes actually get there, it seldom, if ever, gives any better satisfaction than its predecessor.

Workmen and artisans will, I believe, generally testify to the fact than the workman or the artisan who happens to become a capitalist and an employer is the hardest kind of man to get along with, the most exacting, the most tyrannical, the least lenient to the faults and shortcomings of his workmen, and the man who is readiest to grind them down in wages just as close to the starvation point as they can possibly endure. He is a man, also, most ready to discharge them on the least symptom of dissatisfaction on their part, even if he has to supply their places with men less efficient, but more servile and subordinate. He conveniently forgets or ignores his record when he was a laborer himself, and was perhaps one of the loudest declaimers against the despotism of the capitalists and employers. The experience of the workman with trades-union " bosses " is similar. There are of course many employers and "bosses" who have risen from the ranks, far removed from any of these contemptible feelings and practices; but the class above described abounds more largely than superficial observers imagine, and they have a wretched tendency to keep the workman down, and to crush him every time he attempts to rise a little higher. Therefore, if the laboring men are to ameliorate their condition to any great extent, they must begin by reforming themselves.

A partial cure for the evils, thus apparently now inherent in the position of employer and the office of "boss," would be found in a more extensive system of coöperation, under which the workmen would each be employer and employed, capitalist and wage earner in one. There would be no boss authority except that delegated by the workmen themselves, and nobody to blame but themselves either for low wages or bad treatment.

If a whole nation can hold together and be prosperous, organized on the principle of coöperation, and if the component parts of a nation, such as the various states, counties, and municipalities, can successfully organize on similar principle and similar lines, it would seem to follow logically that any number of sovereign citizens of such a country should be competent to organize themselves in a similar fashion for an object even more closely connected with their welfare than citizenship; namely, the means of making life comfortable, enjoyable, and worth living, rather than a disagreeable burden, and a perpetual struggle for a poor livelihood.

CHAPTER XXX.

THE PHYSICAL FORCE ANNIHILATORS.

Several species of this genus, including socialists, nihilists, anarchists, and communists. — A retrospect of their plans and purposes for the regeneration of mankind and the reconstruction of society, after going through a few preliminaries, such as the suppression of rulers, and the extinction of capitalists. — According to the programme, the scheme will imply wholesale assassinations and universal plunder to begin with. — After purposes indefinite. — A problem for the socialistic reformers as preliminary to success.

THE men whose peculiar characteristics and purposes I mean to discuss in this chapter, are not such objects of dread as their name, " Annihilators," might seem to indicate. The safety of both themselves and their intended victims is secured by the magnitude of the task they have undertaken, compared with the paucity of the means proposed to accomplish it.

Their proposed scheme is nothing less than the annihilation of society and its reconstruction. In the reconstructed state it is presumed that everybody will be able to enjoy leisure, after performing about an hour's easy work daily.

" Annihilator " is a generic term comprising several species, the principal of which are communists, anarchists, and nihilists. There may be a few others, but they are of minor importance, and, at present, I shall confine my remarks to those named. They wish to destroy everything and to build up anew. This purpose may include themselves in the general annihilation, and they may think that, like the phœnix, they can again rise from their ashes, — a supposition not more preposterous than some of the feats in the way of transforming society which they propose to achieve.

The annihilators think that they are very much oppressed in

this country, but they are under a delusion. The large majority of them have come from countries where the people are oppressed by military rule, and where the one-man power is predominant; and they think that the same condition of things exists everywhere. They do not pay any attention to the study of our constitution and the nature of our government. If they did, they would discover that there is no place in the world where the laws and institutions, regarding personal liberty and the right of free speech, approach those of this country; and no place where the annihilators themselves would be afforded the opportunity of earning as good a living as here. The enjoyment of such privileges is fully demonstrated by the fact that but few of them are in our prisons, — probably not any greater proportion than there are of our other citizens. This exemption in itself is a privilege they could not enjoy in other lands, as many of them know from hard experience.

If they would only conduct themselves decently for five years after arriving, they might have the chance of rising to the highest positions in the land, except that of president; and their sons born here would be eligible even for that eminent office. There is no other place in the world where such aspirations find any such encouragement or possibility of realization. Yet this country is probably first in wealth, second in area, and third in population, being excelled in the last only by China and Russia.

Just think of the son of a poor, miserable, starving creature who was born in slavery, under the heel of an effete despot of Europe, being able to become a greater executive in power and influence than the imperial tyrant whose serf his father was born! A few centuries ago an historic possibility like this would have been read in Europe like a fairy tale, classed with such stories as Cinderella and the Glass Slipper, or some of the tales in the "Arabian Nights' Entertainment."

Such, however, is the ingratitude of human nature, that the very people admitted to the full fruition of these inestimable benefits, purchased by terrible struggles, are ready to turn, serpent-like, and destroy the social and political fabric reared at so much expense and suffering, and which munificently confers the great boons of protection and sustenance on the downtrodden portion of humanity from every clime, on the most agreeable and easy terms.

They have only to fall in with our facile customs and benign laws and perform a sufficiency of manual labor, or brain work if they are capable of it, to keep their bodies and minds in a healthy condition. In return for this they are fed and clothed better than some of the nobility whose servants they were; and yet they are not happy. Are such people fit for freedom? Not except on the principle laid down by Macaulay, who said that the best way to regulate discontent, arising from what may be considered too much liberty, is to grant more liberty. Macaulay may be right, but he never had European annihilators, transplanted to American soil, to deal with, or he might have thought differently. I do not think, however, that we have anything to fear from these destructive elements in human form. They do not thrive on this soil; they are not indigenous to it. They are exotics, and poisonous ones, but the fact that the poison is labeled in sight of all men is the best protection against its fatal effects. The few native or naturalized converts that these pernicious missionaries may bring over to their way of thinking, or raving, have no influence on the body politic in general, and only show by the ease with which they have been captured that they are not qualified to enjoy and exercise the prerogative of the citizenship bestowed upon them. Such easy subjects to the hypnotic influence of the annihilators do not count for much as members of our political system. They are excrescences upon it, and have to be endured in accordance with our generous system of government, by which drastic measures are seldom resorted to except in the last extremity.

This mild treatment may work to the detriment of our system in some instances, on the principle that forgiveness sometimes only encourages sin; but the country is strong enough to afford a large measure of benevolence, even at the risk of having its benignant rule of action imposed upon. The rule has worked tolerably well in practice for over one hundred years, and it would hardly be prudent to change it except in the face of clearly demonstrated necessity.

Germany seems to have been the birthplace of socialism, but the present German organizations, and especially the scattered portions that have been transplanted to our soil, have departed materially from the principles held by the older brood in the fatherland. The latter believe in prosecuting their ends by constitutional, semi-constitutional, and educational methods; but the new brood proposes first to demolish the existing system, and that without anything to put in its place. These people seem to think that, when chaos has come through this act of demolition, reorganization on a basis of social equality will be effected in some mysterious way. When the question, How? has been asked at any of their big conventions, the effort to formulate a plan has frequently ended in violence among the very people who propose to organize the world as one happy family and harmonious brotherhood. This was notably the case in the Congress at The Hague in 1872.

Two divisions were formed out of that secession, one called the " Black " and the other the " Red." The Blacks were the most uncompromising annihilators, and proposed the destruction of all existing governments by physical force. They were the full-fledged nihilists, and took their name from the Latin word " *nihil*," — nothing, or " having no foundation in truth." The latter meaning, given in the Latin dictionary, seems to be peculiarly significant, as the system itself has certainly no foundation in truth; but the organization which had itself baptized by this name evidently meant that " nothing " should remain of any government when they got through with it. Their special field was Russia, where, it must be admitted, they have worked so as to make their influence felt.

The " Reds " were inclined to work by constitutional and educational methods, and at that time devoted themselves chiefly to Germany; but their idea also was to make the annihilating brotherhood universal.

The nihilists have probably not been so powerful or compact

for the purpose of general mischief in Europe since that dissension. At that time the crowned heads were beginning to
stand in awe of them, and the division in their ranks was regarded as a good omen by the royal families and rulers of
Europe. Bismarck is reported to have said : " Crowned
heads, wealth, and privilege well may tremble should ever
again the ' Black ' and the ' Red ' unite."

It was recently reported that there has been a secret reunion,
and also that the more rational portion of the annihilators propose to make the United States a camping-ground and prepara-
tory field where the sinews of war can be collected for the
purpose of overturning the thrones and decapitating the rulers
of Europe. They may decide on using this country for that
purpose until the European conquest is accomplished, before
turning their dynamite on us. There are a few able heads
among them who have seen military service on the other side
in all three armies, Russian, French, and German. There are
also some Italians of the Carbonari type, and a small sprinkling
of Spaniards, but very few English or Irish.

Some of the more enthusiastic ones imagine that the revolution can be made general and simultaneous on both sides of
the Atlantic with the same facility that the telegraphers' strike
was inaugurated at the same moment all over the country a few
years ago by a whistle in the Western Union Building. These
sanguine annihilators think that they will communicate with all
their centers of activity through land and cable telegraph at
the same instant, thus giving the command for the universal
holocaust, when the armies of Europe, America, and Oceanica
will be pounced upon mercilessly and become the prey of
dynamite, no quarter being allowed except to those who are
quick to embrace the destructive tenets of the annihilators.

This part of the contract, however, is considered too vast by
the more rational leaders, and especially by the " Reds," who
favor the tactics of dividing and then conquering. While the
" Blacks " consider the old method too slow and antiquated, the
" Reds " think it is better to make sure of the victory even at
the expense of a little delay, than to take risks by precipita-

tion. The anarchists, too, are rather inclined to be on the conservative side; but the nihilists are uncompromising, and want to get into action with their dynamite bombs and the murderous machinery of nitro-glycerine on the very shortest notice. In fact, the anarchists seem to be coming back to the original idea of their organization indicated by their name, "without government," which was used then in the sense that every man shall be a law unto himself, as predicted by some of the old prophets. This prophecy has yet to be fulfilled, for there is no record of any experience of its realization. It is supposed that the anarchists might have tried it on these lines with the favorable opportunities offered in this country at the time of the Chicago strike; but Governor Altgeld of Illinois, being stronger with the nihilists than with the anarchists, was opposed to the views of those who advocated this theory, and they had to succumb, as Altgeld and his adherents had the "pull" in politics, and were bent in the first instance on the crippling of the trunk line railroads.

As to the communists, who are members of the same annihilating family under consideration, there has been little heard of them since the sacking of Paris after the German invasion. From this long quietude of the commune we learn a lesson of great interest and significance to our own republic. Annihilators cannot multiply on republican soil. It is too rich for them, and they become plethoric upon it; so, in order to avoid death by apoplexy they are obliged to emigrate, if they can find any place on earth that will harbor them. If they cannot, they await their inevitable fate where they are. Sometimes they even see the error of their ways, reform, and become peaceable citizens.

John Most is now as gentle as a cooing dove and seldom makes an inflammatory speech; the two terms in prison, one in London and the other in New York, cured him. And the name of Justus Schwab of this city, who was so prominent a few years ago as a red-hot socialist, is seldom mentioned. Why? Simply because he has accumulated some money by selling beer, sauerkraut, and quick lunch, and now owns some real estate, including the house in which he lives. Consequently he is unable to see why he should divide up the fruit of his hard earning and frugality with the fellows who spent all their money in his saloon, while he was collecting it carefully and putting it in property to be divided among his children when he goes to the happy hunting grounds of the social reformers. He encouraged the socialists and the newspapers to advertise him and his place until he became independent, and then he did not have much use for either. The socialistic slate has been broken years ago, and the man who used to proclaim in the language of Prudhomme that "all property is robbery," now adheres firmly to the plunder which he was then amassing. Justus Schwab is a whole object lesson in himself, when the fiery Justus of seven or ten years ago is contrasted with the sedate and tenacious property owner of the present time.

John Swinton is another of those who have been careful to adhere to a fair share of the good things of this life, and, though he has been fairly consistent and has contributed according to his means both materially and intellectually to the cause of socialism, yet he has never been known, I believe, to let his own supply of loaves and fishes run short. John Swinton has always been the first consideration with him. Even when he started a newspaper he called it John Swinton's paper, so much was he in favor of giving John the preference ; and probably the name helped to kill it, for socialists are very jealous about individual honors, though their theory is the reverse.

These eminent failures, and many others similar in kind, go to show that the proposed revolutionary system of reform must be sadly lacking in the elements of cohesion, popularity, and permanency. The great problem which these reformers have yet to solve is the exclusion of the selfish principle in human nature. In that they have apparently made very little headway in half a century, and without this solution their socialistic schemes are so many ropes of sand.

CHAPTER XXXI.

THE ANNIHILATORS' METHODS.

For the regeneration of society. — A closer examination of the remedies which the various destructive fraternities entitled to this common appellation propose for the inequality complained of, and how they would work in practice. — Where will they get the men to help them to demolish thrones and break up present political organizations? — They could put down the present tyranny only by establishing a greater. — Failure of all previous attempts to establish communities. — Our ballotbox and existing law are ample to maintain the strictest equality, to remedy all wrongs and redress all grievances.

IN another chapter I have sketched a general outline of those restless, reckless, and revolutionary spirits who may be classed under the general appellation of "annihilators." They propose to abolish private property and suppress the motives for its acquisition. Of the various types of these revolutionists the only kind that seem to have a clearly thought out and analyzed programme of reconstruction after the destruction, are the scientific socialists. The anarchists and nihilists, as a rule, have only vague ideas of the detailed course of action of humanity after the emperors and presidents and legislatures and police are abolished; they have boundless faith in luck after the universal disintegration; but they make no provision that the same things which they now hate shall not happen again. Therefore it seems to me that those two kinds, anarchists and nihilists, are to be regarded by sensible people only as pestilent disturbers, who deserve no respect because they have not even a plausible programme to offer.

But socialists have a pretty well-arranged plan of reconstruction. The governmental socialist is an evolution from the early communist; but in the spirit of enforced equality, —

equal sharing of everything without regard to merit, — they are alike. Let us begin with the governmental socialist, and examine the programme he offers us. Those who hold his views, like the revolutionists, propose to abolish the heads of all governments, European kings, presidents, and governors of states, also the various houses of legislation. Then they propose to establish a system of compulsory equalization. In their own words they mean to have, " instead of the capitalistic and individualistic system of production and distribution, a system of governmental coöperation and governmental production and distribution. The whole people of a country in their collective capacity shall produce and distribute everything, like a great joint stock company, only more equitably." The new government is to control railroads, telegraph lines, and all kinds of industrial forces. In this scheme there will be no room for, or incentive to, individual enterprise. Every person is to work under no other stimulus than that the fruits of his labor are to be divided equally among the members of the community to which he may belong.

These people, while making high-sounding statements regarding the happiness sure to result upon the adoption of their principles, are quite reticent as to the means for effecting the transformation, although it is to be the most radical change and on the largest scale that has ever been attempted. "Socialism," they say, " would abolish poverty by preventing it, by removing its causes. As poverty is the cause directly or indirectly of nearly all crime, therefore, by the abolition of poverty, crime would become almost unknown, and with crime would disappear all the ' leeches,' 'vampires,' and ' vermin ' that fatten on its filth, — such as the entire legal fraternity, soldiers, police, judges, sheriffs, priests, preachers, and many others."

Now, this is very well as a description of society in its metamorphosed condition, but how we are to get there is another matter. The socialists point to a development through the trusts, forgetting that between the largest aggregation of commercial trusts and the smallest attempt to give to every member of the community an equal share in the general profits,

there is a great gulf to be jumped. Not one of the four leading species of annihilators gives any satisfactory explanation of
this. They all seem to take it for granted that the only thing
necessary will be to send around the cards of the new candidates for the committee on reorganization, and the latter will
be elected unanimously. No allowance seems to be made for
the possibility of any opposition to the new régime. It is
thought to be so attractive in its nature that everybody must
irresistibly embrace its doctrine the moment it is presented to
them.

Why the reformers, or rather the upsetters, have a right to
expect this sudden change in human nature is not stated. It
is not considered necessary to state it. It is one of those
things that are supposed to be self-evident. Yet when one
begins to canvass the opinions of the community anywhere,
he finds that this change, or rather transformation of mind,
and this desire for another condition of society, have very
few adherents. There is not one person in twenty, or perhaps
in a much greater number, who would not set the individual
down for a crank or a crazy person who began to talk on the
subject of the impending revolution and the new state of society
and politics, where nobody would desire to get the money he
earned, but would be willing to have it put into a general fund
to be divided equally at the times set apart for such division.
It is safe to say that not one out of a thousand would listen
for a moment to any such extraordinary arrangement for the
disposal of the fruits of his or her labor.

Where, then, are the converts to the new régime to come
from? Can the annihilators manufacture them? When Marshal Ney sent to Napoleon for more men at Waterloo, the
answer of the chief was, " Does he expect me to make them ? "
The annihilators seem to have some such expectation. They
appear to think that some unseen power will make these men
to order, fully imbued with the ideas of a new dispensation,
and prepared to enforce it despotically upon society as it exists
at present.

That the change proposed is not adapted to the nature of

mankind, as the latter has existed from time immemorial, will be readily understood if we go back a few thousand years to the patriarchal age when people lived in tribes. This was communism on a small scale, and if it had been consonant with human nature to adapt that mode of existence to a larger scale, then was the most appropriate time to begin the operation. But instead of this being the social purpose at the period in question, the tendency was all the other way. This may have been owing to the perversity of human nature, its general inability to discern what is for its best interests, and its natural proneness to evil; but it is a "condition, and not a theory, which confronts us," and in considering this question in all its bearings, we are obliged to take both human nature and society, as at present constituted and as it formerly existed, in the concrete, not the abstract. In other words, we are obliged to take it in the most practical sense in which any scheme of organization or reorganization must deal with it. We may people the world with imaginary beings, and work out Utopian theories for our own amusement and the entertainment of others who delight in that kind of theorizing; but in practical life such theories will prove of the most delusive character, and leave us eventually the sorry victims of our own folly and overheated imaginations.

One of the most interesting features of the proposed new social state, in which everybody is to be supremely happy in the thought that he is working for the benefit and maintenance of everybody else, is the currency idea. This part of the programme outshines anything that has been suggested by either silverites or Populists. It is to be a new currency, of course, based upon the credit of the new state. The material has not yet been agreed upon, but it will be neither of the precious metals. These are tabooed, and the unit of value to start with will be a hundred minutes of labor for one dollar, or a cent a minute when the minutes are fewer than a dollar's worth, and there will be no means of measuring the quality or quantity of labor performed except by the conscience of the laborer.

Nothing is to be taken note of except the time, and it is

to be left to the good will and option of the individual himself whether he works or "loafs." As he will get as much
for one as for the other, there can hardly be two opinions
as to which any but a very few conscientious ones will choose.

Here again the presumption is that all people will be conscientious philanthropists.

This is presuming an entire change in the feelings and
desires of the beings who are to be citizens of the New Utopia,
and an utter absence of every incentive and motive which now
prompts the individual to labor and lay up for the future.   It
is easy to see that such a condition of things, if possible, would
stop all development, and a state of stagnation would be the
inevitable result.   Then for generations there would be perpetual war between the rising generation and that which would
then be passing away after having introduced these felicitous
changes in human economy.   The transmission of the selfish
ideas of the old Adam would be certain to come up from time
to time in the younger offspring, thus perpetually disturbing
the harmony of society.   No power could suppress this evil
tendency for many generations, as it is inherent in human
nature itself and one of the mysteries hitherto beyond the reach
of solution.   With a finer development and the entire suppression of selfishness, the secret may be discovered and the problem solved by some philosopher of the future school of thought.

But here again we are met with another difficulty, when we
speak or think of development of thought.   How can such
a thing exist in the sphere of the annihilators' future?   It would
be entirely superfluous.   "Eat, drink, and be merry, for to-
morrow we die," would be the motto of that social state.   The
only serious consideration would be to get sufficient work out of
the members of the community to maintain the eating and drink-
ing.   The chief incentive to work, namely, profit, having been
taken away, what kind of pressure would supply its place so as
to keep the various communities up to the point of sustenance?
It must be remembered that the "robber class" who, from the
most selfish purposes, now deal in futures and thereby lay up
stores against famine, would all be extinct.   Thus far there has

been no provision made to supply their place in the provisional work which they now perform by the law of natural selection.

Suppose that on the brink of a crisis of this kind the communities should take a notion to go on a strike, being prompted by a spirit similar to that which of old seized the Israelites when Moses restricted them to a manna diet and they longed for the " fleshpots of Egypt," — what method of discipline would be resorted to in such an emergency ? It seems to me that people would be placed in such a quandary that they might be obliged to cast lots and resort to a tiding-over experiment in the way of cannibalism until the clouds of famine should roll by and the demoralizing influences of the food panic pass over.

Then the selfish spirit of the forefathers would begin to rebel, and by and by get uppermost, involving the biggest insurrection that the world has ever seen.

Now, I have taken one illustration from ancient history, that of the tribal organization, to show that the communistic idea was wanting in the seeds and attributes of permanency. The system evidently had not come to stay with those good people, and they did not transmit it to their modern posterity, who have embraced the selfish marriage of man and wife, together with their other backslidings. The family, as understood by the ancients, being simply a modification of the tribe, no longer exists in the civilized portions of the globe. It is still extant in China, and also, with various modifications, in other Eastern nations and among certain tribes of Africa; but wherever its existence lingers, one of its characteristics is that the people are poor and ignorant. It was tried, and in course of time rejected, by a few of the ancient nations who stood highest in the scale of what we understand by civilization ; but it is significant that, as the idea died out after various experiments, people began to grow more humane, and what is designated " civilization," for want of a better term, developed among them. They began to improve in their habits, a higher standard of morality began to prevail, domestic comforts were improved, more even-handed justice was dispensed, and provision against the emergencies of life became a subject of personal and individual concern, and conduced largely to a higher dispensation of happiness in the " selfish " family circle. Under this progressive state of evolution great discoveries have been made, for which there could be no inducement in a socialistic system. And the world, especially the republican portion of it, is making considerable progress toward the highest plane of happiness and prosperity ever dreamed of, except by annihilators.

In quoting instances and illustrations of historical experiments in communism and socialism, there is one that should not be passed over in silence, as it is probably one of the most prominent of examples, and the only successful one. The community to which I refer was that formed on the day of Pentecost, of which the record is found in the New Testament, in the second chapter of the Acts of the Apostles. It seems to have been organized by the twelve apostles, on the occasion of a meeting in Jerusalem to promote the spread of the gospel. There was a large assemblage, composed of the representatives of various nations, many of them Jews, mostly dwellers in Jerusalem, then the metropolis of Palestine. According to the narrative written by St. Luke, the assemblage was touched by a miracle which caused the disciples to speak in the tongues of the foreigners. Some of the audience were astonished, and were curious to know the meaning of it, while others mocked and said, " These men are full of new wine." The Apostle Peter, however, sustained the theory of the miracle in a powerful sermon, and a large number of the people must have agreed with him, for he succeeded in organizing an association or church of three thousand members, the result of the initiation being the sale of everything that the person possessed, the proceeds to be put in a common fund, and the members of the community — " all who believed " — to have " all things in common." The narrative goes on to say that these people " sold their possessions and goods and parted them to all men as every man had need," and furthermore, that " the Lord added to the church daily such as should be saved."

Now, this community was established under what must be

considered the most favorable auspices, and under divine protection and guidance; yet there is no account that I have seen or heard of concerning the prolongation of its existence beyond a short period.

Where the church or community organized by the Apostle Peter and his eleven holy brethren of the same community did not succeed in transmitting that system to posterity, what chance is there for miserable, wicked creatures, who are constantly breathing fire and slaughter against capitalists, to establish a permanent organization of a communistic character that has any guaranty of becoming a popular success?

To put the question thus clearly and plainly, is, I think, to answer it. There cannot possibly be any hope of such an experiment succeeding in a civilized community, and its success, if possible, would institute the worst system of slavery with which the world has ever been cursed. It could not be organized in the first instance, except by the strongest and most cruel kind of tyranny. It would relegate humanity to a state of the most selfish savagery.

All the modern experiments, likewise, have failed, and most of them were of a mild and civilized character. Robert Owen, a Welshman who made a fortune in the cotton trade, spent about a quarter of a million dollars in eleven experiments in attempting to establish communism by rational methods, and through reason and education. One of these was New Harmony in Indiana. His son, Robert Dale Owen, who had been induced for a time to assist his father in these abortive attempts to transform human beings into the similitude of angels, gave up the business, became an ordinary member of civilized society, and put his very liberal education and bright intellect to useful purposes as an author and a magazine writer. He also had a short but honorable career in Congress, and died in 1877, deeply lamented by a large circle of friends and admirers. His father died in 1858, at the age of eighty-seven, after having spent fifty years and $300,000 in the unsuccessful effort to establish communism on a healthy and permanent basis.

Robert Owen was a great philanthropist, highly respected in

the highest circles in England, and a special favorite with the royal family there, despite his radicalism. He once lent William IV., Victoria's uncle and predecessor, £10,000, and when the king handed him a promissory note for the amount, he threw it in the fire. When men of such high purposes and plenty of money to back them up fail to succeed in the experiments under consideration, what must be the fate of men whose theoretical morals, at least, are of the lowest type, and who have no money to put any enterprise under way — hardly enough even to print their inflammatory and traitorous platforms?

These people talk about defending the laborer while they propose to rob the capitalist, apparently forgetting that capital is the fruit of labor, and is quite as necessary as labor in any plan of coöperation, large or small. Man in his present state of civilization is more helpless without capital than a wild monkey of the forest; and capital cannot be preserved and increased to the point of doing its greatest possible good and reaching its highest aims and purposes without the coöperation of its natural ally, labor. There should be no disruption or discord, therefore, where such vital interests are mutually indispensable to the health, happiness, and prosperity of the whole people.

Neither the system of Owen, nor that of Fourier the Frenchman, seeks the destruction of any property, but rather the building up of it. The destructive idea is quite modern. The Fourier system was tried in this country on Brook Farm, at Roxbury near Boston, Massachusetts, from 1841 to 1846, and several of the most prominent literary personages of a little over half a century ago went through the mill of experience on this famous farm. Among them were Horace Greeley, George William Curtis, William Ellery Channing, George Ripley, Albert Brisbane, and Charles A. Dana. These men, with a few clever women (of whom Margaret Fuller was one), as might be expected from their high intelligence and honesty of purpose, soon demonstrated the futility of the experiment and gave it up. Brisbane was probably the only one who adhered tenaciously and publicly to the opinions and platform of Fourier after the farming experiment failed. He translated Fourier's works and wrote books and comments upon them until near the time of his death a few years ago. Fourier died in 1837, leaving a host of disciples on both sides of the Atlantic, who are now nearly all dead. Brisbane was probably the last of the enthusiastic ones on this side.

Those communities that have been organized on the ostensible foundation of religion have had fair material success during the lives of their leaders and organizers, but the gross immorality which has characterized most of them soon planted the seeds of their decay, and the successors of the original leaders were seldom able to continue the full authority bequeathed to them. This has been the result with the Oneida Community experiment at Oneida, New York, over which a man named John Noyes ruled with a rod of iron for many years. After his death the community collapsed. The Salt Lake experiment in Utah, organized by Joseph Smith and Brigham Young, has been handicapped by the strict execution of the laws passed by Congress against polygamy. Young was a man of extraordinary personal power, with great individuality and marvelous magnetic influence over his deluded followers. He found Utah a barren wilderness and left it a fertile garden. He built a temple larger than that of his polygamous prototype, Solomon, although the gold was hardly so abundant in the Utah structure as in the sacred edifice of Lebanon built by the wise king of Israel. At last the nation became disgusted with the whole system, and suppressive enactments were passed by Congress designating polygamy a crime.

My strictures as to immorality do not apply to the Shakers, who have, perhaps, come nearer to success than any modern movement. Even they, however, lack vitality and are rapidly dying out.

One of the great elements of disintegration in all of these efforts to organize a community on a permanent basis arises from the dissatisfaction inseparable from the idea of the fruits of one's labor being devoted to persons who put forth no effort to assist the community. This and the strong desire implanted in the human mind for hire and profit as the reward of labor appear to overcome all the broader intentions of elevating the standard of the whole community and of making the individual sacrifices necessary to accomplish the end. That self-preservation which is the first law of nature would thus seem of itself capable of frustrating every effort to establish a community where the earnings are to go into a common fund, and where the most industrious and frugal individual, as well as the genius, is to be depressed to the working level of the lowest human animal.

The drones are the chief disintegrators of all these social schemes, but the tyranny of the "bosses," which always develops with the possession of power, is a potent factor of destruction by inciting rebellion. The worm will turn when trampled on.

In conclusion, I would say that the privileges connected with the ballot-box make provision for equality and equity as near perfection as any theory that the annihilators can prescribe. With regard to the abuses of trusts and other corporations, the legislation already on the statute books, both national and in most of the different States, together with the provisions of the common law, are pretty nearly sufficient to deal with these matters so as to remedy and correct all abuses.

Part IV.

WALL STREET AND INTERNATIONAL AFFAIRS.

CHAPTER XXXII.

PEACE AND PROSPERITY.

Some reflections on the horrors of war. — How it ruins material prosperity and degrades humanity. — Remarks on the efforts of the six European powers to put Europe on a peace footing. — The favorable influence which the success of the movement would exercise on trade and commerce. — Plans for an Anglo-American reunion discussed. — Captain Mahan's views. — A defensive alliance of all civilized nations against a possible invasion of barbarians.

I TAKE the title of this chapter, "Peace and Prosperity," to be the union of two words that in their meaning can scarcely be disunited. The apparent prosperity that war sometimes brings must be dearly paid for, either by the parties themselves or their descendants, as in the case of our own Civil War, the debt of which is not yet paid.

Napoleon I. brought the continent at large to a condition of bankruptcy in which France herself was overwhelmed, despite the immense plunder secured by the unexampled avarice of the conqueror; and England, though she emerged victorious out of that terrible struggle, did so only at the expense of a permanent debt, which by certain statesmen has been considered a national blessing, as a means of investment. To me it seems rather that a national debt, instead of being a national blessing, is a national curse of inherited taxation incurred to gratify the ambition of a few individuals, — who probably never have to abate one of their luxuries in consequence of their errors, — or of being the instruments of so much entailed misery to millions.

Yet we hear people constantly talking about the glorious achievements of war and the prosperity which attends it. War, in the nature of things, can never bring prosperity except to a comparatively small number of individuals at the expense of taxing an exceedingly large number, together with their off-spring for generations. These remarks apply more especially to wars of conquest, wars for sustaining imaginary dignity and wars for prolonging the power and prestige of the reigning monarch or executive when the people are tired of him and he wants some excuse or plausible plea to revive his popularity. Such to a large extent was the Franco-Prussian War provoked by the necessity and ambition of Napoleon III. and the Empress Eugénie, and such would have been the war which might have been fomented with Great Britain by President Cleveland, when with overweening zeal he espoused the cause of Venezuela under the questionable plea that the Monroe Doctrine was dangerously menaced.

It has now been amply demonstrated how easily that Anglo-Venezuela misunderstanding could have been settled by arbitration, without causing the least disturbance to the business interests of either of the nations concerned; yet before this was made manifest our country had to pass through an expensive panic, which also reflected a very unfavorable influence for a time on the business interests of Great Britain.

Looking at the subjects of peace and war through the medium of business experience, to say nothing of the far greater questions of human happiness and misery involved in their consideration, it is a healthy sign of the times and a forecast of a higher development in civilization to witness the action in the interests of peace and prosperity taken by the six great powers of Europe in the Turko-Grecian affair. Its success proves the possibility of what has been regarded as an impossibility, — the harmonious coöperation of the leading powers for the settlement of critical international disputes, even concerning matters in which their interests conflict. This is largely a new function in diplomacy, and what was accomplished in the case of this war shows how valuable a concert of this nature may become for the future maintenance of amicable international relations. The concert of the powers has introduced an important element favorable to the creation of permanent political confidence. More than this, it is a great gain for quieting the disturbed state of Européan politics that the six states directly interested in the long dreaded Eastern question thus were able to discuss freely its involvements and agree upon a common policy to prevent its being made an occasion of common quarrel.

The business interests of every civilized country, and of some that are not civilized in our sense of the term, are so related to one another through the expansion and development of trade and commerce that war has become a far more extensively disturbing element than ever before, and every year of progress renders it more and more so. We have thus arrived at an era in the advance of trade when an outbreak in even the smallest of the nations or a hostile collision with its neighbor is felt as a shock charged with forebodings of evil throughout the civilized world. No matter how free we ourselves may be from the immediate interests and bearings of the quarrel, and no matter how we may be able to profit by it temporarily, owing to its stimulating influence in certain departments of our exports, we nevertheless feel it as a premonitory symptom antagonistic to the interests of business in the long run.

It is to be regretted that the United States Senate did not entertain a more cosmopolitan opinion of the great question of arbitration between this country and Great Britain. In view of the efforts which have recently been exerted to put the nations on a peace footing, it would have been a great honor to this country to have taken the initiative in such a grand international enterprise. The very effort to promote such a laudable design is a record to which future generations will point with pride, and which will illumine the history of that great nation which has so distinguished itself when most of the passing events, now regarded as of the highest importance, shall have been quite forgotten.

The idea of a great union of civilized nations for mutual defense is rapidly developing in the minds of thoughtful people. We may perhaps say that its first impetus was given at the international conference at The Hague, but more recent events have tended to the crystallization of public opinion upon this subject, in unmistakable shape.

China's reactionary defiance of the civilized world has set the people to thinking, and as a result we are about to witness the subjugation of barbarianism by the combined forces of civilization. It is of course earnestly to be hoped that this may be accomplished with little bloodshed, but that it must be accomplished, even at high cost of life and treasure, is apparent from a glance at the following summary of the population of the countries now interested in common cause : —

United States	75,000,000
Germany	55,000,000
France	40,000,000
England	40,000,000
Japan	40,000,000
Russia	80,000,000
Total	330,000,000

as against, say, 400,000,000 Chinese. The time has evidently come for the step to be taken. The Yellow Peril is a very real one, when we reflect that year after year since the Chino-Japanese War the armies of China have undergone thorough regulation and drill in the use of the most modern arms and appliances of warfare.

Although an invasion by these Mongolian hordes, similar to the descent of the Goths and Vandals upon the Roman Empire, is not to be considered probable, still it must be granted that such a vast nation under one strong central government is a menace to the peace and prosperity of the rest of the world.

To my mind, the best solution seems to lie in the decentralization of the Chinese government, — the division into principalities, autonomous in the government of internal affairs, but under the tutelage of the great powers now having territorial interests there. But the United States should insist that perfect good faith be kept in the pledges of an " open door " policy agreed upon by all the interested nations. A successful termination of this present serious trouble will, it is to be hoped, form a lasting bond of friendship between all the great powers, and bring appreciably nearer the fruition of the Czar's great humanitarian proposals.

The subject of an alliance of the English-speaking people has been very extensively discussed during the past few years by some of the ablest writers and thinkers of the day, and some have gone so far in accordance with the foregoing suggestions as to advocate an alliance of all civilized nations. Among these may be mentioned Captain Alfred T. Mahan, formerly of the United States Navy, who is, perhaps, one of the greatest marine tacticians in the world, and a man capable of taking the widest range of vision of all that relates to the sea, both from a military and a commercial point of view. His ideas, therefore, on the possibilities of an Anglo-American reunion are worthy of the most careful consideration, and will furnish an excellent guide to any one pursuing the study of the influence of that reunion on the financial affairs and prosperity of the proposed reunionists, and especially on those of the United States.

Among others who have recently made most valuable contributions to this department of literature may be mentioned Captain Lord Charles Beresford, of the Royal Navy of Great Britain ; also Sir George Clarke, Mr. Arthur Silva White, and Mr. Andrew Carnegie.

Captain Mahan dwells at length on the necessity of America taking a deeper interest in the sea, which he regards of far greater importance than the land. He thinks that the time is past forever when any single nation can control the domain of the boundless deep, but suggests that an Anglo-American alliance could do so to the great interest of both parties, and to the union and the benefit of humanity at large. His great apprehension of the future seems to be a possible inundation by countless hosts of outside barbarians, while he does not forget the inside ones in the shape of anarchists and socialists. He believes in the firm maintenance of the military system for accomplishing the highest objects of civilization. In the prospect of a possible barbarian invasion, Captain Mahan thinks that the United States will be obliged to play a prominent part in the defense, and, to quote his own words, "to cast aside the policy of isolation which befitted her infancy, and to recognize that, whereas to avoid European entanglement was once essential to the development of her individuality, now to take her share of the travail of Europe is but to assume an inevitable task, an appointed lot in the work of upholding the common interests of civilization." He predicts that against this possible invasion the only barrier will be the warlike spirit of the representatives of civilization, and adds with patriotic fervor, backed by good argument, "Whate'er betide, sea power will play in those days the leading part which it has in all history, and the United States by her geographical position must be one of the frontiers from which, as from a base of operations, the sea power of the civilized world will energize." In urging the just recognition of the superiority of the sea to the land, this able author says, "Control of the sea by maritime commerce and naval supremacy means predominant influence in the world, because, however great the wealth of the land, nothing facilitates the necessary exchanges as does the sea."

If Captain Mahan and other great thinkers and tacticians who hold the same or similar opinions are correct, then our navy cannot be enlarged too soon nor too extensively.

It may be asked, How will this accord with the peace theory and the holding forth of the olive branch to the nations? It will be perfectly consistent with that, as all preparations for defense, and defense only, are. Savages and barbarians bent on plunder do not understand anything about the significance of the olive branch until they are first made to feel the power behind it. Then they become docile. It may require such a display of strength as Captain Mahan supposes, to reduce these nations outside of civilization to a state of mind in which they will feel disposed to reason, so far as they are capable of reasoning. But in order to accomplish this great purpose, the necessity for which may still be far distant, a pacific alliance among all civilized nations, irrespective of language, will be an indispensable preliminary. Such preparation would certainly be the best guaranty for universal peace and prosperity, thus enabling the human race to apply its best energies to its own development instead of to its degradation and destruction.

CHAPTER XXXIII.

THE BARING FAILURE.

The true story of the cause of that astounding collapse told for the first time. — The great Baring boom, and what the scaling down of the interest on British consols had to do with it. — The Duke of Marlborough's hand in it. — Sensational acts of the hypnotic gentleman who captivated the Argentine beauty, and through her captured all the Barings' business in the South American republic. — Magnificent executive ability displayed by Mr. Lidderdale in the rehabilitation of the firm. — Amazing gratitude of the benevolent friend who assisted Lord Revelstoke with five million dollars. — The future money center of the world.

THERE have been many versions of the Baring failure and its causes, but the true story of the latter is here told for the first time.

The means to obtain the money which caused the big Baring boom, first in the securities of Guinness's XX. and afterward in the properties, real and imaginary, of Argentina, originated in the act of Parliament, a few years ago, which scaled down the interest on the British consols from 3 to $2\frac{3}{4}$ per cent., and that act of Parliament originated in a casual conversation between the Duke of Marlborough and myself.

When the Duke, who married Mrs. Lily Price Hamersley, now Lady Charles Beresford, was in New York, he and I became quite well acquainted, and had frequent conversations on financial questions and other subjects, in all of which I found him an exceedingly brilliant talker, thoroughly informed on all subjects that came up.

One evening the conversation was diverted to a comparison of the market value of our government bonds with that of the British 3 per cents., or " consols " as they are called. These securities had been called "consols" by way of abbreviation since the time of the Consolidated Act in 1757, in the reign of George II., by which the debts of the nation, including annuities, were consolidated or brought together into one scheme, an average rate of interest being struck at 3 per cent. This rate had never been changed, and it was therefore natural for the idea to get into the British mind that it was destined to be perpetual.

As these "consols," or the British consolidated fund, are kept in account in the Bank of England and virtually form the great bulwark of its deposits, the decrease in the rate of interest was regarded as an injury to the credit of that mighty financial institution, which had been established in 1694 on the first national loan of £1,200,000, to William III.

I said, "Your Grace, the English consols in comparison with our government's ought to be reduced to a lower rate of interest, as 3 per cent. for such a high grade security is too high, and the premium at which our bonds are now selling makes the credit of the United States higher than that of Great Britain," — for our bonds were then on the basis of $2\frac{1}{2}$ per cent. per annum or thereabout.

Marlborough appreciated the criticism at once, and remarked that his government ought to stand on an equal footing with that of the United States. He added, "The comparison from your point of view, with which I coincide, has never, I think, been presented to the British Parliament; but I will call the attention of some of my political friends to the subject as soon as I return home."

The Duke remembered this resolve; the attention of Parliament was called to the subject, and the result was that the interest on consols was cut down to $2\frac{3}{4}$ per cent. by an act of Parliament, with the understanding that there should be a further reduction to $2\frac{1}{2}$ per cent.

When the fact was announced that the rate of these time-honored and most reliable securities had been reduced one quarter of 1 per cent., the surprise and astonishment of their holders in England could hardly have been greater if they had been struck by a cyclone; and if some of them had known that the Duke was at the bottom of it, Blenheim Castle might not have been the best place for him to seek repose and shelter.

To the American mind one quarter decline in the interest of any security appears of but small account ; but if we take into consideration the result to the steady-going life of the average Englishman, with his income adjusted to a certain mode of living just so as to make both ends meet, we can easily imagine that this decline of one twelfth was sufficient to produce a shock. If it deprived him of only one or two luxuries, it was yet a hard matter ; but this cutting off of one twelfth of their income was to plunge many of them irretrievably into debt. Consequently they became desperate, and in the moment of their partial frenzy they determined to part with their holdings and buy into others that would yield more.

This was the opportune moment when the Barings resolved to put upon the market the Guinness's Stout Corporation securities. Guinness's XX. was a commodity known and appreciated by everybody in Great Britain and her colonies who had arrived at the years of discretion, and the shares were known to have for their basis one of the best properties in all the British dominions. Consols were, therefore, rapidly changed into cash, and invested in this new and promising security. The Barings took in the money with such rapidity, and the accumulations became so large, that the fiction of Sindbad the Sailor in the Valley of Diamonds might have seemed more true than the reality.

While the tide of this wonderful prosperity was still rising and threatening to overwhelm all other multi-millionaires, a young man with a strong resemblance to Adonis in features, and an Apollo Belvedere in form, was roaming through South America eking out a precarious existence by selling, for a noted New York chemical firm, a new pill warranted to cure fever and ague and several other malarial ills to which flesh is heir in sultry climes. He was also equipped by the same firm with samples of the famous Florida water, which was presumed to exercise about the same healing influence externally that the pill possessed internally. He was by birth a natural hypnotist, improved by art, and had been a pupil of the famous Charcot, the French hypnotist, but was not particular about his master's advice never to take advantage of his power for selfish purposes. This young man had been employed by the firm, and was intrusted with the South American mission on account of his linguistic abilities and his amazing hypnotic power in convincing the people of every tongue and clime that the pill and the water were exactly what he represented them to be, only a little superior in quality, perhaps, modesty being one of his many personal characteristics.

The wanderings of this disciple of Æsculapius over the pampas of South America would afford material for a new Odyssey, but I will omit most of his adventures, and confine myself as closely as possible to those more immediately connected with the Baring failure. He did not meet with any particular siren or other enchantress, to my knowledge, until he arrived at Buenos Ayres, where he encountered one of nature's loveliest daughters, a Venus of the pampas. The hypnotist was bent on combining business with pleasure, and lost no time in securing his newly found prize against the possibility of recapture by leading her to Hymen's altar. He went through the formality of politely asking the consent of her father, who was the head of the firm of Barings' agency in Argentina, and who at first objected to the marriage on such short acquaintance ; but he soon surrendered to the irresistible influence of the hero's magnetism, and his new son-in-law became a member of the firm.

This modern Ulysses, taking Shakespeare's advice, threw his pill and Florida water to the dogs, and went into another line of business. Like a dutiful son-in-law, he exhibited gratitude toward his bride's parent by taking the burden of managing the firm off his hands, and through the same hypnotic propensity became manager of the concern, showing that, like Ulysses again, he was " a man of many resources." He visited London just at the time the Barings were looking out for new financial worlds to conquer, saw Lord Revelstoke, who was then at the head of the house, as well as one of the directors in the Bank of England, and pictured to his lordship the new imaginary worlds in the Republic of Argentina.

Revelstoke had some doubts at first as to the magnitude of Argentina's wealth, and in order to remove these, he sent an agent to Argentina with our hypnotic hero who, like Elijah with Elisha, threw a double portion of his persuasive spirit upon the agent, sending him back to Revelstoke with a story of prospective wealth, compared with which the exaggerated accounts first given seemed mild and unassuming. Revelstoke no longer hesitated, but began to organize these newly discovered properties, adding the new securities to those of Guinness's XX.

But Englishmen are proverbially conservative. As soon as purchasers became aware of the fact that the properties behind the fresh securities were not virtually gold mines and valuable concessions in Argentina, but rather castles in Spain, they began to realize quickly on all Barings' securities. The result can be easily imagined. The Baring riches began to take wings. The Barings tried hard to impede their flight, and might have done so with the $100,000,000 of Russian gold which was still in their vaults; but the astute Rothschilds, it is alleged, or somebody in their interest, informed the Czar of the firm's unfortunate situation, and his Imperial Highness of Russia ordered that gold transferred from London to the vaults of the Rothschilds at Frankfort-on-the-Main, and elsewhere.

Down went the great house of Baring, as if struck by lightning.

Now comes the second part of this chapter which describes one of the greatest feats in all the history of financiering. It was performed by Mr. Lidderdale, Chairman of the Board of Governors of the Bank of England, who had been for a considerable time a resident of New York, representing the great mercantile firm of Rathbone and Company of London. By his able work at this crisis he averted a panic which, but for his timely intervention, would in all probability have been world-wide.

At that time merchant ships on every sea with their precious cargoes were relying on the Barings to credit their bills of lading. Merchants and business men everywhere were depending on the house for credit to tide them over. Then there were thousands upon thousands who had Barings' paper, which had hitherto been considered as good as gold everywhere.

When we take a retrospect of these things, we can imagine the Herculean task Mr. Lidderdale had undertaken; viz., to stand in the place of the broken-down Barings, to act as substitute for them, to answer all immediate claims, and to pay all immediate demands until the clouds should roll by and the Barings again be put upon their feet. It took seven million pounds sterling, equal to $35,000,000, to essay the mighty task, and this he procured from the Bank of England through his great influence with the governors of that institution. In fact, the majority of the banks and bankers in London also lent their aid in the work of rehabilitation.

Perhaps there was no man in England qualified to attempt the gigantic operation except Mr. Lidderdale. Where did he learn how to do it?· It had never been done in England before. There was no attempt in the case of Overend, Gurney and Company, in 1866, to ward off the blow by such means. Mr. Lidderdale must have learned his *modus operandi* from his experience in the methods of the New York Clearing House, particularly its mode of warding off panics by the issue of certificates. This famous transaction on his part, therefore, reflects the highest credit upon New York banking management, and acknowledges the managers of our united city banks to be in the foremost rank of the world's financiers.

There are certain circumstances connected with the reorganization of the house of Barings heretofore known to but few, which are of the most interesting character. How the firm got so suddenly on its feet again has puzzled many financiers, who thought they were very clear-sighted in such matters and could see through almost anything in the financial world, no matter how dense it might appear to others.

It was not the Bank of England that did it, though most people think it was. That institution carried over only the outstanding obligations, though this operation undoubtedly was a great deal for the bank to do, and, as previously stated, it averted a panic the extent of which, from the nature of things, must have been world-wide. But setting the Barings on their feet again, and making them once more conspicuous in the eyes of the world and as fully trusted as before, was wholly another matter, and cannot be confounded with the operation so ably managed by Mr. Lidderdale.

Some people may infer that it must have taken a powerful syndicate to perform this work. I admit that such an inference would be quite natural, for the task was a huge one ; and if the event had occurred in New York, the chances are that only a syndicate with millions at its back would have essayed the undertaking. It may therefore seem to the reader that I am taxing his credulity too severely when I ask him to believe that the reorganization of the Baring Brothers into a limited liability company was accomplished by one man. He came forth from a well-earned retirement and placed his whole fortune, a million pounds sterling, $5,000,000, at the disposal of the Baring Brothers. He was simply a relative of the family, but alas ! how few are the relatives so unselfish as he proved himself to be. In fact, many relatives would, in the circumstances, have brought railing accusations against the unfortunate ones and played Job's comforters. This man was not of that stamp. He was one of nature's noblemen. What a lesson such a man teaches to those cold-hearted, grasping misers, who hold fast to their wealth even on the brink of the grave. He had made a fortune in the old house of the Barings and had retired to enjoy it in the evening of life. He was a bachelor, well known in financial circles in New York, and had lived here several years, being a member of the banking firm of Ward, Campbell and Company, 52 Wall Street.

These are the bare facts, the mere outlines of a financial episode of real life in our own times, and I believe it is hardly an exaggeration to say that they would afford material to an imaginative author, which I make no pretense of being, for the production of a most thrilling fiction.

The great firm of Barings was the result of the growth of a

hundred years, during which its ramifications extended all over the world, but the blooming of this great century plant of commerce in South American fields overtaxed the strength of the parent stock, so that it must needs have a period of recuperation.

The position occupied by this great house was unique in the history of the world. Decade after decade had fostered the establishment of the greatest credit ever accorded a private firm. Its activities were world-wide. Through this ever increasing confidence its bills were accepted without question and without limit, as equivalent to cash the world over.

The merchant at Hong Kong, at Yokohama, at Melbourne, at Cape Town, or at Rio de Janeiro, who in return for his shipments received their documents, no matter whether these were dated at two months, three months, or six months, had the immediate equivalent of cash. Such a credit virtually provided an addition of many hundreds of millions to the world's currency.

It may be considered doubtful if such a position will ever again be held by any single private concern ; at least, it is not likely in our time. Still, it is a source of very great satisfaction that the old house has, since its rehabilitation, again advanced in popular confidence.

> "You may break, you may shatter the vase if you will,
> But the scent of the roses will hang round it still,"

is peculiarly applicable. The fragrant odor of a great and honorable name has not suffered destruction, while the vessel has been cemented together. An effect of the tremendous shock which their misfortunes caused may be observed in the course of the London money market since 1890. Prior to that time, for years the maximum interest rate scarcely ever exceeded 3 per cent., ruling almost invariably at a much lower rate. Since then, however, London discount rates have been subject to the wider fluctuations of other money centers. Does not this unsettling of stability presage a shifting elsewhere of the great money center of the world?

And if so, why not to New York? We have here the metropolis of what is acknowledged the richest country in the world — a city rapidly becoming as cosmopolitan as London, financial institutions and great business firms which rival those of the Old World, and in addition a geographical position at the very gateway of this continent which places it, in that respect, beyond rivalry. All these factors tend toward the establishment here of that necessary foundation of stability which fosters commercial and financial supremacy.

CHAPTER XXXIV.

THE VENEZUELA MESSAGE PANIC.

This panic one of the most far-reaching and most disastrous in its consequences. — It was a surprise, and hence its great power for mischief,
especially at a time when prosperity was just under way. — An utter
collapse of credit, both foreign and domestic, aggravated by foreign
holders returning our securities. — The Monroe Doctrine and how President Cleveland construed it. — Simply an outburst of honest and over
weening patriotism on his part. — His misapprehensions regarding the
nature of so-called international law, and what constitutes a *casus belli*.
— The President's just cause for offense at Salisbury's hauteur, but still
the Monroe Doctrine not applicable to the case. — How the message
and its consequences played into the hands of the free-silver faction and
helped to make the candidacy of Bryan possible.

THE Venezuela message panic was probably farther reaching and really more disastrous than any in recent times,
primarily for the reason that it was sudden and unexpected.

The rumblings of the silver panic were distinctly heard in
the distance ; so with the tariff panic, and also in the case of
the currency-reform panic. Disaster growing out of the last-
named was due to the apprehension that State banks were
going to supplement the national banks with all the horrors of
wild-cat currency associated with the name of those institutions
in former years, the great variety and large volume of whose
notes, together with their numerous and bewildering counter-
feits, had complicated finances prior to the Civil War.

But let us examine the circumstances associated with the
Venezuela message panic more closely. They are of the deepest interest to the people of this country, and show us the stern
necessity of an Executive acting with the most diplomatic discretion where international affairs are involved, and where a rash
or false move may in an instant let loose the dogs of war and

ruin business. It is like playing with fire, when the head of a nation touches rudely a point which may be made a *casus belli* by some sensitive people. Happily, Great Britain was not very sensitive on the matter in question.

The candid intention of Mr. Cleveland was a patriotic defense of the Monroe Doctrine, but the time and the occasion were inappropriate. For several months prior to the date of this diplomatic document business had been reviving, and confidence was being gradually restored. A fresh impetus was visible in the channels of trade all over the country, and a general feeling of cheerfulness, which had not been discernible since 1893, pervaded the masses. Stocks had gone up very considerably, dry goods were selling at a more lively rate, with advancing prices from the jobbers to the retail merchants, and quite a prosperous business all around had been successfully initiated.

At this juncture news came from Washington, and was duly distributed by the news agencies, to the effect that Mr. Cleveland had gone off on another duck-hunting tour. This, too, was a reassuring feature of the times, bearing upon the subject of prosperity. It was naturally inferred that if the President felt at liberty to go off on a tour of recreation, his mind must be in a state of agreeable composure so far as public affairs were concerned, and that he, too, was enjoying a full share of the beneficent influence of the improved condition of business.

After a few days' absence from Washington, the nation was informed, to its great satisfaction, that the President was having unprecedented success in his sport and that he seldom missed his aim. Then, in an evil hour, he returned to Washington and sprung that ill-starred Venezuela message on Congress and the civilized world.

It was December 17, 1895, when the blow fell. The effect was instantaneous, and the panic spread like wildfire all over the Union, and wherever our credit relations in Europe existed the same feeling of distrust and dread of coming calamity seized the minds of the people at large. There was a wild rush to sell everything on the very shortest notice, and to get gold if possible, for the dreadful specter of war admonished the people that the yellow metal would be their tower of strength in the event of hostilities. Credit was broken down to an extent that the country had not witnessed since 1873, and there was scarcely a household throughout the length and breadth of the land where the baneful effects of this war scare were not felt. In fact, the whole country lay prostrate in presence of the phantom of "blood and iron" which the people had conjured up from the depths of their own fertile imaginations, because there was nothing in reality to justify half the excitement which the occasion developed. With the exception of the last two paragraphs or so, the language of the message was almost as mild and inoffensive as the one delivered to Congress by President Monroe on December 2, 1823 ; and that message was a model of smoothness and politeness, the Monroe Doctrine itself, so called, being couched in such harmonious and conciliatory language as not to offend the most fastidious taste.

The whole pith of the Monroe Doctrine is contained in the following clear and admirably constructed sentence, —

"With the existing colonies or dependencies of any of the European powers we have not interfered and shall not interfere ; but with the governments who have declared their independence and maintained it, and whose independence we have on great consideration and on just principles acknowledged, we could not view any interposition for the purpose of oppressing them, or controlling in any other manner their destiny, by any European power, in any other light than as a manifestation of an unfriendly disposition toward the United States."

This is a very long sentence, but at the same time the language is clear and comprehensive. It is smooth, non-committal, and diplomatic in every happily chosen word. There is a peaceful tone even in its rhythm, and yet when you read between the lines you find that beneath the conciliatory and peace-loving surface there is something in it which says, " If you don't heed this admonition, but intend to bring on the armies of your Holy Alliance to recapture Brazil for a worthless king who will cover the Atlantic with fleets of pirates and commit wholesale murder and robbery, the United States will fight." Viewed in this light, the Monroe message was virtually more belligerent than the Cleveland message. Yet the words of the sentence are so well put together that it is difficult to construe it so.

In reading Mr. Cleveland's message carefully in its entirety, one can see where it was quite natural and easy for him to fall into the error which provoked the threat in the last three paragraphs, and especially in the final one. Mr. Cleveland inferred that the very act against which President Monroe mildly admonished the European powers had been actually committed in the Venezuela affair. He labored under the impression that the English claim as to the boundary line was simply a pretext for extending the English system to this hemisphere in violation of the Monroe Doctrine. The following short paragraph explains the logic on which Mr. Cleveland leaned for the justification of this opinion : —

"If a European power, by an extension of its boundaries, takes possession of the territory of one of our neighboring republics against its will and in derogation of its rights, it is difficult to see why, to that extent, such European power does not thereby attempt to extend its system of government to that portion of this continent which is thus taken. This is the precise action which President Monroe declared to be 'dangerous to our peace and safety,' and it can make no difference whether the European system is extended by an advance of frontier or otherwise."

This reasoning appears very plausible from Mr. Cleveland's standpoint, but it is not conclusive nor broad enough in its scope to take in the whole situation. It seems to overlook the fact that the land in dispute had belonged to Great Britain by prescriptive right and adverse possession for sixty years, whereas twenty years would have been sufficient, according to the laws of most countries, to establish permanent ownership. Having got this idea fully impressed upon his mind, and reasoning on these premises, it is easy to see how he arrived at the panic-breeding and hostile conclusion which he honestly thought was indispensable to maintain the honor and integrity of the nation whose " peace and safety," as the Monroe Doctrine expresses it, he considered endangered. When in connection with this interpretation we consider the somewhat supercilious and haughty refusal of Lord Salisbury to submit the matter to arbitration, it is not so difficult to discern the exasperating causes that moved him to treat Salisbury as cavalierly as his lordship had treated our President and Mr. Olney, the Secretary of State.

These are certainly extenuating circumstances, panic or no panic, for that imprudent part of the message which caused the financial upheaval. The following and concluding parts of the message are self-explanatory on these points : —

" The course to be pursued by this government, in view of the present condition, does not appear to admit of serious doubt. Having labored faithfully for many years to induce Great Britain to submit this dispute to impartial arbitration, and having been now finally apprised of her refusal to do so, nothing remains but to accept the situation, to recognize its plain requirements, and deal with it accordingly. Great Britain's present proposition has never thus far been regarded as admissible by Venezuela, though any adjustment of the boundary which that country may deem for her advantage, and may enter into of her own free will, cannot, of course, be objected to by the United States.

" Assuming, however, that the attitude of Venezuela will remain unchanged, the dispute has reached such a stage as to make it now incumbent upon the United States to take measures to determine with sufficient certainty for its justification what is the true divisional line between the Republic of Venezuela and British Guiana. The inquiry to that end should of course be conducted carefully and judicially, and due weight should be given to all available evidence, records, and facts in support of the claims of both parties.

" In order that such an examination should be prosecuted in a thorough and satisfactory manner, I suggest that the Congress make an adequate appropriation for the expenses of a commission to be appointed by the Executive, who shall make the necessary investigation and report upon the matter with the least possible delay. When such report is made and accepted it will, in my opinion, be the duty of the United States to resist, by every means in its power, as a wilful aggression upon its rights and interests, the appropriation by Great Britian of any lands or the exercise of governmental juris- diction over any territory which, after investigation, we have deter- mined of right belongs to Venezuela.

" In making these recommendations I am fully alive to the responsibility incurred, and keenly realize all the consequences that may follow.

" I am, nevertheless, firm in my conviction that while it is a grievous thing to contemplate the two great English-speaking peoples of the world as being otherwise than friendly competitors in the onward march of civilization, and strenuous and worthy rivals in all the arts of peace, there is no calamity which a great nation can invite which equals that which follows a supine submission to wrong and injustice and the consequent loss of national self-respect and honor, beneath which are shielded and defended a people's safety and greatness."

Another error into which Mr. Cleveland incidentally fell, and which stimulated him to arrive at the conclusion that a *casus belli* had been committed by Great Britain, is contained in the following excerpts from the message : —

" Practically, the principle for which we contend has peculiar, if not exclusive, relation to the United States. It may not have been admitted in so many words in the code of international law, but, since in international councils every nation is entitled to the rights belonging to it, if the enforcement of the Monroe Doctrine is some- thing we may justly claim, it has its place in the code of interna- tional law as certainly and as securely as if it were specifically mentioned ; and when the United States is a suitor before the high tribunal that administers international law, the question to be determined is whether or not we present claims which the justice of that code of law can find to be right and valid.

" The Monroe Doctrine finds its recognition in those principles of international law which are based upon the theory that every nation shall have its rights protected and its just claims enforced."

Unfortunately for these opinions there is no code of inter- national law except by a figure of speech highly inflated. In a well-regulated world there ought to be such a code, and doubtless there will be after the millennium ; but so long as the lion and the lamb lie down together, according to present custom, with the lamb inside the lion, the prospects for an international code are not very bright.

Nor is the Monroe Doctrine a law either national or international. It is simply a policy or another Declaration of Independence. Henry Clay tried hard to make it a law, but Congress tabled his resolution, and the subject was dropped. The Monroe Doctrine, however, is universally respected in the sense just stated, and Marshal Bazaine was quick to recognize it in the interest of his imperial master, Napoleon III., when our troops were sent to the frontiers of Mexico soon after our Civil War. The French politely withdrew, and bloodshed was thereby prudently avoided. Other cases less conspicuous might be quoted, but this will do for an illustration.

The theory laid down by Mr. Cleveland, that every nation shall have its rights protected by international law, is simply a cosmopolitan chimera, yet a very beautiful and poetical idea. Every nation is obliged to fight its own battles. If the theory were true, Cuba would not so long have sustained the struggle single-handed against the power of Spain.

It remains now to state briefly the origin of the Monroe Doctrine. England was chiefly responsible for it, as she suggested the idea through George Canning, her famous statesman and diplomatist, then Secretary of State for Foreign Affairs and afterward Prime Minister. The Holy Alliance had resolved to restore to Ferdinand VII. of Spain his former colonies in South America ; and England, seeing that that would be a serious menace to her shipping interests and her " rule of the waves," nipped in the bud the despotic scheme. Canning proposed that England should join the United States in the declaration ; but Monroe was too shrewd a diplomatist for that, as his French training while minister at the Tuileries, together with his personal associations with Washington, Jefferson, John Adams, and James Madison, had taught him to be very circumspect in diplomacy.

The Holy Alliance, I scarcely need to state, was organized

by Russia, Austria, and Prussia shortly after the battle of Waterloo in 1815, for the ostensible purpose of pacifying Europe, maintaining the purity of religion, — hence "holy," — returning to the rightful owners some of the plunder of which Napoleon had deprived them, and of being prepared for the contingency of another possible Napoleon. Other nations of Europe joined it; but England, through Canning, was the first to perceive that its real object was conquest and despotic rule. She therefore withdrew, taking self-protective action, as has been stated. France followed England's example a year or two afterward, and the Alliance was broken up a few years later, all its ambitious schemes being dissipated; after which Europe became comparatively tranquil for a season.

The last paragraph or two in which Mr. Cleveland's threat is contained, and which caused the panic, are said to have been composed as an addendum to the original document as agreed upon by Mr. Cleveland and Mr. Olney. Perhaps the idea of this unfortunate addition to the message entered the brain of Mr. Cleveland while on the duck-shooting expedition. His notion seems to have been that if Great Britain got an inch in Venezuela she would take an ell, put to rout the existing government, and set up the English system in its place; and if it had been manifest that this was the intention of Great Britain, then the Monroe Doctrine would have been applicable in the case, as with the French in Mexico. Under such conditions, the belligerent language of the President might have been justifiable, but hardly so until all attempts at arbitration had been exhausted. There is no evidence, however, that England had any intention of conquest; neither had she committed any overt act that the United States could consider "dangerous to its peace and safety," which would be necessary to create a *casus belli*, according to another clause in Mr. Monroe's message. Consequently, to say the least, Mr. Cleveland was rather precipitate in his patriotic purpose, and his rash and premature action cost this country about $2,000,000,000 in the shrinkage of all securities and the almost total suppression of credit, or more than two thirds of the amount of the national debt at the close of the Civil War.   Credit paper became of little or no value or use, thus contracting the medium with which we do most of our business at least 75 per cent.   Nothing would pass but coin or its convertible equivalent, and so business was brought to a general condition of stagnation.   As all the nations of Europe regarded the concluding part of the message as a menace of war which England must regard either by accepting or by showing the white feather, business with foreign nations was also largely blocked, and all our foreign relations became immediately strained.   We were almost as much isolated for a short time, in a financial sense, as if we had been surrounded by a Chinese wall.

The worst feature of the predicament was that the message was popular before the people began to think and reflect upon it, and this feeling was further fomented by Congress catching the "Jingo" contagion.   Speculators and investors were tumbling over one another in their excitement to get rid of their securities and to obtain gold, no matter at what sacrifice, for the purpose of hoarding it in safe-deposit boxes against threatened business disaster and the probable upheaval of thrones and kingdoms in prospect; for if war should break out between two of the greatest civilized nations in the world, there was no knowing where it would end.   Money, in consequence of this state of affairs, became stringent, and our securities were sold by European holders as fast as they could get rid of them, the gold meantime flowing from our shores in a steady and rapid stream.   The United States Treasury reserve of $100,000,000, melted away like snow before the noonday sun until it fell to $49,000,000, and the faster it decreased the more the panic increased, and the tighter grew the money market, so that there was scarcely a spot in our whole broad land that the panic did not cover.   Failures of bankers, brokers, and merchants were reported daily and sometimes hourly ; there was a tremendous run on nearly all the savings banks, and general disorganization in the whole financial world seemed imminent.

Lord Salisbury may have felt like William Pitt at the breaking out of the European campaign of his day, when the powers of

Europe were beginning to league themselves against Napoleon. "Roll up that map of Europe," said Pitt, "it will not be required for the next ten years." His words were truly prophetic, and the thought of his prophecy being fulfilled, as it was afterward, is said to have caused his death. There was no fear of such a fatal result, however, in the case of Salisbury. He is not so sensitive; yet the circumstances afford food for very serious reflection to the people of the United States, when it is considered that Mr. Cleveland's *faux pas*, made with honest intentions and but slightly wrong in theory, cost this country nearly one half of the aggregate debt incurred by England during her fifteen years' war with Napoleon, including the period that she assisted the allies with money and munitions of war when she was not actually in the field herself.

This country had never before met such a sudden revolution in business. The panic of 1873 had hitherto been considered quick and expansive in its action, but it hardly compared with that of 1895. This latter reduced business transactions generally to a retail basis, a kind of hand-to-mouth operation, and on purely cash principles. The strained relations between buyer and seller were of a very disagreeable character, making commercial transactions quite irritating, and threatening to sap the foundations of our prosperous system of trade and commerce. Business was thus pent up within exceedingly narrow limits, and profits accordingly must have been reduced to the very lowest ebb. All securities, as a matter of course, experienced a tremendous fall in prices, many of them seeking a lower level than in the panic of 1893. That panic was not to be compared to the Venezuela message panic, because it did not carry with it a total annihilation of credits, which the later hobgoblin of war did.

The paralysis in business that ensued, growing out of this terrible disaster, was continued without much visible abatement up to the time of the Chicago Free Silver Convention, July 9, 1896. The agony had been endured by the most long-suffering people on the face of the earth from December 17, 1895, the date of the message. It is not an exaggeration, I think, nor am

I guilty, I believe, of attaching too much importance to that part of the message productive of the panic, when I say that it was mainly due to it that a few men, some of them quite obscure previously and others notorious for their revolutionary predilections, were enabled at Chicago to organize the new democracy.

CHAPTER XXXV.

OUR NATION'S CREDIT.

Why should this credit, as illustrated in the market value of our bonds, not be on as high a plane as the credit of other nations ? — A plea for the Sherman Silver Law and how it was instrumental in tiding the financial world over the Baring panic. — A brief retrospect of bond issues and cognate subjects of national interest.

REGARDING the credit of our nation there seems to have been a great deal of misconception and loose thinking in the past. I here reproduce a few points which I published some time ago on this and kindred subjects, viewing them from that common-sense point of view which everybody — the ordinary business man, the farmer, and the mechanic— can understand as easily as the professional financier. There may be, however, certain college and other financial professors, men who have been in the habit of bending and torturing statistics to dovetail with preconceived opinions and theories, who will not understand the subject from my point of view.

Though I am an uncompromising advocate of the gold standard under existing conditions, yet I am not afraid to do justice to silver and silver legislation internationally considered, through fear that some cranky critic, who looks superficially on financial subjects, should charge me with inconsistency.

The Sherman Silver Law, for instance, served an excellent purpose that could probably not have been achieved at the time by any other instrumentality, but it was right to repeal an objectionable part of it when through altered circumstances and the march of events it became really objectionable. Whether the time of repeal was exactly opportune or not is a point which has afforded scope for controversy, and which I have discussed in another chapter and need not therefore

refer to further ; but the law was justifiable in itself and exhibited great legislative wisdom in its author.

The highest credit nations of Europe are England and France.
They have never issued promise-to-pay obligations bearing less
than 3 per cent. interest, except when England, years ago,
reduced the rate on a part of her consols to $2\frac{3}{4}$ per cent.,
which was the initial cause of the Baring failure.

Almost everything that has gone wrong financially on this
side since that memorable failure of the Barings has been
charged to the Sherman Silver Law, especially so as to the
return of our securities and the large shipments of gold. The
charge is far from being well founded. The Sherman Law certainly did not have anything to do with the Barings' disaster,
and it was that catastrophe which sent our stocks and bonds
back, for money had to be raised in England by the holders of
these properties, because they were almost the only ones that
could find a ready market. The Silver Law did not enter into
the question ; it was simply a matter of raising money. These
people had Argentine, Brazilian, Turkish, Spanish, Russian,
Egyptian, and numerous other securities of like character, but
they were unsalable, so there was no alternative but to sell
their American stocks and bonds ; therefore the gold that
went to pay for them did not go because of the Sherman Silver
Law or from the fear of its consequences at that time. No one
will say that the Sherman Silver Law had anything to do with
the Panama swindle and scandal, which came so near creating
a revolution in France. The fear of this caused the French
people to draw their money from the banking institutions and
hoard it, the Bank of France being compelled thereby to
recuperate her gold reserve by buying gold from America and
drawing vast sums from us in consequence. Who can possibly charge that the Sherman Silver Law was the incentive
to Austria for selling her 4 per cent. bonds, and with the
proceeds buying our gold at a premium, and in that way
taking it from us as so much merchandise to be bought by
weight?

Having given the causes as above for our gold shipments, —

namely, the natural sequence and after effect of the Baring failure panic, the threatened revolution in France growing out of the Panama scandal, and last but not least, the Austrian scheme for placing that nation on a gold basis, — I unhesitatingly assert that these were legitimate and substantial reasons to account for the departure of the yellow metal, and not the Sherman Law.

What, then, are the actual facts? When summed up, they are these : the Sherman Silver Law, as a matter of fact, did excellent service, and without it an immense number of banking institutions, railroad companies, and merchants in this country would have come to grief; in other words, the credit is due to the Sherman Silver Law for not only carrying us through trouble, but for helping England, France, and Austria. The new money created by the sanction of the 1890 Silver Law made it possible for this country to sustain itself, and at the same time to send gold to foreign countries.

Notwithstanding, however, that the Sherman Silver Law has done so much for us as a nation, I am of the opinion that it was wise legislation to repeal the purchasing clause of the said law, for we have enough of that kind of money in circulation now.

The leading nations have come down to a business basis, requiring international action as the remedy for their difficulties. It has become necessary to utilize their resources in the best possible way, and money as a power is now recognized as the most potential influence in connection with national alliances. Every country has its own products, some more or less than others, the surplus or deficit of which is destined at no distant day to be regulated by commercial reciprocal treaties. Such interests will be more influential and powerful in cementing friendships between nations than are armies and navies, the change being from one of force to that of mutual interests. War methods belong to the past, and after present troubles are adjusted, will soon, by common consent, be relegated to the rear to make way for offensive and defensive reciprocity commercial treaties, which will insure prolonged peace and prosperity. The true spirit between nations should be to exchange commodities with each other, and not bullets; and not to engage in the endeavor to grab each other's gold by its purchase or other sharp methods. There is gold enough for all if mutual consideration and forbearance are exercised. Mutual confidence and a fair spirit of reciprocity between nations will make the world's supply of gold ample to provide for all legitimate exchanges, internally and externally, with the nations now on the single standard basis; but not to provide for a selfish spirit of hoarding at the same time. To prevent the excessive shipments of gold periodically, the five great nations — England, France, Germany, Russia, and the United States — should adopt an international note currency or a $1\frac{1}{2}$ per cent. gold bond issue, not to exceed say $500,000,000, each to issue $100,000,000, the five nations to be equally responsible for the principal and interest by a mutual agreement. These obligations, backed by such high credit, would take the place of gold exports and imports. Gold would be no better as a remittance — as a matter of fact, not nearly as desirable. The notes or bonds would be an international currency, and would provide a substitute for gold in a settlement of balances between nations. It would do away almost altogether with the present clumsy method of shipping gold from one country to another, and a few weeks afterward bringing it back again, as is now the usual practice. It has really come to be a matter of dollars and cents with nations, especially with those that are overburdened with debt, which includes most of them. These increasing burdens must eventually make it imperative to abandon the large standing armies and navies, and to substitute commercial treaties.

CHAPTER XXXVI.

OUR NATION'S NEW DEPARTURE.

The influence of our recent victories on the minds and purposes of other nations. — Significance of the Czar's note on disarmament. — Was our war with Spain justifiable? — The part played by the President and Congress in the war. — The problem of our new possessions. — What shall we do with them?

ON New Year's Day, 1898, it would have been difficult to imagine that this country in so short a time could have exercised such an immense influence on the financial and political concerns of the world at large as it does to-day. One great manifestation of this universal influence is the recent Peace Congress at The Hague which met in May, 1899, at the request of the Czar of Russia.

It is evident that the war of the United States with Spain forced this movement to manifest itself much sooner than it would have done if international affairs had gone forward in the old channels. The idea of the United States becoming an empire, in power if not in name, has given the nations fresh impetus for thought, and has very probably affected some of them with feelings of alarm.

The formation of an empire, anywhere, has always been a disturbing element to the rest of the world. It was so with that of ancient Rome, also with that of Charles V. of Germany, with that of Napoleon I.; and, though the empire of Great Britain has been of gradual formation, its extension has been a prolific cause of serious unrest to the nations, and especially to Russia.

In the latter instance the feeling of uneasiness has been mutual, and a constant source of irritation to both nations, despite the soothing influences of family relations and intermarriages between the two royal houses; and this feeling and those strained relations have been particularly emphasized since her Majesty, Queen Victoria, assumed the title of Empress of India.

Now that an alliance between the United States, Russia's best friend, and Great Britain, Russia's greatest possible enemy, has been suggested, and considering the evidence that the United States has recently given to the world of its great possibilities in the way of martial development and power on both sea and land, it is not to be wondered at that Russia, whose statesmen and diplomatists are the most subtle and far-seeing in the world, should advise the wisest course in diplomacy to avert unhappy collisions between any of the civilized nations in the future.

Europe may laugh at the Utopian idea of young Nicholas; but he is, in all likelihood, only the mouthpiece for the expression of the concentrated wisdom of his advisers. The idea of the happy and prosperous state of things that would ensue were the Czar's suggestion put into practice, is so overwhelming in the vastness of its conception and the multitude of its blessings to humanity, that minds accustomed to think of nations in arms can hardly grasp the nature of the proposed change.

Let us try to conceive of a burden of $1,000,000,000 taxation being at once lifted from the shoulders of 350,000,000 of people, and at the same time 5,000,000 of the flower of these people turned to the arts of peace and profitable production, instead of living on the production of those less eligible for toil, and that simply for the purpose of being in constant training to kill their fellow-men with the greatest possible rapidity.

The theory that the statesmen of Russia are opposed to the views of the Czar does not appear to me to be tenable. The late Count Maravieff and some of his colleagues may have only acted that part for the sake of effect, pursuant to some secret purpose.

The formerly avowed policy of France on the question of Alsace-Lorraine was of a very narrow character, although natural; but the outcome of this conference has already given breadth to her national views, as well as to those of other nations. It must be remembered that the provinces about which France felt so patriotically sore were wrested by her from Germany less than two centuries ago.

The conference would have been foredoomed to failure, if the settlement of boundary lines had been a preliminary part of the programme, — a principle that was well illustrated at the Congress of Vienna in 1815. At that time the representatives of the nations of Europe had just succeeded in getting into a complete muddle on the boundary question, when they were suddenly relieved by the escape of Napoleon from Elba, which upset all their plans and calculations and postponed this question indefinitely. If there is any hope for the Czar's plan for a paradise on earth, present boundaries must be held sacred. Any boundary line settlement that could possibly be proposed would leave international affairs in as bad a condition as that in which they now stand, and would entail a series of settlements running back to the days of Julius Cæsar, and then even there would arise a new starting-point, calling for the redress of older grievances back to the Creation, perhaps, or at least as far as the Deluge.

It may be of national interest in contemplating this magnificent reform, or rather peaceful revolution of the nations, to take a retrospect of the contribution of our own country to the proposed change ; but before discussing this matter it is proper to place before the mind of the reader the exact utterance of the Czar.

The press at first jumped to the conclusion that he actually proposed disarmament, though his words were only suggestive of it. He simply suggested that the powers of the world should have a conference on the subject of reducing armaments and lessening their expenses. The full text of the note was as follows : —

"St. Petersburg, August 24, 1898.
By Count Maravieff, as Foreign Minister :

" The maintenance of general peace and the possible reduction of the excessive armaments which weigh upon all nations present themselves in existing conditions to the whole world as an ideal toward which the endeavors of all governments should be directed. The humanitarian and magnanimous ideas of His Majesty the Emperor, my august master, have been won over to this view in the conviction that this lofty aim is in conformity with the most essential interests and legitimate views of all the powers; and the imperial government thinks the present moment would be very favorable to seeking the means.

"International discussion is the most effectual means of insuring all peoples benefit — a real, durable peace, above all, putting an end to the progressive development of the present armaments.

"In the course of the last twenty years the longing for general appeasement has grown especially pronounced in the consciences of civilized nations; and the preservation of peace has been put forward as an object of international policy. It is in its name that great States have concluded between themselves powerful alliances.

"It is the better to guarantee peace that they have developed in proportions hitherto unprecedented their military forces, and still continue to increase them, without shrinking from any sacrifices.

"Nevertheless, all these efforts have not yet been able to bring about the beneficent result desired — pacification.

"The financial charges following the upward march strike at the very root of public prosperity. The intellectual and physical strength of the nation's labor and capital are mostly diverted from their natural application and are unproductively consumed. Hundreds of millions are devoted to acquiring terrible engines of destruction, which, though to-day regarded as the last work of science, are destined to-morrow to lose all their value in consequence of some fresh discovery in the same field. National culture, economic progress, and the production of wealth are either paralyzed or checked in development. Moreover, in proportion as the armaments of each power increase, they less and less fulfill the object the government has set before themselves.

"The economic crisis, due in great part to the system of armaments '*à l'outrance*,' and the continual danger which lies in this massing of war material, are transforming the armed peace of our days into a crushing burden which the people have more and more difficulty in bearing.

"It appears evident that if this state of things were to be prolonged it would inevitably lead to the very cataclysm it is desired to avert, and the horrors whereof make every thinking being shudder in advance.

"To put an end to these incessant armaments and to seek the

means of warding off the calamities which are threatening the whole world — such is the supreme duty to-day imposed upon all States.

" Filled with this idea, His Majesty has been pleased to command me to propose to all the governments whose representatives are accredited to the imperial court the assembling of a conference which shall occupy itself with this grave problem.

" This conference will be, by the help of God, a happy presage for the century which is about to open. It would converge into one powerful focus the efforts of all States sincerely seeking to make the great conception of universal peace triumph over the elements of trouble and discord, and it would at the same time cement their agreement by a corporate consecration of the principles of equity and right whereon rest the security of States and the welfare of peoples."

In this connection the following table speaks for itself : —

ARMED POWER OF EUROPE.

LAND FORCES.

PEACE FOOTING —

	Germany.	France.	Italy.	Austria-Hungary.	Russia.	England.	Turkey.
Men	607,308	559,260	216,235	277,192	1,743,244	220,199	228,574
Horses . . .	108,800	192,200	58,760	67,400	176,600	——	33,400
Guns . . .	2,967	3,480	1,986	2,712	2,672	720	696

WAR FOOTING —

Men	5,166,592	4,849,572	2,181,790	1,767,087	5,008,284	637,863	1,061,862
Horses . . .	201,200	192,200	55,800	86,740	295,718	——	90,600
Guns . . .	4,588	5,024	1,986	2,712	6,084	——	696

NAVAL POWER.

	England.	France.	Russia.	Germany.	Italy.	Austria-Hungary.	Turkey.
Armored ships	88	49	60	42	25	19	18
Guns	3,298	1,627	1,343	898	925	488	312
Cruisers and gunboats .	188	110	37	23	25	18	20
Guns	3,086	1,547	530	380	547	75	121
Torpedo boats	293	266	230	192	209	87	42
Men	79,947	80,920	40,532	21,513	21,724	13,313	22,276
Reserves.	83,000	84,350	45,000	37,000	19,600	2,000	36,000

This is a statistical view of the formidable forces which cause such a terrible drain on the resources of Europe, and keep the greater number of the people in bondage to support it. A study of the figures and of the possibilities in expense, human suffering, and slaughter which they imply, is sufficient to appall the stoutest heart, whether it beats in the bosom of the proudest autocrat or the most humble laborer.

Let us return now to the part which our own country has played in prompting the note of the Czar, suggesting permanent relief from this overwhelmingly oppressive condition.

In the first place, we have set a noble example to the world since our own Civil War by the reduction of our armaments to a point that demonstrated our temerity more than our prudence, a fact which the late Spanish War clearly showed. Though we came out of that struggle victorious, yet, a few years prior to the sudden reorganization of our navy, Spain's superior fleet might have made it entirely practical for General Weyler to have carried out his proud boast of invading this country with two hundred thousand men.

We had a providential escape, coming out triumphant beyond precedent in the history of wars, despite the fact that our army was overtaken by disease in Cuba, which, on account of our hasty and inadequate preparations for war, we were not prepared to meet until its fatal effects had been severely felt.

That incompetency should have been displayed in some parts of the commissariat and the medical department of an army so hastily organized for foreign service as was ours, is not to be wondered at. Such accidents are likely to occur in the best regulated armies, as with the British, for instance, in the Crimea in 1854, when the greater part of Lord Raglan's command were starving and half naked for days, while plenty of food and clothing was within a few miles of them. A similar mishap, only on a much larger scale, occurred to the French army in the campaign which ended disastrously at Sedan in 1870. Errors, either of oversight or by lack of full preparation, are seemingly bound to occur in connection with nearly all military operations, most especially those which are unduly hastened by a rapid march of events. Complaints have been numerous during the South African campaign.

Some persons are inclined to lay the blame for the mistakes in our service on President McKinley; but it was impossible for any man to exercise the superhuman individual foresight necessary to detect the incompetency of untried subordinates in every department of a rapidly mobilized military service ; while his calmness, courage, and promptitude, so far as the conduct of the war itself was concerned, were well-nigh faultless.

The President counseled peace at any price not inconsistent with national honor, and left every possible loophole in his power for Spain to escape from the trouble which she had brought upon herself, without entailing further disgrace to Spanish arms and humiliation to Spanish chivalry ; but Spain in her irrational pride ignored all such opportunities, and interpreted what was meant for her best interests into an insult to her historic greatness and invincible valor. Her answer to all amicable and soothing propositions was, " No ! we will fight to the bitter end." When she did yield for a brief period to the appearance of reason and a possible settlement on rational principles through the scheme of autonomy, she was not sincere, but only playing at diplomacy to deceive our people and gain time with the hope of European intervention. This was fully revealed in the private correspondence of Minister de Lome to the editor of the *Madrid Herald*, which was accidentally discovered by a Cuban and handed over to our government.

In that correspondence Señor de Lome ridiculed our Congress and statesmen, and used very disrespectful and abusive language concerning President McKinley. He was therefore regarded as *persona non grata*, and before notification to this effect could reach his government he prudently resigned. On his way home, however, he stopped in Canada with the object of concocting mischief against this country, until he was informed by the government of that country that his presence in the Dominion was undesirable.

About this time, February 15, 1898, was perpetrated that horrible crime, the blowing up of the battleship *Maine* in the harbor of Havana, where she was anchored on a friendly visit. That tragic event, in which 266 out of a crew of 404 of our brave sailors and marines, including two officers, perished, caused a shock of consternation and horror throughout the civilized world. It was then demonstrated to every right-thinking mind that patience with Spanish treachery and cruelty had ceased to be a virtue, and our eighty millions of united people joined with one voice in a cry for retribution. Public opinion everywhere pointed to Spanish officials of Cuba as the perpetrators of the dastardly deed. A court of inquiry consisting of Captain W. T. Sampson, Captain F. E. Chadwick, Lieutenant Commander Potter, and Lieutenant Commander Marix investigated the matter for six weeks. They found that the explosions happened externally, and that there had been no carelessness on the part of the crew of the *Maine;* but the court was unable to fix the responsibility. This had no effect, however, in removing suspicion from the Spanish officials, and the whole country became impatient with the President because he did not declare war against Spain at once.

The destruction of the *Maine* was undoubtedly the crowning crime which precipitated the war, though the cause was diplomatically and officially attributed to the cruel domination of Spain in Cuba and her refusal to relinquish the island. That the war was justifiable on account of Spain's misrule in Cuba, most of the nations of Europe admit. It is not difficult, however, to produce positive evidence in order that the justice of Uncle Sam's intervention may be made clear to all men.

I shall pass over the details of the case of the *Virginius,* in 1871, in which Spain's officials in Cuba defiantly shot down more than thirty American citizens. No punishment was inflicted by Spain on these colonial assassins, and we had no modern navy then.

Every attempt at autonomy in Cuba during the succeeding years, up to 1896, was a failure and generally a farce. In the last of the several wars waged for Cuban independence, Captain General Campos, one of the most humane officials ever sent out by Spain, acknowledged that all efforts to reduce the Cubans to subjection had failed, and he returned home at the beginning of 1896. The chief complaint against him was that he was too humane. He wished to adhere as closely as possible to the rules of civilized warfare, and that policy was insufficient to subjugate Cuba.

So Campos was succeeded by a man who had gained a bad preëminence for human butchery and nameless cruelties among the semi-civilized and savage population of the Philippine Islands, from whom he had also replenished his own coffers to the extent of several million dollars, filched from the natives and politicians of those wealthy islands. The name of this man is Valeriano Weyler, called by way of distinction "Butcher Weyler," a cognomen which his actions in Cuba, to say nothing of his notorious career in the Philippines, fully justify.

Weyler conceived one of the most fiendish schemes that has probably ever entered into the heart of man, for the purpose of putting Cuba fully in the power of Spain. It was nothing less than extermination by starvation of half a million of people, most of whom were peaceable and uncomplaining, and who were tilling the soil industriously for that portion of its product barely sufficient to maintain them, the residue being undoubtedly divided among Weyler and his political colleagues, except a small surplus that was sent to Spain. This scheme of wholesale assassination excited universal horror and indignation when the nature of it became known ; but prior to that more than 100,000 had died in the agonies of hunger and the diseases caused by starvation. These people were driven into the cities and walled in by cordons of soldiers until they found relief in death. The total number in the six provinces that perished in this way probably exceeded 300,000. The idea was to starve the *pacificos*, in order that the Cuban insurgents might no longer be able to obtain food to enable them to continue the war. Spain herself became so disgusted at this villainous mode of warfare, and ashamed at the universal outcry against it, that she ordered Weyler home, and then an effort was made through General Blanco, who succeeded him, to save the remnant of these miserable people, called *reconcentrados;* but many more perished before relief could reach them, though several expeditions were sent from the United States with food, money, and medicine.

In this last dire extremity it is worthy of note that those truculent volunteers, the Cuban soldiers of Spain, exhibited their fiendish spirit in a diabolical manner toward the poor *pacificos*. When these starving people were seeking some wood to cook the food which we had sent them, the volunteers would not permit them to have the fuel, but told them sneeringly to let the " Yankee pigs " who sent them the food supply them with wood, and shoved the miserable creatures aside with their bayonets.

These cruelties and numerous others were laid before the world in their naked deformity by newspaper correspondents, chiefly of the United States and Great Britain, and corroborated by consuls from each of the six provinces, as well as by Consul-general Fitzhugh Lee, and by several of our own congressmen and senators who visited the island. So the cup of Spain's iniquity was full to the brim prior to the *Maine* horror; and when that occurred both Houses of Congress were so moved that they were unanimous in their resolution empowering the President to declare war. It was not a case of emotional action on the part of either Congress or the President, but the united expression of a humane indignation and an intelligent purpose resulting from a careful consideration of the facts, that purpose having the approval of nearly the whole people of the United States and subsequently of the world at large. The people urged Congress and Congress urged the President, who, in the interest of peace, struggled against the inevitable almost to the very point of inciting popular displeasure and distrust.

The mind of the President was made up on the subject shortly after he received the report of the Court of Inquiry, and this, together with the consular reports from Cuba, convinced him that there was but one way of settling the trouble between Spain and the people of the island. He sent a message to Congress April 11, 1898, in which he stated that armed intervention in Cuba by the United States was the only means that could be devised, in view of the barbarities practiced on the people of the island by Spanish authority.

Congress immediately drew up a set of joint resolutions stating that Cuba was, and should be, free, demanding that the government of Spain relinquish its authority in the island, and withdraw its land and naval forces from Cuba and Cuban waters, and directing the President of the United States to use the land and naval forces of the United States to carry these resolutions into effect.

The President signed these resolutions, April 20, 1898, and immediately sent an ultimatum to Spain, quoting the resolutions and requesting her to withdraw her army and navy by noon on April 23. The Spanish government did not await the ceremony of receiving the ultimatum at the hands of Minister Woodford, but immediately sent that gentleman his passports without the usual Castilian politeness and its dilatory ceremony, thus taking the initiative in the declaration of war prior to the time set by President McKinley's ultimatum. Minister Woodford notified all our consuls in Spain, and immediately set out himself for Paris, after handing over his official business to the British minister at Madrid.

President McKinley then issued a proclamation dated April 22, 1898, in pursuance of the joint resolution of Congress, to the effect that a blockade be established and maintained on the entire northern coast of Cuba in accordance with the laws of the United States and the law of nations applicable to such cases. This action was approved by Congress, and a call for 125,000 volunteers was issued, and immediately responded to with enthusiasm from all parts of the country, showing that the response for a million men would have been made with as great alacrity.

On the very morning of the day of this last proclamation the first gun was fired by our navy, from the *Nashville* which captured the first Spanish prize, the steamship *Buena Ventura*.

On April 25, Congress, at the instance of the President, passed a bill declaring that " war exists between the United States of America and the kingdom of Spain," and moreover that war had existed since April 21, the date on which Minister Woodford received his passports. The bill further provided " That the President of the United States be, and he hereby is, directed and empowered to use the entire land and naval forces of the United States, and to call into the actual service of the United States the militia of the several states to such an extent as may be necessary to carry this act into effect."

From these considerations it would seem that if ever there was a justifiable cause for war, our recent troubles with Spain most assuredly come under that head.

The war had virtually begun as above described, but thus far it was slow until that memorable May morning in Manila Bay when the greatest surprise and the most wonderful victory in the history of naval warfare took place : the quick and complete destruction of the Spanish squadron of eleven ships under the command of Admiral Montojos, by Commodore Dewey's squadron, without the loss of a single American life or ship.

This sketch of events leading to the recent war is intended simply as a retrospect of the great work accomplished in so short a time, with the view of obtaining a more correct appreciation of the destiny of the United States consequent upon its new departure. Never were 114 days filled with events more momentous in their consequence ; not even the famous " one hundred days " beginning with the flight of Napoleon from Elba and ending with Waterloo. The destruction of Cervera's fleet off Santiago was Spain's Waterloo.

Some persons are anxious to know how we are to manage the new possessions and discharge the new obligations forced upon us. Those who can conquer territories usually know how to govern them, though Spain has proved a glaring exception to this rule.

The best opinion that I have seen on the subject emanated from a Spanish source before the treaty of peace was signed, and is contained in the following article : —

"Those who say that colonies are nothing but encumbrances, and that the loss of Cuba and Puerto Rico will prove beneficial to our trade and to our merchant navy ; those who believe that distant territories merely serve for having our banner there, and as an outlet for the refuse of our political parties, are now deeply concerned over which it would be best for us to retain, if possible, Puerto Rico or the Philippines.

"Neither the one nor the others.

"It is true that Puerto Rico, in due honor to the lamb on her shield, has always remained loyal to Spain, but Puerto Rican fealty is not much to be relied upon since the day when Señor Moret took there the spirit of discord. As to the Philippines, the magnitude of the affair is evident to all. An army of from 50,000 to 60,000 men and ample political reforms would be indispensable to conquer the island of Luzon. Have we got the means to go into this colossal undertaking? Do we feel inclined to face it? One of the morning newspapers says that friends of the government have expressed the opinion that the sending of these reinforcements would be very difficult, not to say impossible.

"It would certainly be difficult; by no means impossible. But before throwing upon Spain the weight of such an enormous undertaking, we must seriously consider whether we are ready to reform our methods as regards colonization. If so, let us keep the Philippines, for there are in those islands enough riches to compensate for all our losses. If not, let us not insist upon retaining them, because they would be an evil rather than a boon to the nation.

"It would be a great thing for us if somebody were willing to take the islands and assume our colonial and war debts. This would, perhaps, be the only way to save interests that are now imperiled.

"There is considerable talk concerning these debts. It is said that the United States will compel us to pay them, and that an international conflict will thus be provoked. In the first place, the United States will not compel us to pay anything, because this is none of their business. They will merely declare that they will not pay or recognize them, and that will be all. In the second place, we ought to consider that the payment of those debts would have devolved upon us even in case autonomy had been a success, and that war with the United States had been averted.

"The Cubans, and also the Spanish residents of Cuba, never agreed to pay more than one fifth of the debt. The remaining four fifths was to be saddled upon the nation.

"The Cubans reasoned with perfect logic. 'This debt,' they said, 'was contracted not in order to build bridges or highways, or railroads, but forcibly to oppose our claims. If the justice of these claims was fully recognized by the autonomy decree, how are we to be compelled to pay the debt?'

"Thus peace will not cost us more than that fifth part of the debt which the Cuban autonomists had consented to pay, and which the United States are now said to reject.

"We refuse to consider the possibility that the debt question may give rise to an international conflict in our favor. The Cuban and Philippine debts are guaranteed by Spain's Treasury, and all that the foreign holders of said debts have to do is to come to us in order to be paid, when the Cubans refuse to pay them.

"Let us accustom ourselves to see things as they really are, for our habit of fancying about them has cost us too dear."

Although there is a great variety of opinion regarding our duty and obligations in the matter of the Philippines, the con-census of the best opinions seems to be that we have virtually assumed obligations of which we cannot honorably divest ourselves, and that we are responsible for giving the islanders a settled form of government.

To have handed the government of these islands back to Spain was, from either a humanitarian or political point of view, not to be thought of ; while according to the opinions of eminent European statesmen, to have turned them over to a European power for cash considerations would much resemble selling them into slavery, and at the same time furnish the possible cause of a European war over the direction of what we had been frightened out of accepting by the bugaboo of imperialism, so-called. We are not, and will not become, an imperialistic nation. The idea of democracy is too firmly intrenched in the minds of the people ever to allow a departure from the Constitution. But we are expansionists, in the very best sense of that word. The name of the Great Republic is synonymous with the expansion of learning, commerce, wealth, and all else that make for the betterment of the human race.

Under the new responsibilities that have devolved upon us, through the acquisition of the Philippines, public opinion is steadied, with a tendency toward the relegation of partisan prejudices to the rear. The aims and intentions of the government in regard to these islands, so wisely set forth by President McKinley, leave no just cause for cavil.

Through the unforeseen results of war, the task of conferring the benefits of civilization upon several millions of human beings is laid, perhaps most fittingly, upon the most progressive nation. We shall not shrink from it, but, as a preliminary, order must prevail.

Beyond this aspect, the strategic value of our new possessions is very great. They form the natural outer bulwarks of defense, and are powerful for the maintenance of the dignity of our position among the nations of the earth. From a commercial point of view, these islands are vastly important. As New York is the gateway to our continent, so the Philippines form the natural gateway to Asia, with its 800,000,000 of people. They are commercially strategic for warehousing purposes.

Recent events have clearly demonstrated the insecurity of the warehousing of materials upon the mainland of China, where they are at the mercy of irresponsible mobs. But our merchants are enabled to store their surplus upon these islands, free from the dangers of revolution or pillaging, and ready at a moment's notice to be sent forward to supply the enormous demands of these myriads of Asiatics. The immense advantages of our position in this most important regard, together with our freedom from territorial entanglement upon the continent itself, place in our hands a commercial power hard to overestimate.